Anne Marbury Hutchinson
American Founding Mother

Christy K Robinson
author of The Dyers series

*A*nne *M*arbury *H*utchinson

American Founding Mother

*C*hristy *K* *R*obinson

Books by Christy K Robinson

We Shall Be Changed (editor)

"This is a book that I will use year after year and it is on point with me every day. I get food for my soul along with a little laughter as well. Life is worth living when I see I am not alone; there are others that have their trials as well."

Mary Dyer Illuminated
Mary Dyer: For Such a Time as This
The Dyers of London, Boston, & Newport

"Christy's writing is presented on a framework of reliable, detailed history, so there is abundant information to be gleaned, and in an entertaining way. Her compelling narrative greatly aided in making Mary Dyer a real person to me. These are fascinating books that deserve a much-expanded exposure. They are simply outstanding, a feast for lovers of history and good writing."

Effigy Hunter

"What an adventure! *Effigy Hunter* breaks the mold; it is time-travel writing, history, genealogy, yet it takes the reader to the United Kingdom, Paris, and other places in Europe giving new insights to those places. Try this book!"

Anne Marbury Hutchinson:
American Founding Mother

- "Congratulations to you on a fine opus. I love it!"
- "I am most impressed by the clear and concise style, filling the reader in with important contextual material as you go."
- "I cannot wait to read your book. I love your excitement about people and their stories."
- "From what little I have known about Anne Hutchinson, she's a worthy subject for your writing – and our reading."

Anne Marbury Hutchinson

American Founding Mother

Christy K Robinson

Book cover and book design by Christy K Robinson

Front cover image: original banner painting
"Mistress Hutchinson" © 2016 by Valerie Debrule,
used by permission.

Editornado Publishing
ISBN-13: 978-0-692-19081-4

In respectful memory of

the Titans of New England

who left everyone and everything they held dear, their heritage and history, to risk their lives and fortunes to serve God and build a new society.

They were ordinary people:
cloth merchants, midwives, ministers, seamstresses, brewers, farmers, mariners, shoemakers, teachers, haberdashers, servants.
Mothers and fathers, elderly grandparents, infants and children, widows, orphans, unmarried women, soldiers, prosperous businessmen.
People of faith, excommunicates, dissidents, saints, heretics.
The people in this book were not born heroes — they became heroes.

Introduction

Anne Hutchinson was despised for her quick mind, her ability to think on her feet and her willingness to defy university-trained theologians. She was unflinching, though she had a premonition of danger to come. She lived four-fifths of her life in her native England but is world famous for her years in early colonial America. She was a woman of valor. She persuaded scores of families to leave their homes, businesses, the church that was their ticket to eternal life, and to create a new colony in the wilderness.

She was straight out of Proverbs 31:10, a virtuous woman. In the words of the 1599 Geneva Bible she studied and probably wore holes in the pages of: "Who shall find a virtuous woman? for her price is far above the pearls. The heart of her husband trusteth in her, and he shall have no need of spoil. She will do him good, and not evil all the days of her life."

Both in Lincolnshire and Massachusetts, "Her tongue is as a book whereby one might learn many good things: for she delighteth to talk of the word of God."

Except for the hostile witnesses who wrote their accounts of her and trial transcripts, she left few clues about herself.

Archaeologists don't study the single pit or trench in which the team is digging and sifting for a few weeks in the summertime. They survey the landscape for miles around, comparing ancient and space-age maps, geological features, a broad selection of written histories and oral traditions, epidemiology, monarchs and local chieftains, descendants and their DNA. As Captain Renault said in *Casablanca*, they "round up the usual suspects": friends, neighbors, and enemies of the people they're studying.

Similarly, historians, genealogists, and authors don't just rehash the known – or what we assume is known – facts about historical figures like Anne Hutchinson, but we discover more about who they were by creating spreadsheets on the activities of the people around them. We study the climate and the epidemics, the laws and customs, and who might not have been visible in the journals of the day, but who had a financial stake in the situation, also known as "following the money," or what might have been said – but not recorded – that changed the course of history.

"Scholarship about the past is not scientific: one cannot rerun the past in laboratory conditions in order to test predictions about it. History has few certainties: it is a structure of probabilities and possibilities and conjectures that would not meet the exacting standards required by a court of law or a forensic science laboratory, but does not have to."

Tom Davis, 'The Practice of Handwriting Identification' in *The Library: The Transactions of the Bibliographical Society*, Volume 8, Number 3, September 2007, p. 269.

We weren't there – but we historical researchers and authors will try to take you there by back roads, satellite views, dusty out-of-print tomes, explanations of ancient scriptures, deciphering and dissecting 400-year-old dialect and handwriting. We'll show you the ends of stories whose threads lead back to Boston, and further back, to England.

Marc Morris, author of *William I: England's Conqueror*, wrote that recovering the characters of individuals who have been dead for nearly a thousand years is sometimes impossible, even in the case of kings and other subjects of the chronicles. Without journals or correspondence to show their thoughts,

...we can perceive them only through the words of others and, in the 11th century, this means the words of contemporary chroniclers, who are invariably partisan. Most of the main sources for the politics of this period are what we would nowadays regard as propaganda and all of them were written by churchmen, who were inclined to interpret the events they described as part of a divine plan. *William I: England's Conqueror*, by Marc Morris. Allen Lane/Penguin Monarchs, 2016.

We see a similar problem with trying to research figures such as Anne Hutchinson, Mary Dyer, Quaker founder George Fox, the Puritans and Pilgrims, and a host of other people and sects. The reporters and authors had their biases, and they were entitled to them, but we should research and interpret them with that in mind. Seventeenth-century figures thought that natural events like earthquakes and eclipses meant that Christ's second coming would happen within months or years, during their lifetimes. Contemporary authors reported monsters when women miscarried deformed fetuses, and they bent facts to draw moral lessons – but then those words have come down to us as historical truth. When researching my Mary Dyer books, I saw that some of the seventeenth- to nineteenth-century writers were using public relations and marketing editorial techniques to juice up their cause. One of the most interesting and fun things about historical research is finding instances of humanity revealed – and people, deep down, just don't change.

Understanding the religious feud between Anne Hutchinson and her many accusers in Massachusetts Bay Colony is not simple, partly because the English language has changed significantly, but also because most of us don't have significant training in theology.

The terms "Puritan" and "Antinomian" were labels applied as insults in the sixteenth and seventeenth centuries. Puritans as we know them considered themselves reformers of the Church of England; when they moved to New England, they called themselves "Church of Christ" or "Congregationalists." Antinomians were not an organized sect, either: the name was one of several labels applied by – ahem! – Puritans. For a list of active religious groups of the time, see this book's Appendix, "Heretics, Seducers, and Nudists, Oh My!"

In an article in *The Atlantic*, Tara Isabella Burton, an Oxford University alumna, wrote: "But when scores of people were willing to kill or die to defend such beliefs – hardly a merely historical phenomenon – it's worth investigating how and why such beliefs infused all aspects of the world of their believers."
https://www.theatlantic.com/education/archive/2013/10/study-theology-even-if-you-dont-believe-in-god/280999/?utm_source=atlfb

To tell as true a story as possible, we have to lay aside our twenty-first-century views and try to see it their way. We have an increasingly secular society, but theirs was intensely religious, black and white and never gray. Even the law-breakers recognized their misdeeds and expected to go to hell. Most people took natural events, including tragic pregnancies, as messages from God. On the other hand, working with stereotypes and labels makes the controversy of the 1630s and -40s easier for us to relate to.

For the people who had left the corruption of the Old World behind them, and had sacrificed their very lives to build the new holy city in America, there was no toleration of pluralism, of beliefs other than their own.

What was "the foundation of all other errors and abominations in the churches of God"? Toleration! answered the Rev. Thomas Shepard. If you follow religious liberty news in

American government today, that sounds familiar, in the mouths of members of Congress and state legislatures, some religious advisers, and religious institution lobbyists. If tolerance is a bad thing, and intolerance is celebrated, the door is wide open to discrimination, bigotry, and ultimately, persecution.

It's been said that there are two people one should never trust: a religious leader who tells you how to vote, and a politician who tells you how to pray. As you'll see in the experience of the Hutchinsons and Dyers and many others, the marriage of religion and politics, church and state, ecclesiastical and civil, is oppressive – and deadly.

The colonial Puritans, like fundamentalist Christians today, wanted to live in an Old Testament model of government, with strict laws that were a reaction to the fear of a return, either dramatic or subtle, to the Catholicism (idolatry) of their parents' generation. Good-versus-evil, law-versus-chaos, saved-versus-damned – these ideas were a safety net to many. Having an intellectual religious experience trumped having a heart experience or personal relationship with God. In practice, it meant that one was saved by *knowing* the Truth, not by faith in God's desire to save everyone who accepts him.

The unorthodox Antinomians, Anabaptists, and Familists were less black and white and more indistinct shades of gray. Puritans, in their rigid belief system, saw that as heresy.

I never expected to discover the seventeenth-century theory that the Boston theocratic (political plus clerical) government might have plotted or set in motion the 1643 massacre of Anne Hutchinson and many members of her family.

So when a colleague asked if, after so many historians and experts had written so much on Anne Hutchinson, I thought I could add to the story, I answered "Yes" without hesitation. And now, with this book, you can judge the answer for yourself. This will most certainly not be the last book written on Anne, and I hope there will be more insights and discoveries in libraries, archives, and attics.

Because this book is written topically, you'll find that some facts and events overlap with other chapters, especially because you'll glimpse the events through the eyes of several eyewitnesses and journalists of the time.

Anne Marbury Hutchinson
American Founding Mother

Chapter 1

A Founding Mother

Even founding mothers were once children and teenagers. Anne Hutchinson was not only in the business of bringing babies into the world, but of helping to deliver a secular democracy to the New World, a century and a half before America became the United States of America.

Queen Elizabeth I was relatively tolerant of Protestants in her realm. The "Puritan" dissenters were Anglicans who desired a greater purification of the Church from anything that they'd inherited from the Catholics, including the *Book of Common Prayer*, certain rituals in the liturgy, and what constituted a sacrament.

Francis Marbury, Anne's father, had been imprisoned several times for clashing with religious authorities. An alumnus of Cambridge University, he didn't consider himself a Puritan, but he seemed to align with them when he criticized his superiors for placing ill-educated ministers in the pulpit.

The Bishop of London, John Aylmer, said of Francis at a trial, "Thou art a very ass, an idiot, and a fool" and an "overthwart [crosswise, from side to side], proud, puritan knave."

But after three prison confinements over several years (his survival was a miracle, considering conditions there), he settled in as a minister and schoolmaster. He married Elizabeth Moore and they had three children. After Elizabeth's death, he married Bridget Dryden and had numerous children. As a newlywed, Francis would be placed under house arrest one more time, during which two of his many children were born – including Anne in 1591, his third child with Bridget.

A minister with a large household needed an income, so he taught school in addition to being minister at the Alford church, St. Wilfrid's. Schools were for boys, but Anne and her siblings were literate, and, better than literate, they had been taught to think critically.

Francis Marbury's at-home family was reduced by infant and child mortality, older children marrying or going to college, and leaving home while the younger children were being raised and educated.

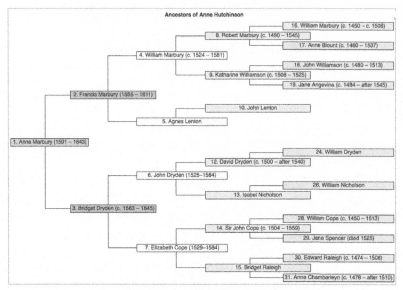

Anne Marbury's pedigree to four generations
Source: Wikipedia

Francis Marbury's first wife Elizabeth Moore's children:
- Mary I (c. 1584–1585)
- Susan (1585-1656) married Mr. Twyford
- Elizabeth I (c. 1587–1601)

Second wife Bridget Dryden's children:
- Mary II (1588-1643) married Bartholomew Layton
- John (1590-1591)
- **Anne** (1591-1643) married William Hutchinson
- Bridget I (1593-1598)
- Francis (1594-1656)
- Emma (1595-1614) married John Saunders
- Erasmus (1596-1627) matriculated at Brasenose College, Oxford
- Anthony I (1598-1601)
- Bridget II (1599-)
- Jeremuth (1601-1623) matriculated at Brasenose College, Oxford
- Daniel (1602-1611)
- Elizabeth II (1605-1614)

- Thomas (1606-1656)
- Anthony II (1608-1645) matriculated at Brasenose College, Oxford
- Katherine (1610-1687) married Richard Scott

Queen Elizabeth, who had tolerated some Catholic practices within the Anglican Church, died in March 1603 and was succeeded by James VI of Scotland, her first cousin twice removed. In addition to epidemic disease, the government and monarchy were threatened by the Gunpowder Plot of November 1605.

From about 1594, Rev. Marbury was given guest speaking appointments and was the preacher at several Anglican churches in London. He and Bridget and the tribe moved to London on a permanent basis in 1605.

There had been severe plague outbreaks in 1602 through 1604, so death and disease were not unknown risks of living in the crowded city. If you notice the short lives of the Marbury children, Anne experienced many losses of close family members, though we don't know the cause of death. The Marbury siblings' lives spanned from 1584 to 1687, late Elizabethan through the Stuart age.

In 1608, in the middle of the Little Ice Age, there was a "Great Frost," which was so severe that many domestic animals and people died of disease and hunger. Down south in London, the Thames froze so hard that they could hold a Frost Fair and have horse-drawn wagons out in the middle of the river. There was little fuel for heating or cooking, and we can imagine the Marbury children huddled in probably two beds. When spring and summer came, the cold and the rain killed or stunted crops, which would certainly drive up prices. More on this in later chapters.

Francis Marbury died in 1611, only in his fifties, leaving 13 living children, from age 26 to infant. Bridget Dryden Marbury, the midwife and mother, married Rev. Thomas Newman, moved to Berkhamsted, Hertfordshire, and lived until 1645. It's conceivable that Bridget's children, including Anne, corresponded over the years. Bridget was 81 when John Winthrop's book about Anne was published in London in 1644.

Anne's childhood

Francis Marbury was a schoolmaster during the years he was silenced from the pulpit. Though girls were homeschooled, Anne must have had a first-rate education from her father in several subjects, including handwriting. Many people could read, but not all could write, and Anne did have that skill. (A chapter of this book explains what education was like at the time of Anne's education.)

The family moved to London when Anne was a young teenager. She was exposed to religious and political thought in the remnants of Elizabeth I's reign and the first years of King James' reign. She would have been well aware of books like *Daemonolgie* (the King's witchcraft identification manual where more than nine of ten people accused of witchcraft were women), political discourse including the recent Guy Fawkes Gunpowder plot, Shakespeare's and Marlowe's plays and poetry, and a flowering of arts and sciences. Publishing took off like a rocket as a new renaissance flourished in the Early Modern Age.

As a "preacher's kid," she would have attended more church services than most young people. To set an example for the family, she would have been an expert at the catechism, both the nursery version, and the more detailed one with its precise answers and proof texts. Until 1611 and the publication of the King James Authorized Version of the Bible, the Bible that was read and studied was the Geneva Bible, which was of a size and price range that most people could afford and could carry with them. It had helpful notes and illustrations in it and was considered to be a scholarly translation of early biblical manuscripts. It was the commentary that King James thought seditious and inspired his new version.

London, as it was in the sixteenth and seventeenth centuries before the Great Fire, was a place of unchecked floods which left mold and rot in building timbers, and the freezing and thawing of the Thames. There were repeated epidemics of spotted fever (typhus), plagues including *yersinia pestis*, flux (dysentery), the King's Evil or scrofula (tuberculosis), measles, the French Pox (sexually transmitted diseases), and death by Teeth (dental abscesses), not to mention the lung diseases exacerbated by the use of coal for cooking and heating.

But not many people could afford a stick of wood or shovel of coal, no matter how cold the weather. They just had to tough it out, whether in the city or the country. You'll see that in a later chapter on the Great Frost.

Young Anne Marbury married the cloth merchant William Hutchinson in 1612, and the couple moved back to their childhood home of Alford and began their own large family.

Anne's and William's children

- **Edward** (1613-1675) died in Massachusetts of wounds received in King Philip's War
- **Susanna I** (1614-1630) died of plague in Alford
- **Richard** (1615-1670) died in London
- **Faith** Hutchinson Savage (1617-1652) died in Boston after seventh childbirth
- **Bridget** Hutchinson Sandford Philips (1619-1698) died in Boston
- **Francis** (1620-1643) died in Eastchester, NY
- **Elizabeth** (1621-1630) died of plague in Alford
- **William I** (1623-1624) died in Alford
- **Samuel** (1624-1677?) married and had one child in Boston
- **Anne** Hutchinson Collins (1626-1643) died in Eastchester, NY
- **Mary** (1627-1643) died in Eastchester, NY
- **Katherine** (1629-1643) died in Eastchester, NY
- **William II** (1631-1643) died in Eastchester, NY
- **Susanna II** Hutchinson Cole (1634-1713) the last child born in England, died in Rhode Island
- **Zuriel** (1636-1643) Born in Boston, died Eastchester, NY

Life in Lincolnshire

William and Anne lived in the small town of Alford, about 20 miles northeast of Boston, where Rev. John Cotton had just been named the preacher at Boston's St. Botolph's, a huge parish church.

Boston, near the east coast of England, was the seaport from which the Pilgrims had escaped to the Netherlands just a few years before the Hutchinsons married.

In good weather over a period of 20 years, the Hutchinsons traveled to Boston to visit St. Botolph's. Not only did they become friends with John Cotton and his first wife, but they would have known scores or even hundreds of people who lived in the area and with whom they did business. When Rev. Cotton fled persecution to the new Boston in 1633, ten percent of the church followed him.

Alford's St. Wilfrid Church was the center of life for the Marburys and Hutchinsons for generations. Babies were baptized, children and parents buried, couples married there. The current building dates to the end of the 13th century, and both families would have contributed to its building and maintenance over more than 300 years. The upper room over the entry porch was Francis Marbury's schoolroom.
Source: Alford church group website

Anne Hutchinson wasn't the only person to hold home church meetings between visits to John Cotton's church. The meetings were called conventicles, and in a time when travel was difficult for many reasons, men and women would hold single-sex meetings at home in their villages to discuss the theology and practicalities of what God required of them for salvation. As a well-educated woman and daughter of a clergyman and granddaughter of a Member of Parliament, Anne would have been a natural to host a women's conventicle. Further, as a midwife or a sort of "elder" of Christian women, she had another avenue to reach women of the parish: the days and nights of a laboring mother's confinement.

In the past, Boston's river that ran down to the North Sea was a major market center for the wool trade with Flanders, but the river silted up and was less useful for larger ships. King Charles I, who came to the throne in 1625, demanded Ship Money nevertheless, in his quest for tax revenues to pay for foreign wars.

Lincolnshire has zones of gravel ridges and lowland fens, which are wetlands in the winter and spring, and fertile land for growing crops (yellow-flowered rape for animal feed and canola oil is a common crop) or grain, flowers, and vegetables. Towns and villages were built on the higher ground, with the church on the very highest elevation, and the fields, which flooded in season, surrounded the towns.

The churches, some of them built in Saxon times and rebuilt or added to in the high medieval, feudal-baron years, had fenced-off chancels where knights or barons were buried under the floor, and the Mass was celebrated. The nave of the building was the place for guild meetings, markets, social events, a hospital for epidemics, a festival dance floor, and, being on high ground, a flood evacuation site for man and beast. In other words, the *people* being the church, this was the heart of the community. This would be true of the church in Alford as well as St. Botolph's in Boston.

There are scores of images of St. Botolph's massive tower, nicknamed The Stump for hundreds of years. But one that gave a new perspective is on Google Maps. It shows the tower from several miles away in the North Sea, in haze over a white-capped rough waves. That means that the tower could have been used as a lookout over land or sea, or as a lighthouse or landmark for merchant or fishing ships coming into Boston through its river channel to The Wash. Perhaps during John Cotton's tenure at The Stump, his ministry was seen as a beacon of light and hope, both by land and sea.

In the Hutchinsons' time, wool production was just coming down from its peak in medieval times. William Hutchinson was a cloth merchant, so he may have shipped raw wool to Europe for weaving and imported cloth, or perhaps he had looms to produce cloth, and sold it in Boston or Lincoln. He was very prosperous when he and the family emigrated to the new Boston in 1634.

The Black Plague and epidemics of typhoid fever (known as spotted fever) swept through Great Britain every few years, with 1625 and 1630 being the worst. Two of their daughters succumbed to the plague in 1630. Anne, with her midwife and healing skills, may have been a nurse to her community, as midwives often knew far more than doctors did about human anatomy and effective remedies.

Why did Puritans and Separatists leave England?

King James I and his son King Charles I felt the rumble of the middle class shaking the kingdom with new discoveries in science, the brilliant literature of the early part of the century, and not least, the rise of Puritanism in the Anglican church. There was well-founded distrust and fear of Catholicism from reports of brutality, burnings, and hangings across Europe, and there were plots afoot in England and Scotland to place Catholic kings on the thrones. The relatively new Church of England retained some of its Catholic rites and customs, and after Queen Elizabeth permitted toleration of religion as a personal choice, both Catholics and Protestants wanted to gain ascendancy for themselves with the new monarch, James I.

Among other "purifying" beliefs, the fundamental, literal Puritans believed that the Sabbath (Sunday) should be kept sacred, and that they should have services in the morning and afternoon. They were not only doing it themselves, but as we see in today's fundamentalist movement, they were insisting on their neighbors observing their beliefs, as well.

Long story short, King James wrote a pamphlet called *The Book of Sports* and ordered it read aloud by the ministers in their churches. Puritan ministers faced silencing and prison if they disobeyed. The book ordered that after Sunday service, the afternoon should be spent playing games and enjoying themselves with healthful recreation. The Puritans said that that broke the Sabbath. So they fixed on a loophole in the pamphlet that had been meant as a threat: that if they didn't do as the little book said, they should leave the country. They couldn't go to the continent of Europe because of the Thirty Years War raging. South America was controlled by the Spanish and Portuguese, which meant Catholicism and papal rule. That left North America. America, with its first colonies dying of starvation, disease, and Indian attacks, was finally finding its feet.

Rev. Cotton had been invited to Massachusetts Bay several times, and the capitol town of Boston was named after his town in Lincolnshire, as a lure for their young and beloved preacher. But Cotton wasn't willing to go until *The Book of Sports* bumped up against him. He was threatened with prison for disregarding orders, so he and his wife hid with friends for about a year. They both contracted malaria, and his wife died. When he recovered, it was time to go to the new Boston. He married again before his departure in 1633. The

Hutchinsons' eldest son, Edward, went with Cotton, and the rest of the family followed in 1634.

Was Anne a proto-feminist?

When she defended herself at trial, Gov. John Winthrop of the Massachusetts Bay Colony responded angrily: "You have rather been a Husband than a Wife and a Preacher than a Hearer; and a Magistrate than a Subject." She was usurping male roles, and that was clearly heresy to that society.

By Husband, he meant head of household, the family priest, the authoritarian ruler. This was absolutely contrary to the Calvinist doctrine of male headship.

By Preacher, he meant a man ordained by other ordained ministers and elders to preach and teach the members of a church. Usually, ordination involved a service of prayer, preaching, and either anointing or laying hands on the candidate with further prayer. The candidate is charged to dedicate his life to serving God and mankind. The congregation also is charged to support the "ordinand." The ordination was a conferral of spiritual and temporal authority on a man after theological education and a period of on-the-job training or internship. Many denominations today believe that ordination is non-scriptural, and is a human recognition of spiritual gifts that God has already bestowed on a deacon, elder, or pastor. But in seventeenth-century Boston, there was a more stringent standard for ordination. Calling Anne a Preacher was a sarcastic insult.

By Magistrate, Gov. Winthrop was accusing Mistress Hutchinson of assuming the role of prosecutor, judge, and government administrator. Winthrop was a magistrate. So was Anne's husband William.

> Initially responsible for investigating, prosecuting and sentencing felons, by 1603 they [magistrates] ... had the unenviable task of enforcing the constant religious changes, and were empowered to monitor church attendance to enforce the *Book of Common Prayer*, under penalty of life imprisonment for a third-time offender. ... As the century unfolded, local government devolved to justices. In addition to controlling hunting rights, vagrancy and licensing of alehouses, they became responsible for road repairs and redeeming English sailors from Barbary pirates. Their authority extended to apprenticeships and prices, sales of

grain, butter, cheese and flesh, and ensuring nobody sold meat on fish days.

Lambert, Alan, "650 years of the office of Justice of the Peace/Magistrate," *Amicus Curiae* Issue 88 Winter 2011, http://sas-space.sas.ac.uk/4559/1/1668-2126-1-SM.pdf

At Anne's trials, she claimed only to have held meetings for women. But after a while, men began attending one of the twice-weekly conventicles, and when 80 or 100 people were squeezed into the Hutchinson home, the Boston leaders considered that a public meeting, which was forbidden.

Mistress Hutchinson was very popular among the women of Boston and surrounding towns, and they may have felt empowered and enriched by Anne's role and her perspective on religious matters. That was deemed an infectious disease when "revelations" were only supposed to be made by God to men, which meant that Anne's perspective on religious matters was not from God but from Satan.

At least in Alford and Boston, Anne seemed to be a seventeenth-century Puritan woman without being "forward" or violating the role of a woman in society.

Most historians believe that Anne was not a feminist, but she was the first woman in America to be accused of it.

Anne's trial defense

Mistress Hutchinson defended herself at both trials, for sedition and for heresy. In the late sixteenth and early seventeenth centuries,

> Lawyers for prosecution and defense played virtually no role. Defense counsel was forbidden, and prosecution counsel was seldom used. The contemporary legal literature offered many supposed justifications for the rule forbidding defense counsel, which the chapter explores. Trial took the form of an 'altercation' between the accusers (the victim and any other witnesses) and the accused. The main purpose of the criminal trial was to hear the defendant respond in person to the accusing evidence. Contemporaries appear not to have understood how severely the procedure of the time disadvantaged the accused.

Langbein, John H., *The Lawyer-Free Criminal Trial.*
http://www.oxfordscholarship.com/view/10.1093/acprof:oso/9780199287239.001.0001/a
cprof-9780199287239-chapter-1

Was Harvard College founded because of Anne Hutchinson?

A Harvard alumni publication suggested in 2002 that Anne's brilliant self-defense spurred the colony to raise up a college "founded in part to protect posterity from her errors... Anne Marbury Hutchinson, ironically, would be more at home at Harvard today than any of her critics." Rev. Peter J. Gomes, the author, called Hutchinson an "inadvertent midwife" to the college.

The timeline of Harvard's funding, planning, and opening classes, however, began more than two years before Hutchinson was convicted, excommunicated, and expelled.

Powerful communicator

In 1650 Boston, 13 years after Anne's trial, female petitioners for the freedom of midwife Alice Tilley used language about themselves that included weak, humble, childlike, the weakest sex, trembling, poor, etc. Anne didn't use those words in her trial. She spoke in an unexpectedly powerful way, which was one of the chief complaints against her. She spoke to men as equals, and she caught them in their fallacies.

If you read her trial transcripts, you will see the ministers and magistrates become heated and emotional, while Anne, the accused radical, remained in control of her words and demeanor. Surely her heart broke to hear the accusations and final judgment made in the name of Jesus Christ, but there's no record of her angry outbursts or dissolving in a puddle of goo.

Years ago, when I was learning my craft as a writer, I was taught not to "write like a girl." I was not to soften my phrases with emotional words like "I'd like to say that ..." or "I feel that ..." but to make my statement boldly, without preamble. It was difficult to unlearn that timidity but strong writing came with maturity and confidence.

Was Anne born with a sense of power? Did she learn it when her father recounted his own trials and tutored her at home? Did she gain strength from the many personal trials as a girl and a woman? Was she valued and supported by her husband? Did she learn it by observation of others?

Working woman

As most women today will readily comment, which woman is *not* a working woman? This is not only a phenomenon of the late twentieth century, where women were employed outside the home, but has been true of all ages. In my baby scrapbook, my mother pasted a cartoon that showed a woman in her kitchen, preparing supper, tending a toddler, rocking the baby carriage with a foot hooked through the handle, and talking on the phone. Multi-tasking is not a new concept. Between England, New England, and New Netherland, Anne Hutchinson set up households in Alford, New Boston and Mount Wollaston (their farm) in Massachusetts, co-founded Portsmouth, Rhode Island, possibly had a home in Brooklyn-Williamsburg, Long Island, and at Eastchester, New York.

Not only did Anne and her family endure trials, fines, humiliation, triumph, and tragedy, they lived during a peak period of climate change: the Little Ice Age. They didn't know that, of course, but the coldest, most severe climate was happening worldwide during the seventeenth century. The polar vortex was a regular occurrence in New England, and the waters of Boston's bays froze solid enough for men and domestic animals to traverse between mainland and islands. The hurricanes and nor'easters were severe, and the worst hurricane ever to hit New England came ashore in August 1635, while the Hutchinsons lived in Boston.

With the crops destroyed or stunted by late freezes, famines followed one upon the other. And when people were weakened by poor nutrition, stress, and hard work, they more easily fell victim to epidemics of measles, smallpox, yellow fever, malaria, and other diseases. There's no record of the Hutchinsons falling victim to the epidemics of America (though they'd lost two daughters to plague in England), perhaps because of Anne's nursing and home management skills.

As a community role model in both Lincolnshire and New England, Anne was a Bible teacher, the administrator of a large family and farm, a manager of farm and personal servants, a respected midwife and nurse, and eventually, a charismatic leader of both men and women.

Mother of a large family whose descendants...

Anne's and William's countless descendants by her sons Edward and Samuel Hutchinson, daughters Susanna Hutchinson Cole, Bridget Hutchinson Sanford, and Faith Hutchinson Savage, have included U.S. presidents, Supreme Court justices, colonial and state governors, U.S. senators and representatives, military officers, actors, a prime minister of Ireland, and many others of no celebrity, who have held up the cause of freedom in North America. They may also have had descendants in England through their son Richard, who emigrated with his parents, but returned to England and died in London in 1670, but genealogy records show nothing.

Founding mother of secular democracy

Massachusetts Bay Colony was not founded as a democracy where the People govern themselves with elected representatives. Rev. John Cotton wrote:

> Democracy, I do not conceive that ever God did ordain as a fit government either for church or commonwealth. If the people be governors, who shall be governed? As for monarchy, and aristocracy, they are both of them clearly approved, and directed in scripture, yet so as referreth the sovereign to himself, and setteth up Theocracy in both, as the best form of government in the commonwealth, as well as in the church.
>
> ... Purity, preserved in the church, will preserve well ordered liberty in the people, and both of them establish well-balanced authority in the magistrates. God is the author of all these three and neither is himself the God of confusion, nor are his ways of confusion, but of peace.
>
> Excerpted from *The Correspondence of John Cotton*. Sargent Bush, Jr., editor. The University of North Carolina Press, 2001.

When the signers of the Wheelwright Remonstrance (see Appendix) were disfranchised and disarmed by the Winthrop government in 1637, they determined to form a new "plantation," or settlement, outside the Massachusetts charter boundaries. During Anne Hutchinson's second trial, they organized themselves, purchased land, and prepared to move their households. The leading men signed the Portsmouth Compact, which appears to be written in William Dyer's hand. In March 1638, they pledged:

> The 7th Day of the First Month, 1638 [7 March 1638].
>
> We whose names are underwritten do hereby solemnly in the presence of Jehovah incorporate ourselves into a Bodie Politick and as He shall help, will submit our persons, lives and estates unto our Lord Jesus Christ, the King of Kings, and Lord of Lords, and to all those perfect and most absolute

laws of His given in His Holy Word of truth, to be guided and judged thereby.

In the margin are noted three Bible texts, given here for your convenience:

Exodus 24:3-4. Afterward Moses came and told the people all the words of the Lord, and all the Laws: and all the people answered with one voice, and said, All the things which the Lord hath said, will we do. And Moses wrote all the words of the Lord and rose up early, and set up an altar under the mountain, and twelve pillars according to the twelve tribes of Israel;

1 Chronicles 11:3. So came all the Elders of Israel to the King to Hebron, and David made a covenant with them in Hebron before the Lord. And they anointed David king over Israel, according to the word of the Lord, by the hand of Samuel; and

2 Kings 11:17. And Jehoiada made a covenant between the Lord, and the King and the people, that they should be the Lord's people: likewise between the King and the people.

We don't know who suggested or insisted upon the scripture references, which have in common making a covenant with one another before God to obey his word and laws. It may have been William Coddington, who was a magistrate of the Bay Colony and one of the 1630 Winthrop Fleet pioneers who dreamed of building the New Jerusalem that would hasten the return of Jesus.

It appears that the new plantation would have that familiar combination of church and state, and an adherence to the religious laws and government model of the Old Testament.

After some disagreements about what Anne Hutchinson called "the magistracy," a group led by William Coddington moved 10 miles south on Aquidneck Island and founded Newport.

The settlement at Portsmouth, Rhode Island, incorporated itself as a secular democracy in 1639, contrasted with the theocratic governments of the other English colonies – and of England, their native land.

Portsmouth formed a new government, with William Hutchinson elected their "judge," like the Old Testament judges of

Israel before the monarchy of King Saul. Their new compact, signed by William and thirty others, read:

April 30, 1639

We, whose names are under written do acknowledge ourselves the legal subjects of his Majestie King Charles, and in his name do hereby bind ourselves into a **civil body politick**, unto his laws according to matters of justice.

The difference between the 1638 and 1639 agreements is stark. Religious language in the first, civil language in the second. Then, in March 1641, the island's general court resolved,

It is ordered and unanimously agreed upon that the Government which this Bodie Politick doth attend unto in this Island, and the Jurisdiction thereof, in favour of our Prince is a **Democracie, or popular Government**; that is to say, It is in the Power of the Body of Freemen orderly assembled, or the major part of them, to make or constitute Just Laws, by which they will be regulated, and to depute from among themselves such Ministers as shall see them faithfully executed between Man and Man.

Between man and man. They weren't cutting out the relationship between God and man, or their devotion to serving God. But secular democracy for this group, who had fled religious persecution in England only five to ten years before, and theocratic oppression just one year before, was the very freedom they longed for and now had in their grasp. They were the point of a movement. And the movement, beginning with those conventicles in her parlor, was led by Anne Hutchinson.

Chapter 2

Education in the Early 17th Century

Anne Marbury was homeschooled as a girl. Girls could not enroll in schools with boys, but they could be taught by a tutor or by their parent. Though writing was not always part of their education, many girls, particularly the Puritans, were taught to read well enough to understand their Geneva Bibles, which had notes and pictures to aid in study.

Young boys of means would attend grammar school, but at that time, a boy had to be able to read and write before he entered the school, so there would have been home schooling first. Teaching little children to write their letters and numbers involved the child tracing large letters with a dry pen or chalk, writing the figures repeatedly until they'd mastered one letter after the other.

The curricula for the early seventeenth-century grammar school consisted of religion, grammar (Latin and its translation, literature reading, rhetoric/composition), sciences, history, geography, mathematics, and music.

A Welsh professor of education wrote that in English grammar schools before 1680:

> In the sciences, Botany, Zoology, Physiology and Anatomy were differentiated and developed by classifications which marked the scientific movement away from the old Aristotelian authority in the advance towards the modern treatment. Magnetism, Mechanics, Hydrostatics, Pneumatics, Chemistry and Geology began to claim treatment separately... Up to the end of the Commonwealth [1659], the Grammar Schools of England may be regarded as apparently exclusively classical instruction, with the exception – a most important exception – as we shall see, that under medieval Catholicism, and afterwards under sixteenth and seventeenth century Puritanism, they were, in intention and largely in practice, permeated with moral, religious, and pietistic instruction.

The English Grammar Schools to 1660: Their Curriculum and Practice, by Foster Watson, M.A., University College of Wales, Aberystwyth. Cambridge University Press, 1908.

Writing was an extracurricular course. (See Appendix of this book for a tutorial on teaching writing.) Grammar schools required that students speak Latin at school, not English. Schoolmasters appointed observers to enforce the practice. There's no indication that Anne spoke or wrote Latin, but it's possible that she read Greek and Hebrew, with her father's theological background.

Women of the aristocratic class were known to write letters, poems, and personal journals. Those of the merchant class often kept inventory and accounts for their husband's business.

If boys were well-connected and had the money for fees, they attended Oxford or Cambridge University. The merchant class, which rose higher in income and power during the sixteenth century, sent its boys to university or apprenticed them to a profession or trade, including military service.

Anne learned from her father, Francis Marbury, a university-educated minister who taught school during the years he was "silenced" for his Calvinistic, reform theological leanings. Though Anne and her siblings may not have learned the same subjects to the depth of boys in grammar schools and colleges, she was certainly a deep thinker who hop-scotched past the Oxford- and Cambridge-trained lawyers and ministers who were her accusers. Perhaps she was taught not to accept teaching at face value, but to mine the ore and refine it in the crucible. Some young men did that and achieved greatness. When Anne did it, she achieved greatness – and was tried for sedition.

Three of Anne's brothers matriculated at Brasenose College, Oxford University, which was founded for "poor and indignant [possibly meaning indigent rather than aggrieved]" boys, for their education in philosophy, logic, and theology.

One of the battles Puritans like Francis Marbury fought was that Puritan ministers were university educated in theology, whereas the Anglican ministers may have been university graduates – or political appointees by family members or aristocrats, bishops, or the Crown. The Puritans were "silenced" (fired, ministerial credential removed) and sometimes imprisoned when they refused to conform to the bishops, and when their knowledge revealed those with lesser thinking skills and more power or those whose hypocrisy or sin was revealed by Puritan ministers unafraid to point the bony finger of judgment.

Marbury, then, was well-versed (no pun intended) on the Bible in English vernacular, as well as the biblical languages, Hebrew and Greek, that told the story in word pictures. This is undoubtedly where Anne learned to read deeply into the texts, and more importantly, to think.

To date, there are no original documents known to be written or signed by Anne Hutchinson. But that doesn't mean she couldn't write. It means the papers haven't survived, or if they have, no one has identified them as Anne's. A later chapter in this book has an excerpt of Anne's 1643 letter, preserved by a Quaker.

There were other literate women in New England. Anne Dudley Bradstreet was a poetess who was educated in several languages. Katherine Marbury Scott (see her chapter in this book) wrote a letter to John Winthrop, Jr. Mary Barrett Dyer wrote a letter to the Massachusetts General Court, and I have a copy of a deed she witnessed and signed in Newport, Rhode Island.

Snippet of Mary Dyer's handwriting from October 1659.

Margaret Tyndal Winthrop exchanged letters with her husband, the governor. Anne Yale Hopkins, the wife of Gov. Edward Hopkins of Connecticut, was believed to have gone insane not because she inherited madness or was driven to it by illness, injury, fear, or unbearable hardships of first-generation settlers, but because of her scholarship in reading and writing books, and the resulting mental exhaustion.

Anne's and William's eldest son Edward Hutchinson may have apprenticed with his own father, and we see from records of his life that he was part owner of the Boston Town Dock, and an officer in the Military Company of Massachusetts. In the 1650s, he was an attorney. He helped Quakers and Baptists with legal affairs but remained a member of the Congregational (Puritan) church in Boston, and he owned or shared ownership in trading ships. Surely Edward was a product of English grammar school and a thorough home education from his parents. He would have studied law in Boston, as he didn't attend university in England. His contemporary, William Dyer, had a similar career trajectory, though he'd been educated in grammar school and a prestigious guild in London. Dyer moved up the ranks of civil and military service in New England, from clerk to colonial recorder and secretary of state, and attorney general.

When Edward came to America with John Cotton, Thomas Hooker, and Samuel Stone, the three eminent ministers preached three sermons on the ship *Griffin* every day. Then Edward lived with the Cotton family. Did his parents consider a vocation in ministry for their son, or was he there to prepare the business and home for his family when they arrived?

It took more than good connections or money to make your mark in the New World – it also took determination, long hours, proving oneself with excellent work, ambition, the ability to eat crow when necessary, and a solid educational foundation with critical thinking and wide reading. Edward Hutchinson and William Dyer were lucky to have been born at the beginning of the Early Modern Age, when scientific inquiry and knowledge increased exponentially.

Chapter 3

The Great Frost

The Great Frost of 1608 began in December 1607, when a massive freeze descended on Great Britain, Iceland, and Europe.

Francis and Bridget Marbury and their family lived in London when the Northern Hemisphere froze over and people and animals died by the millions. They and their parishioners experienced food and fuel shortages.

The cold enveloped city and country alike, stopping trading ships, sending icebergs on the North Sea between England and the Continent, and freezing seaports so that coastal shipping trade came to a stop for three months.

"The first decade of the 17th century was marked by a rapid cooling of the Northern Hemisphere, with some indications for global coverage. A burst of volcanism and the occurrence of El Niño seem to have contributed to the severity of the events. … Additional paleoclimatic, global evidence testifies for an equatorward shift of global wind patterns as the world experienced an interval of rapid, intense, and widespread cooling." Schimmelmann, Lange, Zhao, and Harvey, abstract, http://aquaticcommons.org/14822/1/Arndt%20Schimmelmann.pdf

The Peruvian silica volcano, Huaynaputina, erupted in 1600, with so much ejecta that more than 12 cubic miles of rock and ash filled the atmosphere. It caused rapid global cooling and catastrophic weather events for a decade, including a Russian famine that killed two million people, epic mud flows in California, great droughts and freezes that affected the Popham and Jamestown colonies in Virginia, and die-offs in European vineyards. The far-off Peruvian volcano affected Great Britain, too.

A succession of hot, dry summers and extra-cold winters in England heralded the coldest years of the Little Ice Age in the seventeenth century. No one knew it then, of course. They just knuckled down and got on with survival.

In January 1607, there were "great floods;" in March it was unseasonably hot; the summer was extremely hot and dry, and many died because of it. But then came December 1607, which many judged to be the coldest winter in memory.

Fruit orchards that would only go dormant in a normal winter split their trunks and died. It cost more to feed livestock than to sustain people on that grain. Birds froze in flight or fell from their roosts.

In London, the River Thames froze solid. According to Meriel Jeater of the Museum of London, the Thames froze 23 times between 1309 and 1814, and then never again. "The Old London Bridge at the time ... had 19 arches, and each of the 20 piers was supported by large breakwaters. When chunks of ice got caught between them, it slowed the flow of the river above the bridge, making it more likely to freeze over. ... When New London Bridge opened in 1831 it only had five arches. The Thames never froze over in the London area again." http://www.dailymail.co.uk/news/article-2524252/How-Londoners-celebrated-River-Thames-freezing-frost-fairs-ice.html#ixzz4r7J3ptFu

Perhaps to profit from the phenomenon of a once-in-a-lifetime cold spell, an anonymous author wrote a 28-page book, *The Great Frost: Cold doings in London, except it be at the Lottery, With newes out of the country. A familiar talke betwene a country-man and a citizen touching this terrible frost and the great lotterie, and the effects of them. the description of the Thames frozen over,* which may have a longer title than the interior text. The cover says it was printed on London Bridge (then supporting shops and tenements above the shops), so undoubtedly the book was meant to be sold on the frozen river below. There were two characters, the Countryman and the Citizen, having a dialogue about the first Frost Fair ever held, and the economic conditions of England because of the extended freeze.

In the city, the Frost Fair meant that shops could set up market tents on the frozen river that "shows like grey marble roughly hewn." Merchants sold souvenirs, winter clothing and shoes, and served alcohol from bars on wheels. People gambled on sports or animal baiting, ate hot fair food from fires built on the ice, and took sleigh rides up and down the river. Ice skating was well-known in the Netherlands and Germany, and perhaps the English tried it. They also played football, and shot arrows and muskets. The Citizen said: "Both men, women, and children walked over, and up and downe in such companies, that I verily believe, and I dare almost sweare it, that one half (if not three parts) of the people in the Citie, have been seene going on the Thames."

Right there in London, probably out on the ice on a Saturday, we'd find the Marbury family, listening to musicians and watching dancers, playing, and eating fair food like turkey leg, meat or fruit pies, and gingerbread.

A man golfing on ice, whose clothing style puts him in this time frame.

But at home, they were bundled up against the cold, as much as they'd been out on the Thames. The river was the main artery for shipping food, trade goods, and fuel like coal and wood into the city, and the ships were stuck out at sea, or frozen in ports. Wagons were similarly prevented from moving goods on frozen roads. The Citizen in *The Great Frost* bemoaned the "unconscionable and unmerciful raising of the prices of fuel."

With little or no firewood or coal, people shared beds, mixing up aunties and grandchildren, parents and babies, servants and any guest staying the night. They had cupboard beds or four-posters with a canopy and curtains to keep their body heat and warm breath captive. The large Marbury family would have shared beds and body heat at night. Frances and Anne Marbury conceived their son Anthony during this climate upheaval.

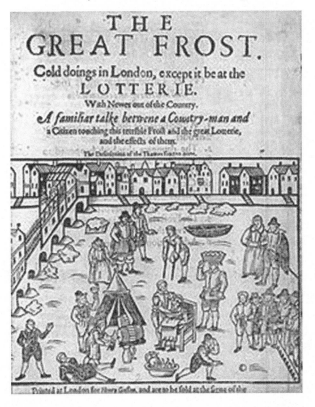

The Countryman commended the city council for having stockpiled coal and wood against an emergency and price gouging.

"Their care for fire was as great as for food. Nay, to want it was a worse torment than to be without meat. The belly was now pinched to have the body warmed: and had not the provident Fathers of this city carefully, charitably and out of a good and godly zeal, dispersed a relief to the poor in several parts and places about the outer bounds of the City, where poverty most inhabiteth; by storing them beforehand with sea coal and other firing at a reasonable rate, I verily persuade myself that the unconscionable and unmerciful raising of the prices of fuel by chandlers, woodmongers, &c. – who now meant to lay the poor on the rack – would have been the death of many a wretched creature through want of succour."

The Citizen responded: "Strangers may guess at our harms: yet none can give the full number of them but we that are the inhabitants. For the City by this means [the closure of the river and roads] is cut off from all commerce."

With commercial traffic stopped in its tracks during the Great Frost, the merchants, warehouses, dock hands, ship crews, and others were forced into stoppages they called "The dead vacation," "The frozen vacation," and "The cold vacation." We can imagine the effect on their economy, especially if they were living hand to mouth.

Coupled with the loss of work and little to sell in the shops, the price of food rose precipitously. "For you of the country being not able to travel to the City with victuals, the price of victail must of necessity be enhanced; and victail itself brought into a scarcity," wrote the Citizen.

The church poor rolls, the parish charity for widows and orphans, would have been stretched past their limits when they experienced weather and epidemiological catastrophes, so of course the Marburys would have been no stranger to hard work, short rations, and sharing small spaces.

The Great Frost was harsh, and it wasn't the only time the Thames froze, but it was the most memorable. It lasted a little more than four months until the ice broke up and life returned to normal. Well, normal for them. Warmer meant...

Plague.

Chapter 4

Signs of the End of the World

The Countryman says to the Citizen in *The Great Frost*, "Your crammed capons feed you fat here in London; but our beef and bacon feed us strong in the country. Long sleeps and late watchings dry up your blood and wither your cheeks: we go to bed with the lamb and rise with the lark, which makes our blood healthful. You are still sending to the apothecaries and still crying out to "fetch Master Doctor to me:" but our apothecary's shop is our garden full of potherbs, and our doctor is a good clove of garlic. I am as lusty and sound at heart, I praise my GOD, as my yoke of bullocks that are the servants to my plough."

It's interesting that the author contrasted city and country, sickness and health, indolence and activity.

In the city, some streets never saw the sunlight because the streets were only wide enough for carts, while the buildings above the shops were built out over the street, so that people on one side of the street could shake hands with neighbors across the street.

The aroma of the city was that of animal offal, human and animal excrement, dead animals, and rotting garbage. It's no wonder that when the weather warmed up in May and June, the plagues returned. *Yersinia pestis*, or Black Death, usually began in ports, as rats and their fleas easily ran on and off boats and ships, and fleas could infest bales of wool, textiles, or animal fodder.

While the Marburys visited and then lived in London, the Black Death, of which there were always a few isolated cases, raged particularly hard in 1602, 1603, 1610-11, and 1625. That wasn't the only disease to fear, though. There were repeated epidemics of smallpox, typhus, diphtheria, influenza, sweating sickness, anthrax, and malaria.

When Anne and William married in London and moved to their childhood home of Alford, Lincolnshire, about 120 miles north, the climate wasn't improved by the latitude, though the putrid smells of the crowded cities would have been replaced by more earthy scents of farmyards and stagnant fens.

In *The Great Frost* booklet, the Countryman painted a dreary picture of country life in England, in the first few years of the new century. Not only were they under a deep freeze in the winter, but their summers brought smaller harvests and greater animal mortality than the prosperous years of Queen Elizabeth's reign.

> "Not only our wives, our children and household servants are unto us a cause of sorrow: but we grieve as much to behold the misery of our poor cattle ... as it doth to look upon our own affliction. Our beasts are our faithful servants; and do their labour truly when we set them to it. They are our nurses that give us milk, they are our guides in our journeys, they are our partners and help to enrich our state; yea, they are the very upholders of a poor farmer's lands and living. Alas! then, what master that loves his servant as he ought, but would almost break his own heartstrings with sighing; to see these pine and mourn as they do? The ground is bare and not worth a poor handful of grass. The earth seems barren and bears nothing: or if she doth most unnaturally she kills it presently [at once] or suffers it through cold to perish. By which means the lusty horse abates his flesh and hangs his head, feeling his strength go from him; the ox stands bellowing, the ragged sheep bleating, the poor lamb [born in April, after the frosts] shivering and starving to death."

We don't know if the author of *The Great Frost* was being melodramatic to better sell his booklet at the Frost Fair, or if that was a true report. We can surmise it's mostly or all true, because of the South American volcanic ash filtering sunshine in the northern hemisphere, resulting in millions who suffered famine and died in Russia.

The plague could be transmitted by flea bites, by contact with the sores or bodily fluids of the plague victims, and by droplets in a cough or sneeze which could be propelled as much as twelve feet across a room.

The Hutchinsons lost their infant or toddler son William to accident or disease between 1624 and 1630. In 1630, they lost two of their daughters, Elizabeth and Susanna, to the deadly outbreak of plague that came north from Italy starting in 1629, and reached London, Cambridge, Lincoln, and Alford in 1630.

In 1625, King James I died, and he was succeeded by his son, Charles I. In February of that year, severe rains, snowmelt, and a super high tide flooded London and much of the low-lying fenlands on the east coast of England, resulting in typhus, dysentery, and a devastating bubonic plague that killed 35,000 people.

In 1630, at the time of the birth of Charles' heir, there was a great, bright comet that caused double shadows at noon: one from the sun, and one from the reflecting comet. For centuries, comets had been associated with war, famine, and epidemics.

In 1618, war had begun between Catholic and Protestant factions on the Continent, and was later called the Thirty Years' War. The plague that broke out in Milan in 1629 didn't take long to infect Europe because troop and refugee movements associated with the battles carried *yersinia pestis* from Italy to the Baltic Sea, and westward to Great Britain. As disease spread quickly in crowded port cities like London, city residents fled to the countryside, where they unwittingly spread the disease.

They had no means of support, so they begged and stole food as society shattered to pieces.

Stephen Bradwell, a London physician, wrote of plague: "Poor people, by reason of their great want, living sluttishly [low standards of cleanliness], feeding nastily on offals, or the worst and unwholesomest meats, and many times, too, lacking food altogether, have both their bodies much corrupted, and their spirits exceedingly weakened; whereby they become (of all others) most subject to this sickness. And therefore we see the plague sweeps up such people in greatest heaps."

Natural disasters, comets, and rumors of war were signs of the end of time, when Christ would return to redeem his chosen, and cleanse the earth with fire.

The Alford parish register for 1630, by the vicar George Scortreth, recorded the first plague death on July 22, and in the remaining days of the month, there were 22 burials. In August, there were 47 burials; in September, 26; in October, 9; November, 6; and December, 3. Statistics suggest that there were probably two "Patient Zero" plague carriers who introduced the plague in Alford just before July 22. The incubation period was one to three days, when the person might experience no symptoms, but could spread the *yersinia pestis* bacteria with a cough or sneeze.

Sometimes the onset of symptoms took several days to worsen, and other times, one could seem fine in the morning and keel over dead in the afternoon. There was no cure or prevention known in that century, but they did practice isolation and quarantine.

About two-thirds of those infected by plague died. Symptoms of plague include swelling of lymph nodes, especially in the groin, armpit, or neck. They also had vomiting, diarrhea, bleeding from sensitive membranes, high fever, and body pain from swellings or decaying skin. Feet and hands could turn black, and fatal septicemia could shut down internal organs.

A plague stone in Yorkshire. The people from affected villages would place their coins in the vinegar to disinfect them for the people who supplied goods or food.

No one knew how the plague was spread, but there were homeless families, singles, and orphaned children on the roads and in the fields, sleeping rough when farmers turned them out of barns or stables. They would be starving and desperate. Based on what the Hutchinsons did only four to six years later in New England (see later chapters), it's reasonable to believe that they took in some adults or children, and that Anne may have nursed people in the village, including relatives and neighbors.

Did the Hutchinsons' acts of Christian charity endanger their own family?

Susanna Hutchinson, 16, was a September 8 victim of the plague. The family must have grieved her loss as she was quickly buried to prevent further contamination. The thirty-nine-year-old mother Anne probably burned the bedding on which Susanna had suffered fevers and convulsions, and perhaps she lime-washed the walls and floor of the chamber to cover bodily fluids.

But three weeks later, as the plague deaths slowed and the weather cooled, eight-year-old Elizabeth was stricken with the same symptoms, and died on October 4. Surely in their despair, the Hutchinson family wondered if other family members, young or old, would succumb to the plague.

Some families were wiped out by the hideous disease. One man, Thomas Brader, and five of his children all died within a fortnight at the height of the epidemic.

Not only humans were susceptible to the plague: cattle, horses, sheep, and other animals died in pens and out in the fields. Death was everywhere, and no one knew where it would strike next.

Two hundred fifty years after the Alford plague visitation, an English antiquarian, Rev. George S. Tyack, B.A., wrote:

> The grounds of Tothby House, near Alford, contain an interesting relic of Bygone Lincolnshire. Beneath a spreading tree that fronts the house, upon the lawn, stands a large stone which has a tale to tell of the deadliest year in the annals of the parish. All through a fatal summer, groups of country folk might have been seen, day by day, wending their way from Spilsby and the surrounding villages to the top of Miles Cross Hill, that overlooks the wide marsh country, and has Alford lying just at its foot. There on the hill-top stood this stone, and on it these good folk heaped bread and other common necessaries of life, which they had brought with them, and retired. Another company has meanwhile toiled up the hill from Alford, and these, approaching as those recede, remove the food and leave money in payment in its place. With such caution, and with such care to avoid all personal contact between buyers and sellers, is all business between the two neighbour-towns transacted – for Alford is plague stricken!

...We are safe in considering that the population of Alford cannot then have exceeded 1,000... In 1630, however, the number of burials entered in the register is no less than 131, while the first two months of the following year contain nineteen more.

Then evidently the disease died out, for there are but eight more interments during the other ten months of 1631.

The early seventeenth century was not the end of the world, as we know. But all the signs were there, for students of scripture.

Chapter 5

William Hutchinson's English Hus-wife

William Hutchinson was a wealthy man for his time, trading in wool cloth and probably raw wool shorn from the millions of sheep that dotted English paddocks.

In past centuries, the River Witham that ran near Lincoln and wound through the shire to Boston, then flowed to the North Sea, had been dredged for barges and small boats that carried agricultural produce between the interior and the North Sea ports, then transferred to ships for transport to London, the Netherlands, and other European countries. But during the early part of the seventeenth century, the estuaries silted with mud and sand, and were not dredged to maintain banks, locks, and proper depths. King Charles I took the throne in 1625, and demanded "ship money" from the ports. He didn't reinvest the money they reluctantly gave up in infrastructure and building or dredging works, but wanted to spend it on continental religious wars. Parliament wouldn't agree, so Charles dissolved them.

The harsh winters and blighted summers would have depressed the English and European economies, making life that much more difficult to endure. Prices rose on food and fuel.

William Hutchinson must have had a good trading and distribution network for his wool and woolen textiles, for his business prospered and he was able to save enough money despite the King's taxes, to move a large family at approximately £100 per person, plus household goods and a few domestic animals, from England to Massachusetts, and still buy farms and a large house in the center of Boston.

His wife must have been a formidable manager of people and time and resources.

Anne and other midwives had great authority from the Church of England and the government, to testify in court regarding rape, infanticide, and bastardy. The latter was a moral crime, but there was an investigation as to the father so he would be forced to support the child, rather than add a mother and child to the poor rolls of the parish. Midwives were admired for their skills and knowledge, and their nursing skills.

Though there's no evidence left for us, perhaps Anne taught her female children and relatives how to read and write as she had been drilled by her father. Teaching two catechisms, one for pre-school children, and one for older children, was a mother's job.

Housewifery was patriotic, for the general good of the kingdom! This is a 1615 publication that Anne Hutchinson probably consulted.

She had her medicinal and food gardens, which need time and labor for planting at the proper time, manuring and composting, pruning and plucking off pests, harvesting, preserving – gardening for a large family and servants would be a full-time occupation, so the children would be busy with chores, and we can figure on local laborers for help there.

There might have been rejected lambs to raise, cattle and calves, horses, goats, hogs, chickens, and cats and dogs to kill pests and herd or guard the beasts. Someone fed the animals, harnessed or saddled the horses for work or travel, milked the cows and goats, mucked out the barn and spread the manure on the fields. The Hutchinsons must have had servants, and servants need management.

Imagine being responsible for so many people and activities – and nursing her own babies year after year.

When the weather was good enough to travel 20 miles to Boston, Anne and William rode horses in what was probably a half-to three-quarters day's journey each way. Did they ride south on Saturday and stay with friends, or get up in the middle of the night on Sunday morning? Probably the former, as the seventh day was called Preparation Day for the Sabbath on the first day of the week. Once there, they could enjoy the fellowship, shared meals, and preaching at John Cotton's large church, where congregants came for miles to hear the brilliant young minister. They would prefer to rest the animals on Sunday as the fourth Commandment called for, then ride home on Monday morning. All that time together on the road and sharing enjoyable activities probably allowed for Anne and William to deepen their friendship as married partners.

Then there were the women's religious studies Anne taught, based on Rev. John Cotton's sermons at St. Botolph's, which required preparation time and refreshments, candles when the day was dark, and benches in the parlor.

People who love God and do such things in his name are people who give, volunteer their time and talents, and work to give a hand up to the disadvantaged. We would probably be correct in thinking that the Hutchinsons were charitable and community-minded, providing jobs to laborers, bakers, laundresses, and shelter to the homeless and food to the hungry. Those are "good works" motivated by love that Jesus endorsesd in Matthew chapter 25.

We glimpse other facets of a good Puritan wife by looking at Margaret Tyndal Winthrop, Gov. John Winthrop's third wife. The Winthrops and Hutchinsons were neighbors in Boston, and Anne attended Margaret's miscarriage.

> It was given to Margaret Winthrop to endure in her fifty-six years of life a far wider and deeper range of emotions and experiences than has fallen to the lot of many women. A sheltered girlhood was rudely shocked by the murder of her father. She ... bravely faced and endured that venturous voyage herself, and encountered with courage the fears and hardships of a pioneer life in a strange savage world. She was brought thither, to use her husband's powerful words, "through the swelling seas, through perills of pyrates, tempests, leakes, fires, rocks, sands, diseases, starvings; and the colony was here preserved these many years through displeasure of Princes, the envy and rage of Prelates, the malignant plots of Jesuits, the mutinous contentions of discontented persons, the open and secret attempts of

barbarous Indians, the seditions and undermining practices of hereticall false brethren."

Earle, Alice Morse, *Margaret Winthrop*, C. Scribner's Sons, 1895

Surely, the seditions and underminings were reference to the Hutchinsons and their followers.

In 1640, when John Cotton had turned against Anne and the church had sent a delegation of men to Rhode Island to get Anne to recant and come under submission of the church that had banished her, the men urged William to force Anne to bend.

William replied, "I am more nearly tied to my wife than to the church. I do think her to be a dear saint and servant of God."

A saint in biblical terms was a person set apart for a holy purpose; all the people who answered God's call to be holy. A servant of God is one who is humble and committed to obeying the promptings in their hearts.

Surely when William Hutchinson said that of Anne in her defense, she would have been energized and filled with love.

Chapter 6

Midwife or Patroness

Today, professional midwives attend several years of college-level classroom and lab instruction, spend hundreds of hours assisting preceptor midwives in clinical and home settings, and take licensure exams. Many midwives are also nurses. There are a few men in the profession, but the majority are women.

Most people think Anne Hutchinson was a midwife, though I've also heard an Ivy League historian say that Anne was not a midwife – she was a high-status patroness and godmother who attended births in more of a spiritual capacity.

Rev. Ros Latham, vicar of St. Wilfrid's Church of England in Alford, says, "The English class system is so strong and Anne's heritage quite aristocratic, particularly her mother, that I see her as being in charge at the birth with a lower class midwife doing most of the messy stuff and following instructions. Anne would take the lead in prayer for safe delivery and spiritual support, establishing her as a recognised spiritual leader and teacher among women."

The majority view, as we've heard for hundreds of years, is that Anne was a midwife. Midwives usually trained with their mothers, who were midwives. Anne's mother, Bridget Dryden Marbury, was named after the patron saint of midwives and babies, St. Bridget.

Rev. John Cotton said of Anne, whom he'd known for two decades, "She did much good in childbirth-travails, and readily fell into good discourse with the women about their spiritual estates."

Anne Hutchinson lost several of her children while living in Lincolnshire in the late 1620s. Presumably, she was the primary caretaker for her daughters who died of plague, and for the son who may have lived between one and a half and four years. Though clerics of the time told parishioners not to become too attached to their children, Anne must have been traumatized by these losses. Her turning to God for answers might have been the turning point between her Anglican upbringing and the more radical Puritanism she espoused under the influence of Rev. John Cotton. Coping with her grief may even have shaped her communications and revelations from God.

Many families of the time experienced a 50 percent or greater infant and child mortality, but Anne's children survived infancy. We're left to wonder if they had remarkable constitutions, or if Anne's nursing and herbal healing skills sustained the family until they were overwhelmed by plague.

Woodcut depicting a tenet of the Puritan beliefs: make babies.

In Boston between 1634 when the Hutchinsons arrived and 1638 when they left, there were several midwives working in the new town, including Anne, and Jane Hawkins. About thirty-five thousand emigrants came to New England through the port of Boston during the 1630s. Because it was a dangerous ocean crossing of eight to twelve weeks and a wilderness with harsh conditions, older people were discouraged from leaving England, and healthy and strong men, and women of childbearing age who could endure hard work, were the ones who would be more successful.

Early-modern midwives possessed more practical knowledge about human anatomy, wound care, and healing than physicians did. Physicians were taught theology and other academic arts and sciences (including anatomy) to take their doctoral degrees, but only learned to practice medicine as apprentices to older physicians.

Midwives cured with herbs and poultices and natural remedies, some of which we'd consider quackery, of course. In the sixteenth and seventeenth centuries, they were supposed to be licensed by an ecclesiastical board in their diocese, but no one today knows who was licensed and who was not.

> ### *For a woman that is new brought in bed, and soundeth (swoons) much.*
> Take mugwort, motherwort, and mints, the quantity of a handful in all, seethe them together in a pint of malmsey [a sweet, fortified Spanish wine] and give her to drink thereof two or three spoonful at a time, and it will appease her swounding.
>
> —*The English Housewife*, by Gervase Markham, 1568-1637

A sixteenth-century midwifery oath required an approved midwife to treat her patients without qualification to wealth or poverty. She couldn't switch babies with another mother, she couldn't use instruments like forceps on the baby and couldn't mutilate a fetus. She would report truthfully on bastardy, and report the baptisms she'd performed. She wasn't to perform or prescribe abortions, birth control, or fertility remedies. Later oaths appear to show a self-regulation of their profession, to respect and cooperate with other midwives, and to report malpractice.

If licensed, they had several tasks to perform. They had authority to baptize a baby if a priest or vicar couldn't get there before the infant died. Even if the mother was married, the midwife had to demand the name of the baby's father during active labor, the better for the Church to punish and make an unmarried father take financial responsibility for raising the child. If the laboring mother refused to name the father, the midwife was supposed to leave her in extremity to force the woman to speak out. They reported the births and deaths (for childbirth was fatal to a large number of mothers every year) to the proper authorities.

There were procedures they were not allowed to do, such as performing surgery. That was reserved for the physician.

Because the mothers were at home in their lying-in period and considered unclean until their purification at four to six weeks, it was sometimes the midwife who would baptize the infant. Puritans weren't very enthusiastic about the "churching" of new mothers because it smacked of popery and was included in the despised *Book of Common Prayer*.

Midwives advised physicians on cause of death and reported the monthly morbidity and mortality reports like Graunt's epidemiological lists that tracked everything from plague to death by toothache.

They also risked being accused as a witch, perhaps because of their natural remedies or their greater success at healing than physicians. Being a "wise" woman was not a compliment – it meant she was possibly a familiar of the devil.

In 1638, Jane Angell Hawkins was one of the midwives of Boston. Gov. Winthrop and the other members of the colonial government exiled Jane on pain of severe whipping if she returned.

> ...It was known, that she [Jane Angell Hawkins] used to give young women oil of mandrakes and other stuff to cause conception; and she grew into great suspicion to be a witch, for it was credibly reported that, when she gave any medicines (for she practiced physic), she would ask the party if she did believe, and she could help her, etc.
> Winthrop's *Journal*, Vol. 1.

If a midwife gave a successful treatment to an illness, she was cutting in on the physician's business, and indeed, John Winthrop practiced physic himself. If the patient died, the midwife must have cast a spell. Either way, it was dangerous to be a midwife in that time.

Changing a baby's nappy:

How the childe must be made cleane...

The Nurse, or some other, must sit neare the fire, laying out her legges at length, having a soft pillow in her lap, the doors and windowes being close shut, and having something about her that may keepe the wind from the child... If he bee very foule, shee may wash him with a little water and wine luke-warme, with a spunge or linen cloth. The time of shifting him is commonly about seven a clocke in the morning, then againe at noone, and at seven a clocke at night: and it would not be amisse to change him againe about mid-night; which is not commonly done. But after hee hath slept a good while do everytime shift him; lest he should foule and bepisse himself.

— *Child-birth or, the Happy Deliverie of Women,* by Jacques Guillemeau, 1612.

Jane Hawkins and Anne Hutchinson were both attending Mary Dyer when Mary miscarried her "monster" fetus. A few months later, Jane and her husband were expelled from Massachusetts Bay at the same time as the Hutchinson party. They died in the late 1650s, leaving three adult sons who had unsuccessfully appealed to Boston's court to allow Jane to return there.

When the Winthrop Fleet crossed the Atlantic in 1630, several women among the thousand passengers were pregnant. At one point, a woman went into labor, and a midwife on another ship in the fleet was hailed and transferred to Winthrop's ship. Sadly, the baby was lost, and Mrs. Dudley wrote that the mother had suffered several miscarriages previously, but she'd recover and perhaps bear a child in the future.

One book written in the mid-seventeenth century (after Anne Hutchinson's death) by Percival Willoughby, a physician, counseled midwives to be gentle with their patients, be soothing, and not stretch the laboring mother or pull the baby from the birth canal.

> And then, and ever, let the midwife forbear to use violence, which hindereth the birth, through much hauling, or pulling, or stretching those tender parts. Such doings create pains, with swellings and soreness, and make the labouring woman unwilling to endure her labour, and the putting down of her throws [contractions]; and, several times, this too much officiousness causeth evil accidents to follow, as tearing the body, sores, and ulcers, or flooding and scouring. All which, in childbed, be found too oft dangerous, and they may prove fatal.

This suggests that some midwives were *not* very good at their jobs.

An Englishwoman named Alice Thornton wrote that before she gave birth for the eighth time, presumably in her late thirties or forties, she prepared her soul in case she died in labor:

> I trebled my diligence and care in preparation, having with comfort received the blessed Sacrament as a pledge of my redemption… After this great mercy in the renewing of our vows and covenants with God, I was fully satisfied in that condition, whether for life or death, having committed my soul in keeping to a faithful Mediator and Redeemer, hoping

for me to live is Christ and to die was gain; when I should exchange sorrow for joy, and death for life and immortality.

People in the sixteenth and seventeenth centuries were earthy and matter-of-fact about sex, childbirth, and body parts, and didn't know the censorship and reluctance to speak of them that came with the nineteenth-century Victorian era. Many of the four-letter words we were taught not to say lest we have our mouths washed with a bar of soap were commonly used though still considered vulgar.

For further information on midwifery and childbirth in the time of Anne Hutchinson, see this book's Appendix for the chapter on *Aristotle's Complete Master-Piece.*

Chapter 7

Here Comes Trouble

About three years ago we were all in peace. Mrs. Hutchinson from that time she came hath made a disturbance, and some that came over with her in the ship did inform me what she was as soon as she was landed.
                                                    –John Winthrop, Nov. 1637

Most of the thousands of English immigrants that came to New England in the 1630s did so because King Charles I had reissued his father's *Book of Sports,* which the Puritans believed commanded them to break the Sabbath (Sunday) to do secular activities, a sin against God. The ministers like Rev. John Cotton who refused to comply were forced to hide and then flee the country, which required finding a ship that wouldn't be stopped by officials. Were he and his pregnant second wife smuggled out of the country? Who arranged to pack the goods, food, building materials, and animals he'd require in the new Boston? Boston had been named after Cotton's city in Lincolnshire. In 1633, when he was on the run, he answered the call of Boston's leaders. Perhaps all was in readiness for his arrival. Twenty-year-old Edward Hutchinson accompanied him.

Anne and William Hutchinsons' daughter Susanna (the second of that name) was a newborn when they left Lincolnshire forever, went to London for a short time, then boarded the *Griffin* in July and began the perilous journey. The Hutchinson family, including siblings of both Anne and William, plus eleven Hutchinson children (Zuriel was not yet born), arrived in Boston on September 18, 1634.

Did they make the required loyalty statement to the King and Church of England to obtain their passports? Or, as a matter of conscience, did they find a way around it? They needed a letter of recommendation from their local minister, and they would have paid the license fees to be allowed to ship out of England. William was a wealthy man, and if he hadn't left by the end of 1634, he'd have paid a stiff tax to get out on top of the fares for passage.

The Hutchinsons and Scotts, though, with the aunts and uncles, the stair-step children and servants, would not have sneaked. They would have been a party of 20 to 30 – more than ten percent – of the 200 passengers.

And the *Griffin* wasn't a little pinnace that sneaked away from England. It was a 300-ton transport ship with at least three masts. It would have carried 20 or more cannons, powder, shot, and small arms, plus the trained sailors, to defend the ship if it were attacked by pirates. In its holds were food for the passage and for 18 months for each passenger, fodder for the animals, building materials, trade goods (William being a cloth merchant), household furniture and farm equipment, seeds, bundled fruit trees, and everything necessary to create a new life in a wilderness without stores and factories. It's possible that the passenger ship sailed in a flotilla with cargo-only ships, as well as smaller, fast ships to scout for pirates or hazards. Even so, 200 passengers plus 70 crew on a 300-ton ship would have been no pleasure cruise.

At least two Puritan ministers were aboard the *Griffin*: Mr. Lathrop and Zechariah Symmes. Mr. Symmes would be one of Anne's accusers, three years later, and their grandchildren would someday marry.

During the voyage of at least eight weeks, and perhaps longer, ships that carried ministers had one or two sermons every day, and those sermons were not 20- or 40-minute lectures. A Puritan minister worth his salt was just warming up at the hour mark. Symmes was known to preach for five hours. To us, who prefer a weekly 15- to 30-minute sermon, that sounds like an ordeal to be endured. To the immigrants without other forms of entertainment, it was desirable. The women could spin wool or sew clothes during the sermons unless it was the Sabbath.

Anne taught or preached to the women on the ship. It wasn't a sin or a crime to do so, but it was frowned on by the male preachers because obviously, God gave revelations to men, and women had weaker minds.

Symmes testified in 1637,

> I came along with her in the ship, and it so fell out that we were in the great cabin together, and therein did agree with the labours of Mr. Lathrop and myself, only there was a secret opposition to things delivered. The main thing that was then in hand was about evidencing of a good estate [he

probably meant Christian good works], and among the rest about that place in John [John 13:34-35, or 1 John 4:20-21] concerning the love of the brethren. That which I took notice of was the corruptness and narrowness of her opinions; which I doubt not I may call them so; but she said, when she came to Boston there would be something seen.

He couldn't pin it down, but he had a vague feeling that Anne was wrong.

Thomas Dudley was the governor in 1634, but John Winthrop continued as usual with his history journal. He didn't mention the Hutchinsons, but he did mention their ship on September 18:

At this court were many laws made against tobacco, and immodest fashions, and costly apparel, etc., as appears by the Records; and £600 were raised towards fortifications and other charges, which were the more hastened, because the *Griffin* and another ship now arriving with about two hundred passengers and one hundred cattle, (Mr. Lothrop and Mr. Symmes, two godly ministers, coming in the same ship,) there came over a copy of the commission granted to the two archbishops [of Scotland and Canterbury, both "favorites" of the King] and ten others of the council, to **regulate all plantations**, and power given them, or any five of them, **to call in all patents**, and make laws, to raise tithes and portions for ministers, **to remove and punish governors**, and to hear and determine all causes, and **inflict all punishments, even death itself.**

There were to be ships and troops to carry a new royally appointed governor-general to New England to enforce the orders. Losing their precious charter and losing control of the colonies and towns they'd planted could mean they'd lose their very freedom or lives and certainly their life savings and investment in building a new colony. The Church of England and its bishops they'd fled would supplant the Puritan society they'd built. It was the worst disaster possible, far worse than a woman teaching other female ship passengers.

A royal takeover was among the Bay's greatest fears. As long as they could keep their patent or charter on the American side of the

Atlantic, they could hold their elections and courts and assign jobs and grant real estate as they liked. With the charter in their possession, they could continue to work out their salvation in the reformed, "purified" Church of Christ rather than what they saw as a corrupt and worldly Church of England. They were very happy for the 3,000 miles of ocean separating them from the King and archbishops.

The English government demanded the return of the charter numerous times over the years. For several years, when the autumn General Court met, they debated complying with the order or using loopholes like "We don't have a quorum of the commissioners you require." What they decided every time was to ignore the demand, build defensive forts, stockpile the powder, muskets and cannon shot, and enlarge, equip, and drill the militia "train bands" up and down the coast.

But what Winthrop and Dudley couldn't know in 1634, when the *Griffin* came with the dread Laud Commission command to return the document and submit, was that only seven months later, in April 1635, "adversaries of this colony had built a great ship [300 tons or more] to send over the general governor, etc., which, being launched, fell in sunder in the midst."

The large warship disintegrated when it hit the water.

Winthrop wrote that the Commission had intended to divide the lands from Maryland to New England into twelve provinces with ten men each to run them for the governor general, "but the project took not effect. The Lord frustrated their design."

If King Charles hadn't been losing power, and the bishops arrested, imprisoned, and executed during the English Civil Wars of the 1640s, the American Revolution might have begun 140 years earlier. Certainly, Boston government built forts to defend their harbor against hostile ships of their own government.

Only six weeks after the Laud Commission orders came, the patriotic zeal was running high, and John Endecott, a violent hothead, cut the red St. Andrew cross out of the British flag, calling it a relic of popery, but insulting King and country. Not wanting the royal wrath to strike them with lightning, the colony apologized and privately disciplined Endecott.

This was the tempest that the Hutchinsons sailed into.

A descendant of John Endecott, Charles M. Endicott, wrote the *Memoir of John Endecott, First Governor of the Colony of Massachusetts Bay* in 1847. He said,

> None but the loftiest and purest motives could have induced our ancestors to struggle with the stern climate and sterile soil of New England. There was no gold mine, or "El Dorado" to allure them. No tropical luxuriance to supply their wants by the spontaneous productions of nature. They could promise themselves no exemption from toil and suffering. – "In the sweat of thy brow shall thou eat bread," was sure to be their portion on this side of the ocean. ... It is the pride of England to trace their ancestry back to the Norman Conquest, to the vassal Chiefs who followed in the train of the Conqueror. But New England traces her origin back to a far nobler conquest – that of principles over tyranny and oppression:
>
> > Among our sires no high born chief
> > Freckled his hand with peasant gore,
> > No spurred or coronetted thief
> > Set his mailed heel upon the floor;
> > No! we are come of nobler line,
> > With larger hearts within the breast,
> > Large hearts by suffering made divine –
> > We draw our lineage from the oppressed.

Anne and William settled their belongings into a house in the town, and organized the farm at Mt. Wollaston (modern Quincy). With a large party of adults who were related by blood or marriage, and a tribe of children from infant Susanna to the young adult Edward, they must have been highly organized to survive one another, let alone life in a small town 3,000 miles from civilization.

They immediately reunited with their friend of twenty years, John Cotton, and when they went to the meetinghouse a few steps from their home, they met former neighbors and relatives, business clients and people they'd known all their lives. With Sabbath services conducted by John Wilson on the first day, and the sermons of John Cotton on Thursday lecture day, they found a new but familiar rhythm in their lives.

This restaurant occupies the site (not the building) where the Hutchinson
Family lived in Boston from 1634-1638.
The building is nearly 300 years old.
David L. Royal, Boston Globe staff

The Congregational model of church membership admission was for the prospective member to be examined by deacons or elders presumably for orthodoxy to Puritan beliefs, who would listen to their testimony of their godly behavior and good works. The prospective member had to tell how and why God had shown them they were among the Elect. The candidates repeated their testimony to the wider church, which voted them in.

Rev. Cotton wrote about the questions put to prospective members of the church:

How it pleased God to work in them to bring them home to Christ? Whether the Law had convinced them of sin? How the Lord had won them to deny themselves and their own righteousness and to rely on the righteousness of Christ? Then they make a brief confession or else an answer to a few questions about the main fundamental points of religion.

Perhaps because of their high economic status, the Hutchinsons were examined by Rev. John Wilson, the senior minister of the First Church of Christ, and admitted to membership in October. William was admitted first, and Anne was allowed to join a week later, after some questions of her words and actions on the ship. Though Rev. Symmes tried to keep Anne from membership, Rev. Cotton vouched for her election to salvation.

Following the pastoral recommendation to be admitted as members, the candidates gave a public confession of their "Christian and sincere affections" to the congregation. They then made a covenant to give themselves wholly (and holy) to the Lord, and received the promise of the pastors to "walk towards you in all brotherly love and holy watchfulness to the mutual building up of one another in the fellowship of the Lord Jesus Christ."

The Records of the First Church in Boston

Joan Drake widdowe.
John Gayle servant to our brother John Button d.[2]
Marie Bonner maid servant to our teacher John Cotton.
Elizabeth Chambers maid servant to our brother Willyam Baulston.
Edward Hitchen a singleman.

The 10th of the same Moneth.

Robert Reynoldes shoomaker.
Edward Hutchinson the younger a singleman.
Dorcas French maid servant to our brother John Winthropp the Elder.

The 26th of the same Moneth.

Willyam Hutchinson merchant.
Beniamin Gillam shipcarpenter.

The 2d of the 9th Moneth 1634.

Anne Hutchinson the wife of our brother Willyam Hutchinson.
Allen Willey a husbandman.
Anne Dorryfall our brother Willyam Coddingtons maidservant.
Nathaniell Heaton mercer and Elizabeth his wife.

The 9th of the same nyneth Moneth 1634.

Thomas Wardall shoomaker.
Richard Hutchinson and Francis Hutchinson the sonnes of our brother Willyam Hutchinson.
Faith Hutchinson one of his daughters.
Anne Freiston one of his kinswomen.

The 6th of the seaventh Moneth 1635.

Willyam Wilson joyner and Patience his wife.

The 20th of the same Moneth.

Willyam Salter a shoomaker.

The 25th of the eight Moneth 1635.

Membership of Hutchinsons accepted in First Church in 1634:
Edward Hutchinson the younger a singleman, October 10
Willyam Hutchinson, merchant, October 26
Anne Hutchinson, wife of our brother Willyam Hutchinson, November 2
Richard and Francis Hutchinson the sonnes of our brother Willyam Hutchinson, November 9
Faith Hutchinson one of his daughters, November 9
Anne Freiston one of his kinswomen, November 9
(William Salter, who was accepted in 1635, later became the jailer of Boston, and applied the whip to prisoners like Katherine Marbury Scott.)

Shortly thereafter, John Wilson embarked on his second trip back to England. He would be gone for nearly a year. Ah, a blessed year when the Hutchinsons were spoiled by two sermons of John

Cotton every week, and Anne could hold meetings in her parlor twice a week: one meeting for women, and one for a mixed company.

Sixteen-thirty-five was a year when scores of ships brought thousands of settlers from England, including Henry Vane, and William and Mary Dyer. The people who came were young and fit and prosperous enough to be successful in trades and to have enough money to outfit themselves in business or on a farm. They had to have enough money to build houses and shops, have enough food supplies until the first crop came in, and to employ servants and possess a few domestic animals. And being young, the immigrants had growing families; the women were pregnant and needed skilled midwives.

Anne became pregnant herself in the summer of 1635, at age 44, with her last child, Zuriel. He or she (the name is masculine) was born and baptized the next March. The unusual name meant "my Rock is God."

It wasn't exactly the calm before the storm. Perhaps it was the quiet buildup of a massive cumulus cloud that was poised to roll off the mountain with a wall of dust and flying debris before the rain fell in torrents.

Chapter 8

The Sound of Trumpets and Drums

In the yeare 1636, the Angels of the several Churches of Christ in N. England sounding forth their silver Trumpets, heard ever and anon the jarring sound of rating Drums in their eares, striking up an alarum to the battell." *Wonder-working Providence*, by Edward Johnson, p. 142

The Thirty Years War, by Jonathan Meyer

"One Mrs. Hutchinson, a member of the church of Boston, a woman of a ready wit and bold spirit, brought over with her two dangerous errors: That the person of the Holy Ghost dwells in a justified person. That no sanctification can help to evidence to us our justification. – From these two grew many branches; as Our union with the Holy Ghost, so as a Christian remains dead to every spiritual action, and hath no gifts nor graces, other than such as are in hypocrites, nor any other sanctification but the Holy Ghost himself. There joined with her in these opinions a brother of hers, one Mr. Wheelwright, a silenced minister sometimes in England." John Winthrop, Sr., *Journal*, October 1636

But Governor Winthrop, remember that *many* of your Massachusetts Bay ministers (including John Cotton) had been silenced in England. Your government named your City Upon a Hill, Boston, after Cotton's Boston in Lincolnshire, to lure him and a large number of his admirers to New England.

In the 1870 book, *The Lives of John Wilson, John Norton, and John Davenport,* author Alexander Wilson M'Clure wrote many pages explaining that historians had hatefully treated his ancestor, John Wilson. They had raked through attics to find letters and journals to find dirt on the minister, but that John Wilson, though not perfect, didn't deserve the bigotry that had attached to his name by people who were religiously and politically polarized. M'Clure wrote,

> The Puritans were indeed remarkably decided in their ways: but they rejoiced in all new light, if it deserved the name, let it shine from what quarter it might. They expected no new revelations: but they did expect, like [the Pilgrim minister] John Robinson, that God would cause more light to break forth from his Word. Accordingly we find that there was scarcely any man of distinction among them but what, like Robinson, he changed his views upon important matters as he increased in years and knowledge.

Rev. John Robinson, 1575-1525 (my ancestor), was an author and theology professor at the University of Leiden after he and William Brewster and the rest of the Pilgrims escaped England in 1609. His farewell to the Mayflower Pilgrims when they sailed to America admonished them to show loving-kindness and grace to the "strangers" or unbelievers in their company, to thereby draw them to God. In other words, preach with their lives, not their words. Robinson was so beloved by the Pilgrims that 40 years later, when his son Isaac became a Quaker sympathizer and then a Quaker, Isaac was not fined or whipped like other men in Plymouth Colony.

If M'Clure was saying that his Wilson ancestor mellowed over the years, and found a way to be popular for his graceful words and acts – that's not how it played out. Wilson was vindictive and sarcastic at the hanging executions of the four Quakers in Boston, including Mary Dyer, from 1659 to 1661. It was he who egged the courts to execute women for believing they'd seen the ghost of their dead child, or who were accused of witchcraft. John Wilson was a warrior in court, in church councils, and in actual warfare, when he was the minister who accompanied the militia to the gruesome Pequot slaughters. Though it might have seemed inconceivable a few years back, we have witnessed the rise of rigid, dangerous authoritarianism in governments and religions around the planet. People just don't change.

Mrs. Hutchinson had enjoyed ten to twelve months, from late 1634 to about August 1635, without the presence of Pastor John Wilson. He'd sailed back as far as the coast of Ireland when part of the convoy of ships had wrecked on the Irish coast. Winthrop's son, John Jr., was one of those traveling with Wilson. They landed safely and made use of their time in Northern Ireland (the part colonized by English, not the Catholic majority) to preach and encourage other reformed Separatists to keep the faith.

Most of the ministers of the colony shared the same doctrines for which they'd risked life and family and property so recently. They believed to their very core. Cotton and Wilson believed similarly and were compatible partners in the Boston First Church of Christ. Wilson seems to have been more judgmental and focused on rooting out sin, not only for the sake of the individual sinner, but for the spiritual health of the entire community. From his participation in the Pequot War massacre, we in the twenty-first century see that he was not particularly soft hearted or full of grace. He'd sailed back to England to bring his wife safely to Boston, but she refused to come to the dangerous wilderness. Wilson tried again in 1637 and was successful. But was Mary Wilson frightened of inclement conditions, or did she prefer living apart from her husband?

Cotton has been billed as a people-person who focused not on God's retribution but upon God's desire to save the one who would keep the letter and the spirit of the godly law. Other research suggests that Cotton was a scholar and theologian who wanted only to be left alone to read and write sermons and books and resented interruptions to minister to the needs of his congregation.

Anne Hutchinson, perhaps from a feminine perspective, sensed the humanist or softer side of salvation that Cotton taught.

But Anne wasn't alone in her views, nor was she the first to promote criticism of most of the ministers. First, there was her husband's brother-in-law, Rev. John Wheelwright. He was a Lincolnshire man who had followed Cotton's theology and developed his own interpretations. Once in Massachusetts, he sought the job of starting a church at Mt. Wollaston (modern Quincy). After his January 1637 sermon at Boston First Church, which was received with excitement by many fine Puritans and horror by others, there was consternation on the part of the government which tried him for sedition. More than 60 prominent young men signed a document called a Remonstrance declaring the innocence of Rev. Wheelwright. (For more on the Remonstrance that blew up in unexpected fashion, see this book's Appendix.)

At that point, the Antinomian Controversy, which started as a women's meeting in the Hutchinson parlor but began to admit men – and women were *not* to teach men – became a battle between theocracy and democracy with words used as musket balls.

Keep in mind that the Puritans didn't call themselves that pejorative name, calling themselves instead the elect or the godly; and Anne didn't consider herself Antinomian, just a dissenter to the dissidents. But for writer and readers, we'll continue with those labels.

To further polarize the Massachusetts colonists, the government was intentionally set up as a theocracy. The "City Upon a Hill" was meant to be the New Jerusalem where Jesus would return to reign on a purified earth and burn the ungodly in a lake of fire. The government melded with its ministers in an authoritarian, rigid society. Church attendance and tithe-paying were required of all community members even if they weren't admitted to church membership. Ministers were paid from the town coffers which meant that they were considered officials.

Ministers who measured up as Puritan reformers were appointed to churches around Massachusetts Bay. If they were too closely aligned with the Church of England, they were dismissed and sent back to England or out to the wilds of York, Maine. Puritan ministers were to interpret God's commands and ensure (or perhaps enforce) that their flock could be presented holy and spotless in the Day of the Lord. To that end, people were expected to report the moral offenses of their neighbors and could drop in on households to test the children on their catechism responses.

> The Puritans insisted that church membership be restricted to the elect, but they sought to dominate the entire population, the whole of life and society, to create a theocracy in which both civil and church leaders, working together, did God's will. Emerson, Everett. *Puritanism in America 1620-1750*. G.K. Hall & Co., 1977.

Rev. John Cotton wrote that:

...the political-religious model for the Massachusetts commonwealth was Israel... [God's] laws were as applicable to Massachusetts as to Israel, "because God, who was then bound up in covenant with them [the Hebrews] to be their God, hath put us in their stead."

Emerson, Everett. *Puritanism in America 1620-1750*. G.K. Hall & Co., 1977.

The meetinghouses, without heat or any comforts but backless benches, were places for public repentance – often with tears – and obedience, as well as community discipline and teaching.

Historians and theologians have spent 370 years trying to understand what the problem was with the Covenant of Works and Covenant of Grace by parsing the words of Massachusetts Bay's ministers and teachers and of John Wheelwright and Anne Hutchinson. They've argued the semantics of the controversy, but don't see much difference between the two camps because both sides claimed that salvation was of faith, not works. The difference was that the "works" people said that evidence of salvation was a changed life of obedience and good works; the "grace" people were hardly flagrant law-breakers but rather believed that God desires our salvation and graciously forgives sin.

Rev. Shepard of Cambridge, one of Anne Hutchinson's primary inquisitors, preached that a minister's role was to bring his flock into unity in a perfect, sinless state because only a perfect man was worthy of the gift of salvation. "No man can stand before God but by perfect holiness, but by doing whatever the Law requires."

It appears to me from reading John Winthrop's books and Anne's trial transcript that it's an issue I've seen in my own lifetime in Christian schools, universities, and churches. Beside the use of words like "justification" (God miraculously and gracefully declaring us righteous in his sight even when we know we've sinned) and "sanctification," (God directing our lives and making us holy over a period of time), there are the Old and New Covenants, the Old Testament law given to the Hebrews at Mt. Sinai, and the New Testament freedom from the law (but how much of the law – part of it, or all of it?), and the belief that Christ (or the Holy Spirit) dwells in believers' hearts – or we're always on trial before a harsh, judgmental God.

Time and again in John Cotton's correspondence with other ministers, and in the Hutchinson trial records, I recognized the controversies I grew up with in churches and denominational schools: the horror of "free grace" not being free, because it was bought with a price – the blood of Christ. "Our kind" (the godly remnant kind who scrupulously examined ourselves for that one unconfessed sin that could keep us out of heaven) did not mix with the people who believed that once-saved-always-saved free grace stuff. If one were assured of their salvation, what would stop them from breaking moral and civil laws and living it up (while we remained soberly miserable and afraid of hell because it was impossible to be perfect)?

One had to study the Bible and church doctrines carefully to extract and memorize proof texts and theological concepts like imputed and imparted righteousness, the significance of the heavenly temple imagery, the 2,700-year-old prophecies that would be fulfilled in our lifetimes, and especially, what constituted proper behavior in every area of our lives, including dress, education, health and foods, keeping the Sabbath holy, sexual mores, and much more. The worship experience must be sedate, letting "all things be done decently and in order" and never contain emotionalism. Like the early Puritans, we studied Protestant martyrology and miracles because we expected to go through a Time of Trouble and persecution before the second coming of Christ.

The zealous Puritan/Congregational legalism has remained alive for 400 years in some denominations.

Perhaps I oversimplified the controversy in my book, *Mary Dyer Illuminated*, knowing that my readers were there for a story, not for a sermon. But when boiled down, I suspect Anne got her theology from the New Testament book of Hebrews, which is a book written by a Jew (perhaps Barnabas or another close follower of the Apostle Paul) to Jewish Christians. The persecuted Puritans of New England saw themselves as a chosen people, the spiritual sons of Abraham, so the Old Testament – including the Ten Commandments and many of the ceremonial and sanitation laws – was their guide.

On one hand, there were the Calvinists clinging to their roadmap to salvation by trying to be perfect, and failing, and knowing that no matter how hard they tried to be good, it would never be good enough for an angry, vengeful God. On the other hand, there was love and grace to forgive one's sin and not condemn the sinner to hell and a God who was eager to save you.

The author of Hebrews was showing them from first statement to last, that in *former* times, they'd been given laws and God's communications through Moses and prophets, *but now* Jesus is our only mediator...

They'd been given the seventh day of the week as a rest day, *but now* Christ embodied the Sabbath rest and peace of salvation every day, all day, especially today...

They'd had a high priest and sacrifices and a temple built by human hands in a place that could be visited, *but now* they had Christ on their side, with access to the very presence of God...

They'd had commandments written on stone tablets, *but now* they had the Holy Spirit teaching and prompting from within...

And the "but now" all pointed to the gift of Jesus Christ, who was both God in heaven and God within our minds and hearts (intellect and emotions).

In Hebrews, which follows a chiastic form like a Hebrew psalm, there are similar passages at front and back of the book, pointing to the middle and most important message, which is that the New Covenant promised in the book of Jeremiah has now been sealed and activated by Jesus at the Last Supper and the next day when he died on the cross.

What is the New Covenant? It's found in Hebrews 8:10-12: For this is the covenant that I will make with the house of Israel after those days, saith the Lord: I will put My laws into their minds and write them in their hearts, and I will be to them a God, and they shall be to Me a people. And they shall not teach every man his neighbor and every man his brother, saying, 'Know the Lord,' for all shall know Me, from the least to the greatest. For I will be merciful to their unrighteousness, and their sins and their iniquities will I remember no more.

A loosey-goosey Covenant of Grace seemed to the Puritan mind to bash their law-and-order foundation of government. How do you codify behavior and punishment for a godly society when the offender can claim that he wasn't subject to the Ten Commandments and he got his law from what his conscience told him? And that because God had forgiven and forgotten his sins, the authorities ought to, also. Talk about trumpets and drums and alarms!

Antinomian means "against the *nomos* (whole law)." That meant not only the dietary and temple regulations, the clean and unclean, and family and societal relationships, but even the Ten Commandments. All were "nailed to the cross," made null by Jesus' death, said Antinomian wisdom, and replaced by the loving instruction of the quiet voice of the Holy Spirit.

"Oh, no, they weren't!" cried the fundamentalist Puritans. "God's words and God's law stand forever! God never changes; he said so himself."

That's the "controversy" part. And remember, they were a black-and-white, polarized culture. There was no middle ground when one's salvation was at stake.

Along with this indwelling relationship of God's spirit and human intellect came personal revelations (according to Hebrews), and Anne, her protégé Mary Dyer, and many others of their company felt the stirring of their hearts and minds with messages from God. This was another rub, because to the Puritan, God revealed his will only to the elect, the pure in heart who were obedient to God's laws and who could discern that will as it corresponded with scripture. And that meant only to men. God, they firmly believed, did not deign to impart his will to women.

Rev. Thomas Hooker, formerly of New Town/Cambridge, then senior minister of Hartford, Connecticut, had many revelations from God, but because he was a trained minister – especially because he was a man – he had the authority Anne Hutchinson claimed came from God. Hooker developed an extreme theology of salvation and conversion that provided a checklist by which to judge one's progress through sanctification. There was no assurance that God would accept a person's virtuous acts (good works to others) as worthy, and no one was without sin, so people lived in terror that they would burn in hell for eternity.

Rev. Cotton argued that worthy acts did not prove that one was saved or deserved membership – that it was faith in God's mercy and grace. This was to get him in deep trouble with the rest of the ministers from early 1637 to spring 1638.

Edward Johnson, in *Wonder Working Providence*, wrote that the Antinomians began to tell people privately, in a sneaky way, that most, if not all the ministers among them preached a Covenant of

Works, and laid a foundation "as near the truth as possible, the easier to deceive." Johnson went on:

> These Sectaries had many pretty knacks to delude withal, and especially to please the Female Sex, they told of rare Revelations of things to come from the spirit (as they say); it was only devised to weaken the Word of the Lord in the mouth of his Ministers, and withal to put both ignorant and unlettered Men and Women, in a posture of Preaching to a multitude, that they might be praised for their able Tongue. Come along with me, says one of them [Gov. Henry Vane], I'll bring you to a Woman [Anne Hutchinson] that Preaches better Gospel then any of your black-coats that have been at the Ninneversity, a Woman of another kind of spirit, who hath had many Revelations of things to come, and for my part, saith he, I had rather hear such a one that speaks from the mere motion of the spirit, without any study at all, than any of your learned Scholars, although they may be fuller of Scripture (I say) and admit they may speak by the help of the spirit, yet the other goes beyond them. Gentle Reader, think not these things feigned, because I name not the parties, or that here is no witnesse to prove them..."
>
> Edward Johnson, *Wonder Working Providence*, p. 127.

> The weaker Sex prevailed so far, that they set up a Priest [Anne Hutchinson] of their own Profession and Sex, who was much thronged after, abominably wresting the Scriptures to their own destruction: this Master-piece of Womens wit, drew many Disciples after her, and to that end boldly insinuated herself into the favour of none of the meanest, being also back with the Sorcery of a second [Jane Hawkins, the midwife], who had much converse with the Devil by her own confession, and did, to the admiration of those that heard her utter many speeches in the Latin Tongue, as it were in a trance. This Woman [Hawkins] was wonted to give drinks to other Women to cause them to conceive, how they wrought I know not, but sure there were Monsters borne [by Mary Dyer and Anne Hutchinson] not long after, as you shall hear in the following History.
>
> Edward Johnson, *Wonder Working Providence*, p. 132.

As I've mentioned, people of the seventeenth century were, by our standards, hyper-religious. How was a person to know if he or she was saved? They considered their earthly existence was a drop in the ocean when compared to eternity in heaven or hell, and they should use their lives to ensure that God noticed their willpower in rejecting sin, and living a holy life (sanctification, the "work of a lifetime") to prove that they were worthy of their election, their predestination to salvation.

What were the qualifications for membership in the church, the only place where one could take Communion and enter that mystical union of God and the human soul; and where one was confirmed by the Christian community as a freeman who could vote, serve on a jury, or be elected to office?

In the 1630s, the Puritan Congregational churches of New England admitted members after an examination by pastors and teachers. They wanted to know the evidence for the applicant's call by God, and what were the fruits of his or her Christian experience. There was probably a review of a catechism, too.

Women were subordinate to their husbands and the men of their church and community. Further, they were subordinate to the government of the colony, who were their spiritual "parents." Anne Hutchinson preached to a mixed crowd of men and women. When she spoke up to the government, she was accused of breaking the fifth Commandment to honor her father(s).

The colonial government became so rigid in granting membership that people resorted to killing their babies or themselves to prevent their children from a hopeless existence before going to hell. They resembled modern people who cut themselves or develop deadly eating disorders in order to feel physical pain and confirm that they exist.

Hutchinson and her followers believed that the divine covenant of forgiveness and reconciliation (grace) could not be earned by legalistic works even if they were good works. Most of the ministers in Massachusetts Bay preached a law-and-order, hierarchical false gospel, the Covenant of Works. Keep the Sabbath perfectly holy before God, obey your parents and by extension your church and government officials, don't steal or lie or cheat on your spouse, don't covet your neighbor's possessions. A holy outward life would be evidence of sanctification of the spirit.

In 1635-36, after he'd acted as chaplain of the militias that destroyed the Pequot Indians in Connecticut, Rev. John Wilson, senior pastor of Boston First Church, went back to England for almost a year. During his absence, Rev. John Cotton, architect of the Covenant of Grace that Anne Hutchinson had studied for 22 years, was pastor and teacher of the church. When he went to another town to preach, he invited ministers from other towns as pulpit guests. That's how Rev. John Wheelwright, William Hutchinson's brother-in-law, was invited to speak in Boston.

As Anne Hutchinson and Rev. Wheelwright saw it, the ministers of the colony were creating a new orthodoxy, one that was based in trying to earn salvation, and was uninspired and needed to evolve toward the light. As the book of Hebrews said, the Old Covenant of Works of trying to keep the Sinai laws, was null and void. The New Covenant of Grace (the gift of forgiveness, intimacy with God, and salvation) was now in effect, but the Puritan churches were living in darkness.

The "orthodox" ministers were now painted as legalists, and the congregations were questioning their authority to teach and judge civil matters. The ministers, along with Gov. Winthrop and Gov. Dudley, could not tolerate dissension and chaos because it could break the delicate balance between the colonial authority and the royal sovereignty back in England. They were determined to keep an appearance of lawful peace and harmony. They responded to the dissenters with the labels of antinomian, libertine, and familist, the latter being a European sect that held plural marriage or "free love," and lived in a commune. (One might draw a modern parallel with fundamentalist Christians calling out liberals as communists, socialists, and baby-killers.)

As 1636 drew to a freezing close, ministers of the Massachusetts Bay Colony grilled Rev. Cotton on his grace teachings. In the absence of John Wilson, Rev. Wheelwright was allowed to preach at Boston First. The church members and guests liked his teaching on grace alone instead of grace plus works. But even with Wilson far away in England, the repercussions sounded loudly in the ears of John Winthrop and the ministers of other towns who were afraid that the evil would spread to their own churches.

Women were not allowed to speak or ask questions in church, so Anne Hutchinson's parlor meetings were growing, and now admitting men. The government, represented by John Winthrop and others, feared the growth of a political movement that would rival or overtake theirs. The ministers saw the theological differences, and felt the heat of the Hutchinson and Wheelwright party's criticism. The key person in the controversy seemed to be Rev. Cotton himself!

Wheelwright supporters had become a powerful political faction that must be put down by the orthodox Puritan government of Massachusetts Bay. At least 60 men, most of them freemen who voted or served on juries and who were members of the church, had refused to financially support the Pequot War, and had insulted Rev. John Wilson by not participating in the war or bothering to send him off with their greetings. Sixty percent of the members of the First Church supported Anne Hutchinson, and that, to Winthrop and his government, was anarchy.

Governor Winthrop wrote about the offenses of the men who were defying the authority of the church and state:

> It is come also into Civil and public Affairs, and hath bred great Disturbance there, as appeared in the late Expedition against the Pequids; for whereas in former Expeditions the Town of Boston was as forward as any others to send of their choice Members, and a greater number the other Towns, in the time of the former Governor [Henry Vane], now in this last service they sent not a Member, but one or two whom they cared not to be rid of, and but a few others, and those of the most refuse sort, and that in such a careless manner, as gave great discouragement to the Service, not one man of that side accompanying their Pastor [John Wilson, chaplain of the expedition], when he was sent by the joint consent of the Court, and all the Elders upon that Expedition, not so much as bidding him farewell; what was the reason of this difference?
>
> Why, nothing but this, Mr. Wheelwright had taught them that the former Governor [Vane], and some of the Magistrates then were friends of Christ and Free-Grace, but the present [Winthrop and assistants] were Enemies, &c. Antichrists, Persecutors.

Gov. John Winthrop, in his *Journal*

John Winthrop wrote in the last entry in his personal journal *Experiencia* that the church was in trouble, but God had refreshed him.

> Upon some differences in or Church about the way of the Spirit of God in the work of Justification, myself dissenting from the rest of the brethren, I had occasion to examine mine own estate, wherein the Lord wrought marvelously upon my heart, reviving my former peace & consolation with much increase & better assurance than formerly; & in the midst of it (for it continued many days) he did one time dart a beam of wrath into my soul, which struck me to the heart, but then the Lord Jesus shewed himself & stood between that wrath & my soul. Oh how sweet was Christ then to my soul. I thought I never prized him before, I am sure never more, nor ever felt more need of him. Then I kept him close to my heart & could not parte with him. Oh how my heart opened to let him in. Oh how was I ravished with his love! my prayers could breathe nothing but Christ & Love & mercy, which continued with melting & tears night & day.

To set it in a time frame, the churches had called another theological convocation or synod to refute Anne Hutchinson's teachings, hammer out their creed and set it in stone. Mary Dyer was in her fifth month of pregnancy with the anencephalic "monster," Anne had a year-old boy, Zuriel, to wean, Gov. Henry Vane had sailed back to England only a few weeks before, the men who had signed the Wheelwright Remonstrance the previous March strongly suspected they'd have to find a new home and were looking at land in New Hampshire to the north and Aquidneck Island (future Rhode Island) to the south, and may have asked John Cotton and Henry Vane to be their religious and civil leaders. (Vane had roomed in the Cotton home for two years, and they were friendly. He'd been part of the Hutchinsonians. He'd lost the reelection bid in May. And between May and July, he'd visited Roger Williams in Providence, possibly with some of the Hutchinsonians and Rev. Cotton. But very suddenly, Vane had taken ship in the first days of August, and if there had been an escape plan, it now had to change.)

John Wilson returned to Boston in late August or September 1637, and that's when the Antinomian Controversy, which had been simmering for months, began to boil hard.

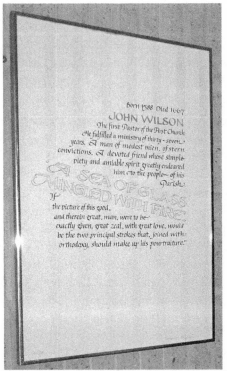

The calligraphic art at what used to be Boston First Church of Christ, and is now a Universalist Unitarian church. Co-founders of the church are memorialized with framed calligraphy at the rear of the sanctuary. This one is on John Wilson, its first preacher.

"John Wilson, The first Pastor of the First Church. He fulfilled a ministry of thirty-seven years. A man of modest mien, of stern convictions, A devoted friend whose simple piety and amiable spirit greatly endeared him to the people of his Parish.
A Sea of Glass Mingled With Fire:
If the picture of this good, and therein great, man were to be exactly given, great zeal, with great love, would be the two principal strokes that, joined with orthodoxy, should make up his portraiture."

Chapter 9

Evangelical Before Their Time

The Puritans of Massachusetts Bay Colony, as with the other colonies of New England, considered themselves a "purifying" sect of the Church of England, ridding the church of its Catholic past and its rituals. Their ministers and teachers had been severely persecuted, and had risked their own and their families' lives, their fortunes large and small, to leave the heritage of centuries and start a new society in the American wilderness. They felt entitled to govern the way they believed. They were zealots. Fundamentalists. Rather unmerciful in their treatment of society's disadvantaged. More Puritan than Puritans in their homeland because of that commitment of their very lives. Enlightened religion, which was still about 150 years in the future, emphasizes the intellect.

But Puritans were far from being evangelical (the Greek root means "good message") with its origins in grace (the Latin root means "gift"). Evangelical religion, also in the distant future, writes religious historian Garry Wills, placed the emphasis on the heart.

The Hutchinsons and everyone they knew in Massachusetts had come over with the same beliefs and the same interest in being part of the New Jerusalem. So what changed? What made them change their minds and hearts? How did the Hutchinson Bible study grow from a women's group to a mixed-gender group of 80 or 100 meeting in their parlor?

Perhaps one reason was what Anne Hutchinson said during her trial about not seeking a theological construct, but seeking Christ. There are always some people who enjoy digging deep into technical explanations, but others prefer the relationship experience.

> Here is a great stir about graces and looking to hearts, but give me Christ. I seek not for graces, but for Christ. I seek not for sanctification, but for Christ. Tell not me of meditation and duties, but tell me of Christ.

Rev. Thomas Weld, one of Anne's chief inquisitors, wrote a long introduction to Gov. John Winthrop's book about the religious controversy in the colony, and published the book in 1644 in London with no byline for Winthrop or himself. Weld described the heresies, the sensational "monsters" of Mary Dyer and Anne Hutchinson, and with crocodile tears pouring from his eyes, the "lamentable" death of Anne and part of her family.

Rev. Weld, though, gave us an idea of how the Covenant of Grace spread through Boston and surrounding towns. Through his accusations, we can discern what Anne Hutchinson was sowing in the field. Notice how Weld subtly uses the words "seduce," "conceive" and "laboring," knowing that Anne attended many childbirths and used the hours or days to teach and influence the women of Boston – and then their husbands.

> Now these, most of them, being so gross, one would wonder how they should spread so fast and suddenly amongst a people so religious and well taught.
>
> For declaring of this be pleased to attend two things.
>
> The nature of the Opinions themselves, which open such a fair and easy way to Heaven, that men may pass without difficulty. For, if a man need not be troubled by the Law, before Faith, but may step to Christ so easily; and then if his faith be no going out of himself to take Christ, but only a discerning that Christ is his own already, and is only an act of the Spirit upon him, no act of his own done by him; and if he, for his part, must see nothing in himself, have nothing, do nothing, only he is to stand still and wait for Christ to do all for him. And then if after faith, the Law no rule to walk by, no Sorrow or Repentance for sin; he must not be pressed to duties, and need never pray, unless moved by the Spirit: And if he falls into sin, he is never the more disliked of God, nor his condition never the worse. And for his assurance, it being given him by the Spirit, he must never let it go, but abide in the height of comfort, tho' he falls into the grossest sins that he can. Then their way to life was made easy, if so, no marvel so many like of it.

That same doctrine of forgiveness and salvation, freely given by God, is what grew the Christian faith from a few thousand believers at Calvary to a world movement. That's what you find in the New Testament's gospels and epistles. But it was antithetical to the Puritan zealots who clung to the Old Testament law, which the apostle Paul termed the Law of Sin and Death.

To assign the best of intentions to the theocratic leaders, they held a sacred calling and responsibility to keep their flock safe from Satan. On the negative side, it's easier to control people by fear than with kindness and perceived weakness. We see this today in political attack ads. If you whip up fear and uncertainty, and pledge to protect, that's where donations and votes come from.

But the actions of the "grace" party puts one in mind of Matthew 4:16 (1599 Geneva version): "The people which sat in darkness, saw great light: and to them which sat in the region and shadow of death, light is risen up."

Weld continued.

And this is the very reason, besides the novelty of it, that this kind of Doctrine takes so well, that you see so many dance after this pipe, running after such and such, crowding the Churches and filling the doors and windows, even such carnal and vile persons (many of them) as care not to hear any other godly Ministers, but only their Leaders. Oh it pleaseth nature well to have Heaven and their lusts too.

Consider their slights they used in fomenting their Opinions, some of which I will set down: as

They laboured much to acquaint themselves with as many, as possibly they could, that so they might have the better opportunity to communicate their new light unto them.

Being once acquainted with them, they would strangely labour to insinuate themselves into their affections, by loving salutes, humble carriage, kind invitements, friendly visits, and so they would win upon men, and steal into their bosoms

before they were aware. Yea, as soon as any new-comers (especially, men of note, worth and activity, fit instruments to advance their design) were landed, they would be sure to welcome them, shew them all courtesie, and offer them room in their own houses, or of some of their own Sect, and having gotten them into their Web, they could easily poison them by degrees; It was rare for any man thus hooked in, to escape their Leaven [sin].

Why, Rev. Weld, that sounds positively horrible! Imagine treating others kindly, humbly, and in a courteous, hospitable manner, and giving them room in your own house when they've been crossing the stormy Atlantic Ocean for 10 weeks and have no home built yet. And for those new immigrant brethren to be grateful for such godly treatment – terrible!

(Because such men as would seduce others, had need be some way eminent) they would appear very humble, holy, and spiritual Christians, and full of Christ; they would deny themselves farre, speak excellently, pray with such soul-ravishing expressions and affections, that a stranger that loved goodness, could not but love and admire them, and so be the more easily drawn after them; looking upon them as men and women as likely to know the secrets of Christ, and bosom-counsels of his Spirits, as any other.

And this Opinion of them was the more lifted up through the simplicity and weakness of their followers, who would, in admiration of them, tell others, that since the Apostles time, they were persuaded, none ever received so much light from God, as such and such had done, naming their Leaders.

As they would lift up themselves, so also their Opinions, by gilding them over with specious terms of Free-grace, Glorious-light, Gospel-truths, as holding forth naked [pure and unadulterated] Christ: and this took much with simple honest hearts that loved Christ, especially with new converts, who were lately in bondage under sin and wrath, and had newly tasted the sweetness of free-grace; being now in their first love to Christ, they were exceeding glad to embrace any thing, that might further advance Christ and free grace; and so drank them in readily.

If they met with Christians that were full of doubts and fears about their conditions, (as many tender and godly hearts there were) they would tell them they had never taken a right course for comfort, but had gone on (as they were led) in a legal way of evidencing their good estate by Sanctification, and gazing after qualifications in themselves, and would shew them from their own experience, that themselves for a long time, were befool'd even as they are now, in poring upon graces in themselves, and while they did so they never prospered; but were driven to pull all that building down, and lay better and safer foundations in free-grace; and then would tell them of this Gospel-way we speak of, how they might come to such a settled peace that they might never doubt more, tho' they should see no grace at all in themselves: & so (as it is said of the Harlots dealing with the young man, Prov. 7.21.) with much fair speech they caused them to yield, with the flattering of their lips they forced them.

They commonly labour'd to work first upon women, being (as they conceived) the weaker to resist; the more flexible, tender, and ready to yield: and if once they could wind in them, they hoped by them, as by an Eve, to catch their Husbands also, which indeed often proved too true amongst us there.

As soon as they had thus wrought in themselves, and a good conceit of their Opinions, by all these ways of subtilty, into the hearts of people; nextly, they strongly endeavour'd with all the craft they could, to undermine the good Opinion of their Ministers, and their Doctrine, and to work them clean out of their affections, telling them they were sorry that their Teachers had so misled them, and train'd them up under a Covenant of works, and that themselves never having been taught of God, it is no wonder they did no better teach them the Truth, and how they may sit till dooms-day under their legal Sermons, and never see light; and withal sometimes casting aspersions on their persons, and practice, as well as their doctrine, to bring them quite out of esteem with them. And this they did so effectually, that many declined the hearing of them, tho' they were members of their Churches, and others that did hear, were so filled with prejudice that they profited not, but studied how to object against them, and censure their doctrine, which (whilst they stood right) were wont to make their hearts to melt and tremble. ...

But the last and worst of all, which most suddenly diffused the Venom of these Opinions into the very Veins and Vitals of the People in the Country, was Mistress Hutchinson's double weekly lecture, which she kept under a pretence of repeating Sermons, to which resorted sundry of Boston, and other Towns about, to the number of fifty, sixty, or eighty at once; where after she had repeated the Sermon, she would make her comment upon it, vent her mischievous Opinions as she pleased, and wreathed the Scriptures to her own purpose; where the custom was for her Scholars to propound questions, and she (gravely sitting in the chair) did make answers thereunto. The great respect she had at first in the hearts of all, and her profitable and sober carriage of matters, for a time, made this her practice less suspected by the godly magistrates, and Elders of the Church there, so that it was winked at for a time, (though afterward reproved by the Assembly, and called into Court but it held so long, until she had spread her leaven so far, that had not providence prevented, it had proved the Canker of our Peace, and ruine of our Comforts.

By all these means and cunning slights they used, it came about that those Errors were so soon conveyed, before we were aware, not only into the Church of Boston, where most of these seducers lived, but also into almost all the parts of the Country round about.

Introduction by Thomas Weld, to book written by John Winthrop, *Short Story of the Rise, Reign and Ruin of the Antinomians, Familists and Libertines that Infected the Churches of New England.* London, 1644.

So, to summarize, Rev. Weld observed Hutchinsonian followers, who, because of their beliefs gained from Anne's sober and wise lectures, practiced being compassionate, kind, merciful, friendly, courteous, welcoming, hospitable, and Christlike. It sounds like they felt assured of their eternal salvation and therefore had joy and peace and weren't embarrassed to share the "good message."

Chapter 10

John Cotton, Patriarch of Massachusetts Theocracy

I f I were to attempt sketching an outline of Rev. John Cotton's life, it would overwhelm the rest of the chapters. There are many books and websites in which to discover important aspects of Cotton, so I'll speak chiefly on the ways he influenced and interacted with Anne Hutchinson.

John Cotton, the second of four children of a lawyer and his wife, was born in 1685 in Derby, in the Midlands of England. He attended grammar school at the Derby School and matriculated at Trinity College, Cambridge University, at age 13. Five years later, he received his Bachelor of Arts degree and began to study for his Masters at Emmanuel College, Cambridge. In 1606, he received his M.A., but continued to study for a Bachelor of Divinity while he worked as a dean and teacher of undergraduates. He was ordained as a deacon and a priest of the Church of England in 1610, and in 1612 was appointed vicar of the huge parish church of St. Botolph in Boston, Lincolnshire.

He married Elizabeth Horrocks in 1613, and it was a life-changing event. As written by his grandson, Cotton Mather, his friend recommended a "pious gentlewoman," the sister of a famous minister in Lancashire,

> to become his consort in a married estate. And it was remarkable that on the very day of his wedding to that eminently virtuous gentlewoman, he first received the assurance of God's love unto his own soul, by the spirit of God, effectually applying his promise of eternal grace and life unto him, which happily kept with him all the rest of his days: for which cause he would afterwards say, 'God made that day, a day of double marriage to me!' The wife, which by the favour of God he had now found, was a very great help unto him, in the service of God; but especially upon this, among many other accounts, that the people of her own sex, observing her more than ordinary discretion, gravity and holiness, [perhaps this included Anne Marbury Hutchinson, who lived in Alford] would still improve the freedom of their

address unto her, to acquaint her with the exercises of their own spirits; who, acquainting her husband with convenient intimations thereof, occasioned him in his publick ministry more particularly and profitably to discourse those things that were everlasting benefit.

Mather quoted by Barry A. Cotton, http://cottondescendants.com/revjohn.html

As Rev. Cotton was known to study for 12 hours each day, he may have relied on Elizabeth Cotton and other women like Anne Hutchinson for reaching the women and children of his congregation, and his assistant pastors to serve the needs of his parishioners when it came to counseling or comforting.

Because the Bishop of Lincoln, John Williams, favored him, Cotton was able to flourish at St. Botolph's Church despite his nonconformity to the requirements of the Church of England. Another Puritan, Samuel Ward at nearby Ipswich, commented, "Of all men in the world I envy Mr. Cotton, of Boston, most; for he doth nothing in any way of conformity, and yet hath his liberty, and I do everything that way, and cannot enjoy mine." Emerson, Everett, *John Cotton*, revised edition, G.K. Hall & Co. 1990.

During the years of Cotton's ministry in old Boston, Anne and William Hutchinson would have made the 20-mile journey from Alford in good weather, to listen to and learn from Cotton. One wonders if they stayed with friends and relatives, if they had a house there in town, and if they brought their children or friends with them.

John and Elizabeth Cotton had no children during their 18 years of marriage. After giving the farewell sermon to the Winthrop Fleet in March 1630, the Cottons returned to the humid fens of East Anglia and Lincolnshire, and were struck down by malaria, which Elizabeth did not survive.

This was also a plague year in England. The population had recently topped five million souls, but the bubonic plague outbreaks of 1625 and 1630 carried away around 450,000 people, including two of the Hutchinson daughters. Surely many members of St. Botolph's parish would have been similarly afflicted, and they believed that the end of time was at hand with plagues, a daytime comet in May 1630, and religious wars on the Continent.

Cotton's pulpit at St. Botolph's would have been filled by less-Puritan and more-orthodox preachers while he was absent for a year, recuperating from his brush with death. During that time, King

Charles I republished his father's booklet, *The Book of Sports*, which, as previously mentioned, commanded that the Puritan members of the Church of England break their holy Sabbath and play games, dance, and have a pleasant afternoon of physical recreation. Breaking the Sabbath meant disobedience to God, and that meant one could not be saved.

In addition, Bishop Laud and his faction were actively hunting Puritan ministers and imprisoning them. English Puritans charged Bishop Laud with subverting established religion, setting up papacy-like superstition, using his power to silence and suspend good men from their pulpits, and installing corrupt ministers in their place.

Cotton's delicate health at the time would never survive the extreme cold, lack of nutritious food, and pestilence of a prison. He went into hiding while now seriously considering the offers that had been made from Boston, Massachusetts.

During that period, Cotton married Sarah Hawkred Story in April 1632, a widow with a daughter, Elizabeth Story, who Cotton probably baptized in 1622. When they boarded the *Griffin* in summer 1633, Sarah was eight months pregnant with their first child; she gave birth at sea in August, and the baby was later christened Seaborn Cotton. John Cotton was 47.

Artist's conception of thatched First Church of Christ,
Boston, in 1634. Church services, teaching, trials, and civil matters all used the
meetinghouse. Anne Hutchinson's second trial, for heresy, was held here.
http://www.firstchurchbostonhistory.org/whichisthefirstchurch.html

John and Sarah Cotton's grandson, Cotton Mather, wrote *Magnalia Christi Americana,* a seven-volume history of New England at the end of the seventeenth century. In the first volume, he wrote that God had called his people out of the corrupt Church of England, "stirring up the spirits of thousands which never saw the faces of each other, with a most unanimous inclination to leave all the pleasant accommodations of their native country, and go over a terrible ocean, into a more terrible desert [the wilderness where Satan ruled], for the pure enjoyment of all his ordinances." Those sufferings were considered the evidence of the godliness of the first generation.

Rev. John Cotton, with Bible in hand,
and his extensive library.
The original painting has been altered.
Connecticut Historical Society and Boston Herald, May 5, 1930

About ten percent of Old Boston's population (perhaps 250 people), and untold tens of thousands of other English people emigrated to New England because of a Puritan ideal between 1630 and 1642. The new settlement of Boston, Massachusetts was named on September 7, 1630; the name was proposed by Thomas Dudley, who had worked for the Earl of Lincoln (the home town of Boston). The naming may have been in honor Lincoln, who hosted John and Elizabeth Cotton during t. and whose sister Arbella Clinton-Fiennes Johnson had die the month after the Winthrop Fleet landed, but others have Boston (an ancient contraction of Botolph's Town) was giv name to induce John Cotton to come to New England.

Among other eminent passengers on the *Griffin* in 1633 we the prominent ministers Thomas Hooker and Samuel Stone, and the oldest child of Anne and William Hutchinson, the twenty-year-old Edward. Though John and Sarah Cotton's escape from England was a closely held secret, the Hutchinsons were intimate enough to be privy to the plans, and sent Edward with their pastor, perhaps for the educational advantage to their son, or because Edward would be an assistant to Cotton, who was still somewhat infirm. On arrival in Massachusetts, Edward lived with the Cottons for the next year until his parents and family emigrated to America.

Cotton's theology, in brief

While Cotton admired European and English theologians and assimilated their teachings into his own, he is best known for promoting Congregationalism, a self-governing congregation, as opposed to the church governed by a hierarchical system of elders (presbyters) or bishops.

> The members as a body have power to admit, admonish, and excommunicate members. The demands of Puritan moral theology were very severe, and those known to have sinned might well be required to make a public confession of guilt in order to maintain their membership.
> Emerson, Everett. *Puritanism in America 1620-1750*, G.K. Hall & Co., 1977.

The church considered itself the moral guardian of its members, and believed in their grave responsibility to present their members to God as pure and spotless. In nature, nothing exists on its own. Individualism was unthinkable. Unmarried people were placed in families. Widows and widowers were urged to remarry. No one struck out into the wilderness and made their own way with a farmstead – a group gathered together a church with a minister, and applied to create a new plantation together. It wasn't only safety in numbers, from raids by Native Americans, but a matter of being a

, their collective mindset, isolation and
ing.

veloped the notions of the Covenant of Works
f Grace, while he ministered at old Boston. It
faming issue in Massachusetts when Anne Hutchinson
studies that the rest of the Puritan preachers spoke
of Works, but Cotton and Wheelwright preached
of Grace. This pricked every minister who was *not*
eelwright.

s book, *John Cotton*, Everett Emerson contrasted part of a
on by Rev. Thomas Hooker, representing the Law, with
Cotton's Covenant of Grace coming to the rescue of sinners with
soft and warm words like Good Father, love for his children, and
gentle Savior. Hooker preached, "Know assuredly that you will burn
for [sins] one day. Your proud hearts were never abased and laid in
the dust. The Lord will ruinate both you and them. Never expect a
good look from God. Set your heart at rest for that."

Cotton said to thousands of Puritans who held little or no
hope of being saved,

> "[P]oor men, yes, yet they were adorned with robes. Had it
> not been enough to say "washed their garments"? What, must
> poor men be set up with robes? Yet robes they have, and
> white robes, and they washed in the blood of the Lamb. So
> that it shows you that the servants of God that come well out
> of tribulations, they get more royal spirits than ever before,
> for robes become [look good upon] royal persons and
> princes. When robes in good earnest are put upon any, they
> put upon them princely majesty; a spirit of glory and royalty is
> put upon them. He carries himself no more like a base drudge
> of this world. He is able to over-wrestle all tribulations and
> afflictions of this world.

There was hope in Cotton's words to his parishioners and it
seemed unique amid the despair preached by other ministers. Their
lives of tribulation, worry, and fear could be redeemed for being
treated by God as royalty.

The Hutchinsons, and hundreds or thousands of colonists
from Lincolnshire, fell in love with that kind of preaching: the
Covenant of Grace.

Cotton corresponded with other ministers in New England, often concerning their confusion about his teachings on grace versus their theological training on obedience to the Laws of Moses. They held several conferences on the subject, and the records seem to indicate that Rev. Cotton walked back his rhetoric and submitted to his professional brethren after two 1637 synods, but carefully returned to his teaching.

According to Sargent Bush, Jr., author of *Writings of Thomas Hooker*, Rev. Cotton was forced to back down on his views of free grace, and in doing so, he was also forced to turn on his followers, the majority of Boston First Church's members.

He considered leaving the Massachusetts Bay Colony for the recently established New Haven Colony, but Gov. Winthrop convinced him to stay and heal the rift in the churches with his modified message. Cotton wrote: "When in a private conference with some chief magistrates and elders, I perceived that my removal upon such difference was unwelcome to them... and so have continued, by the grace of Christ, unto this day."

When his involvement in Mary Dyer's tragic miscarriage came to light, he was questioned. However, with his credentials, position, and gender being respected, later accounts shifted the blame for burying the fetus without reporting it, to Mrs. Hutchinson. Rev. Cotton had followed English law in his involvement, but his critics thought he should have reported so terrible a monster because of its religious significance. His answer that it seemed like a private grief might have stemmed from experience with church members over the last 25 years, or possibly staying silent about a miscarriage by his first wife.

The rest of Cotton's life

After the religious rebels, so many who had been Cotton's supporters and friends for years, made their dramatic exodus from Massachusetts Bay, he had to recover his balance quickly. He answered letters (see following chapters) from those who questioned his theology and his loyalty to the New England Way, and wondered how to proceed with their spiritual journey when their world had been turned upside down.

On the home front, John and Sarah Cotton enlarged and raised their family that included Sarah's daughter Elizabeth, and their children together: Seaborn (1633), Sarah (1635, Anne Hutchinson probably attended as midwife), Elizabeth (1637, born between the Hutchinson trials), John (1640), Maria (1642), and Roland (1643).

Cenotaph for First Church ministers interred together.
The stone may not be the exact location of their remains,
because the construction of King's Chapel disturbed some graves.

In New England, there were no church organs – organs being related to the hated Catholic mass, and drawing attention away from God and to the skills of the performer. At Sabbath meetings of the Massachusetts Bay churches, they sang psalms without musical accompaniment. Rev. Cotton disapproved of (though did not completely disavow) the use of instruments in worship. He wrote:

> We also grant that any private Christian who hath a gift to frame a spiritual song may both frame it and sing it privately for his own private comfort and remembrance of some special benefit or deliverance. Nor do we forbid the use any instrument therewithal: so that attention to the instrument does not divert the heart from attention to the matter of the song.

He was speaking of music composition and musical accompaniment in a private setting, not in public worship at the meetinghouse. At the meetinghouse, it was strictly *a capella* for many decades. In fact, some Christian denominations that are spiritual descendants of the Congregational way still do not allow instruments in their services.

In 1640, three ministers published the first book in the American colonies: a Psalter called *The Bay Psalm Book* that they approved for use in the churches of Massachusetts Bay. It was a text of psalms in rhyme, translated from Hebrew, without musical notation because almost no one was musically literate. The three principal authors were Richard Mather, John Eliot, and Thomas Weld. Cotton wrote the preface to the psalm book.

A few years later, he published the tract, *Singing of Psalms as a Gospel Ordinance*, and wrote:

"We lay down this conclusion for a Doctrine of Truth. That singing of Psalms with a lively voice is an holy Duty of God's worship now in the days of the New Testament. ... As we are to make melody in our hearts, so in our voices also."

One imagines that without instruments or skilled church musicians, the congregation probably sang in a most unmelodious manner.

Cotton (Boston), Hooker (Hartford), and Davenport (New Haven) were asked to contribute their wisdom and guidance to a religious synod called by Parliament at Westminster, London, from 1643 to 1652. None of them attended (Gov. Winthrop didn't want to lose Cotton, and opposed allowing him to go), but Cotton wrote *The Keys of the Kingdom of Heaven*, a book on the New England Congregational model of church governance, which contributed to the discussion. He wrote numerous other books during that period.

The New England churches met to decide how to govern themselves as individual congregations, but unified with similar beliefs, and the Cambridge Platform leaned heavily on Cotton's book.

Hutchinson's son Francis and her son-in-law William Collins were arrested and imprisoned in Boston, and eventually banished on pain of death. It wasn't Cotton who got them released, but Gov. Thomas Dudley.

Calligraphic artwork in the Unitarian Universalist Church that is the successor of Boston First Church of Christ. The text says,

John Cotton

Born in Derbyshire England 4 December 1585. He died in the Colony of Massachusetts Bay 23 December 1652. Fellow of Emmanuel College, Cambridge. Vicar of the Church of Saint Botolph, Boston, Lincolnshire, 1612-1633.

Regardless of Preferment & Conspicuous as a Puritan Divine, He became the object of a Prelatical Persecution. "Unawed by influence and unbribed by gain." He then sought refuge in New England. Ordained immediately on his arrival, he ministered to his death as "Teacher of the Boston Church, 1633-1652."

"Scholar, Theologian, Preacher, Publicist, He gave form & inspiration to the Ecclesiastical Policy known as "The New England Way." Preceptor and friend of Vane. From him Cromwell sought counsel. Living, he was revered as "That Apostle of his Age." Dead, he is remembered as "Patriarch of the Massachusetts Theocracy."

*****

    In 1643, Cotton was one of the ministers and magistrates who voted to execute three Rhode Island men for sedition and heresy, but the vote failed and the men were put to hard labor and then banished on pain of death. (More in later chapters.)

In November 1652, Rev. Cotton preached to Harvard students and ferried back across the Charles River to Boston. He became ill after exposure to winter weather, and died December 23 at age 67. He was the first to be buried in a shared tomb for First Church ministers in the Kings Chapel Burying Ground. Surrounding his grave, his colleagues John Winthrop, John Wilson, Roger Clap, and other notables of early Boston were buried.

Chapter 11

The Roots of Civil Disobedience

In 1636, the rumblings of religious schism were vibrating in the Massachusetts Bay Colony. Anne Hutchinson was holding women's religious meetings in her home that eventually included some men, including the young governor of the colony, Sir Henry Vane. They discussed the sermons on the "Covenant of Grace" preached by Rev. John Cotton, and criticized the other ministers of the colony, who preached what Hutchinson called the "Covenant of Works." Freedom of speech was not a human or civil right at that time. It was considered sedition to criticize and undermine authority.

It's easy to see that the everyday members of the colony were unsettled by religious matters, because they believed they'd left that behind in England, in favor of a Puritan utopia. But controversies were also going on with the elite: the political machinations and egos of the governors and ministers were probably kept quiet, but certainly raised hackles because people noticed and were taking sides. One of those incidents concerned the governors John Winthrop, considered to be too lenient in punishments, and Thomas Dudley, an ultra-conservative authoritarian. The two men had known each other for years, and their children were married, so in his journal, Winthrop calls Dudley his brother and protests of the love between them. The journal was meant to be public, so it would tend to favor its author. More than 200 years after the incident, a Winthrop descendant wrote of a dispute that the very young Henry Vane involved himself in.

> It would seem ... that the only charge arrayed against Winthrop on this occasion was for having "dealt too remissly in point of justice in one or two passages," or, as it is also expressed, for having "failed in over-much lenity." Winthrop was of opinion, it appears, that, "in the infancy of plantations, justice should be administered with more lenity than in a settled state, because people were then more apt to transgress, partly of ignorance of new laws and orders, partly through oppression of business and other straits." But Governor Haynes was of another mind, and so were [Henry] Vane and [Rev. Hugh] Peters. Even the ministers, too –

Cotton and Wilson and Hooker – were in favor of a more rigorous administration of the government; and, upon the matter being referred to them for decision, they delivered an opinion precisely the opposite of that which Winthrop had expressed, pronouncing "that strict discipline, both in criminal offences and in martial affairs, was more needful in plantations than in settled states, as tending to the honor and safety of the Gospel."
Robert Charles Winthrop, *Life and Letters of John Winthrop, from 1630 to 1649.*

"Rigorous administration of the government." And it involved the chief ministers of Boston and Salem, who came up with a 15-point protocol on the proper resolution of disputes, including the intention to speak to the issue, but not in a personal manner.

Yet they did not follow that resolution in dealing with religious dissent, including the Wheelwright and Hutchinson controversies.

Rev. Cotton invited William Hutchinson's brother-in-law, Rev. Wheelwright, to preach a message of salvation by grace at Boston's First Church of Christ in January 1637, while Rev. Wilson was overseas, and the sermon was well-received by many families. However, the sermon was considered heretical and seditious by the colony's magistrates and highest officials, and Wheelwright was tried and banished.

Nathaniel Ward, in his book *Simple Cobbler of Agawam*, wrote, "I dare take upon me, to be the Herald of New-England so far, as to proclaim to the world, in the name of our Colony, that all Familists, Antinomians, Anabaptists, and other Enthusiasts, shall have free Liberty to keep away from us, and such as will come to be gone as fast as they can, the sooner the better."

People are still saying that today about those whose politics they disagree with: "If you don't like it, then you can leave." Today, it's just aggressive, empty talk. Then, banishment was truly punitive. The time between the sentence and banishment might be shunning, home arrest or prison, the offender had his weapons confiscated, and he'd have to leave his employment and home and strike out into the terrifying wilderness.

In March 1637, William Dyer, Mary Dyer's husband of three years, was one of 60 men who signed a Remonstrance to the General Court that appealed Wheelwright's conviction. Thanks to Anne

Hutchinson, the signers were beginning to see why there should be a wall of separation between ecclesiastical (church) and governmental rule.

The Remonstrance was supposed to be read and answered at the May sitting of the General Court, when Henry Vane was to have been re-elected governor. However, former (and future) Governor John Winthrop changed the venue of the Court and its elections from Boston to New Town/Cambridge, where there would be fewer Wheelwright and Hutchinson supporters. Vane's agenda for the day was to read and discuss the Remonstrance, but Winthrop stopped it by saying they'd take care of it after the gubernatorial election – but Winthrop won the seat, not Vane, and when the Remonstrance should have come up on the agenda – *poof* – It vanished as unimportant.

The consequences were only beginning to set in, however. Gov. Winthrop and Gov. Thomas Dudley were not letting go of this. Vane returned to England in August. There was a theological convention about what the Hutchinson/Wheelwright followers were talking about, and Rev. Cotton avoided punishment and professional ruin by siding with Winthrop and others against Anne Hutchinson, his friend and supporter of more than 20 years. She was tried for heresy and set in house arrest in nearby Roxbury to wait out the winter.

*****

The men who had signed the Remonstrance last spring were disarmed of weapons and ammunition, which were required by law to protect themselves and their community from animals or Indian attack. They also lost their freeman status, which meant they couldn't vote or participate in government or juries. Finally, if they refused to submit to the Bay government, they were considered seditious and had to remove themselves and their families from the colony by May 1, 1638 (this allowed them to survive the severe winter under a roof, with food and warmth). Those who apologized for the Remonstrance were given back their arms, but not their freeman status.

During the winter, men who included William Hutchinson, William Coddington, and William Dyer started talking with the recently-banished Rev. Roger Williams, and they resolved to buy

Aquidneck Island (Rhode Island) from the native Americans. When Anne Hutchinson's second trial, for heresy, concluded with her excommunication, Mary Dyer did the unprecedented and courageous act of supporting Anne and walking out together, thus making a silent but very effective condemnation of Boston's policies. Mary suffered the consequences of that act when she was identified as the mother of a "monster" (a miscarried fetus with severe birth defects), which proved her own divine punishment for heresy.

Somewhere between 75 and 100 families left Boston in late March, when the snow still lay thigh-deep, and walked to Providence, then traveled to the north end of Aquidneck, and founded the town that would later be called Portsmouth.

Within a year, they set up a government which they called a democratic "bodie politick." When Winthrop heard of it, he was disgusted with the philosophy and wrote: "a democracy is, amongst most civil nations, accounted the meanest and worst of all forms of government."

This exile from Massachusetts Bay Colony on account of individual religious belief and denial of a government melded with religion was always forefront in the minds of Rhode Island settlers. Always. It was the backbone of their royal charters and the laws that they drafted and approved for themselves.

When the English Quaker missionaries arrived in 1656 and 1657, they were tortured and threatened with death by the other New England colonies (Massachusetts Bay, Plymouth, New Haven and Connecticut). Rhode Island answered a letter from Governor John Endecott and affirmed their intent to allow religious liberty for all people, including Quakers, Catholics, Anglicans, Jews, and others – even those who did not practice religion. They refused to obey the United Colonies' rule because *we may not be compelled to exercise any civil power over men's consciences.*

When Mary Dyer, Marmaduke Stephenson, and William Robinson were sentenced to be hanged in October 1659, it was their choice to hang, their choice to lay down their lives, to call attention to the injustice and horrific behavior of the church-state in Massachusetts. They were given the option of banishment to save their lives. They chose the spectacle to outrage the public, and it worked to a point. Mary was reprieved – against her will. The two men died by hanging. Mary obeyed God's call to give up her life the next spring, and her civil disobedience ending in death really did stir up public sympathy for Quakers and outrage at the government. An English Quaker obtained an order from the newly-restored King Charles II to stop the executions. Meanwhile, the Rhode Island leaders, including William Dyer, were writing a new constitution/charter for the king to approve. The central focus was "liberty of conscience," or religious liberty.

The other huge concern in New England, happening at the same time as the religious controversy, was the Pequot War in Connecticut in 1636-37. The Bay government, as mentioned earlier, was ostensibly in New England on a joint venture of commerce and to be apostles and missionaries to the Indians of the region. The explorers and settlers of the 1620s and 1630s had virtually walked onto tracts of cleared agricultural lands after countless local Native Americans had died of smallpox and other epidemics of European diseases for which they had no antibodies. They didn't buy their lands from the Native Americans, considering the land to be theirs by charter of King Charles I.

But the missionary work with the Indians was primarily performed by Rev. John Eliot and a few others. Eliot undertook to translate parts of the Bible into the Wampanoag language, the tribe that lived near Plymouth. New England tribes, though, were feeling the pressure of being squeezed out of ancestral territories with hunting, fishing, and agriculture. When crimes against the English were committed, Indian hands were chopped off and nailed to doors in Boston. Tensions built through 1636, until an English settler was killed on his boat, presumably by a Pequot tribesman of the Connecticut River Valley.

Anne Hutchinson's supporters, and a large number of the Boston First Church members, refused to send money or troops, so the Pequot War became a joint venture of John Endecott's Salem men and Plymouth Colony. Rev. John Wilson went to the war as chaplain, but the rest of Boston stayed out of it – to the frustration of Gov. Winthrop.

The colonial forces committed what we would consider genocide: men, women, children, and babies were burned to death or stabbed or shot if they tried to escape the inferno. Rivers of blood sizzled in the fire. A few months later, even more Pequots were massacred, until only about 400, who had escaped to Long Island, remained of the tribe.

When the English colonial soldiers looted a village and stumbled on a cache of grain the Pequots had stored for winter, Gov. Winthrop wrote that they should bring it home to Boston. Knowing what trauma even the victors bring home, surely there was post-traumatic disorder after seeing innocents slaughtered and burned.

Of the 100 or so Pequot women and children captured, most of them were enslaved. If they tried to escape, they were hunted and then sent to the Caribbean to be traded for Africans. Several high status Pequots went to Governor Winthrop's house to be domestic servants.

But they weren't servants. They had no choice about their fates.

Captains Mason and Underhill, and former Gov. Endecott, attributed their military success to God's favor. Mason wrote that God "was pleased to smite our Enemies in the hinder parts." Was he saying that God spanked the Pequots, or that the "hinder parts" meant the lands beyond the east coast of Massachusetts?

Having had a hand in genocide, the Bay had a taste for blood. It was not a foregone conclusion that Anne Hutchinson's conviction would not end in her execution by hanging. Jane Hawkins, the midwife she associated with was suspected of witchcraft, and of course, Mary Dyer miscarried a "monster," though that was a secret for five months.

The Pequot War's brutality, combined with the scorn and vitriol heaped on the Anne Hutchinson and her supporters, made Boston, and indeed, all of New England, heartsick, angry, and oppressed.

Chapter 12

Sad Boston 1637

*M*rs. *Winthrop to Her Husband.*

DEAR *in my thoughts, I blush to think how much I have neglected the opportunity of presenting my love to you. Sad thoughts possess my spirits, and I cannot repulse them; which makes me unfit for any thing, wondering what the Lord means by all these troubles among us. Sure I am, that all shall work to the best to them that love God, or rather are loved of him. I know he will bring light out of obscurity, and make his righteousness shine forth as clear as the noonday. Yet I find in myself an adverse spirit, and a trembling heart, not co-willing to submit to the will of God as I desire. There is a time to plant, and a time to pull up that which is planted, which I could desire might not be yet. But the Lord knoweth what is best, and his will be done. But I will write no more. Hoping to see thee to-morrow, my best affections being commended to yourself, the rest of our friends at Newtown, I commend thee to God.*

Your loving wife,

MARGARET WINTHROP.

Sad Boston, 1637. [Probably late October or early November, during the General Court and Hutchinson trial]

To her honored Husband, these be delivered.

The year 1637 was one of war (massacre of Pequot men in Connecticut and the taking of native women and children as slaves), dissent in the churches of Massachusetts Bay, and the gubernatorial coup in May when Henry Vane was outvoted and John Winthrop returned to the seat. Along with it came the hostility of Vane supporters, Margaret Winthrop's final pregnancy which ended in miscarriage, the fall of Anne Hutchinson ending in her trial for sedition, the disfranchisement and disarming of the men who had signed the Wheelwright Remonstrance, the certain banishment of the heretics, and other strife. Food was not plentiful because of failed crops. During the ecclesiastical synod that sat to refute the Hutchinson teachings, Rev. Thomas Shepard, one of Anne's accusers, lost his wife to a fever, and Rev. Hugh Peter, another inquisitor, had lost his wife of twelve years. And the winter ahead, though they couldn't know it yet, would be one of the most severely cold ever documented in Boston.

—

Governor Winthrop wrote back to Margaret from New Town, soon to be called Cambridge.

For Mrs. Winthrop at Boston.
Dear, – I am still detained from thee, but it is by the Lord, who hath a greater interest in me than thy self, when his work is done he will restore me to thee again to our mutual comfort: Amen. I thank thee for thy sweet Letter: my heart was with thee to have written to thee every day, but business would not permit me. I suppose thou hearest much news from hence: it may be, some grievous to thee: but be not troubled, I assure thee things go well, & they must needs do so, for God is with us & thou shalt see a happy issue. I hope to be with thee tomorrow & a friend or 2 I suppose.

So I kiss my sweet wife & rest
Thine John Winthrop.
This 6th day.

Sweet Heart, – I was unwillingly hindered from coming to thee, nor am I like to see thee before the last day of this week: therefore I shall want a band or 2 or 3 cuffs. I pray thee also send me 6 or 7 leaves of Tobacco dried & powdered. Have care of thy self this cold weather, & speak to the folks to keep the goats well out of the Garden; & if my brother Peter* hath not fetched away the sheep ram, let them look him up & give him meat, the green pease in the Garden etc. are good for him. If any letters be come for me send them by this bearer. I will trouble thee no further, the Lord bless & keep thee my sweet wife & all our family: & send us a comfortable meeting, so I kiss thee & love thee ever & rest

Thy faithful husband,
John WINTHROP
This 6th of the 9th [Nov. 6], 1637.

*Winthrop's "brother Peter" was Rev. Hugh Peter, the stepfather of John Winthrop Jr.'s wife Elizabeth Reade.

Chapter 13

The First Trial at New Town

H ave you been to Cambridge, Massachusetts, which was at first called New Town, and wondered where the meetinghouse was, when Anne Hutchinson was tried for sedition in 1637? I've visited when the temperature and humidity matched at 95 percent, and my makeup dripped off my face as we shot a video at Harvard University in late July.

That weather was well known to Gov. Winthrop, because he wrote that the summer was so hot that they could only bear to travel at night (walking, with wolves about). But the other side of the calendar was so cold, so frosty, so blizzardy, that the court could not convene during the winter. If they were going to root out the sedition of Anne Hutchinson and the signers of the Wheelwright Remonstrance, they had to do it quickly: between the August theological synod and the onset of the polar blasts.

Among others like Rev. Wheelwright and those who'd signed the Remonstrance the previous March, Anne Hutchinson was charged with sedition and heresy. Gov. Winthrop wrote in his *Journal* that the general court agreed on November 2 that two "so opposite parties could not contain in the same body, without apparent hazard of ruin to the whole, agreed to send away some of the principal."

Either the court had decided Anne's fate before the trial began, or Winthrop condensed the process when later journaling it.

The trial should have been held in Boston where Anne had committed her "crime" of teaching men and criticizing ministers, but there were too many supporters and friends there to guarantee a conviction, so the venue was moved to New Town, called Cambridge beginning in 1638. The very strait-laced Gov. Thomas Dudley and others lived there, across the Charles River from Boston on the Shawmut Peninsula.

In 1637, former Gov. Dudley actually accused former Gov. John Winthrop of being too lenient on lawbreakers, and the 1636-37 Governor, Harry Vane, that young whippersnapper in his early twenties, intervened. From the tone of Winthrop's *Journal* entries, it's plain to see that Winthrop was miffed at Vane's attempt to reconcile the two older men who had founded the colony. Winthrop knew his

Journal was intended as a historical record, not a personal diary, so he kept his temper. But you couldn't call Winthrop and Dudley bosom buddies, even though his daughter Mary Winthrop had married Dudley's son Samuel and they shared a grandchild.

Another of Anne's principal accusers was Rev. Thomas Shepard, who lived and ministered in New Town. Reverends Thomas Hooker and Samuel Stone, who had previously ministered there, had left the year before to found Hartford, Connecticut, but they remained in correspondence with Rev. Cotton on the issue of grace alone versus grace plus works.

Holding Anne's first trial at the meetinghouse in New Town was deliberately designed to make her defense more difficult. To get there, she had to walk from central Boston to the river ferry, and then from the ferry landing on the other side of the Charles River, uphill to the meetinghouse, in freezing weather the Little Ice Age dished out. A month earlier, there had been a Nor'easter with snow, which wrecked a ship. Anne and her escort (perhaps her brother-in-law Edward Hutchinson or her sons) had to walk in frost and snow, past small farms and frozen marshes before entering the village.

A book about Harvard University pinpoints the location of the original meetinghouse.

> The streets were laid out fairly straight and symmetrical – excepting Crooked Lane, which had to avoid the brook. The first meetinghouse, where the General Court dealt with Anne Hutchinson ... was on the southwest corner of Spring (Mount Auburn) and Water (Dunster) Streets. For a marketplace, there was set aside a plot of ground which is still open: Winthrop Square and the lawn in front of the Pi Eta Club, whose house is the site of Governor Haynes' homestead. Morison, Samuel Eliot, *The Founding of Harvard College*, 1968.

Boston and Cambridge have changed in countless ways over the last 380 years. Beacon Hill was cut down, its soil used to fill swamps and bays. Islands were connected to the mainland by infill or bridges. But though roads can be renamed, sometimes the modern streets and highways follow the original path.

For Bostonians in 1637, it was about five miles from one meetinghouse to the other. In freezing weather, with primitive roads. Not even the rich people of Boston traveled by horse or coach at this time. Farm carts were pulled by oxen. People walked or took boats.

When the town and church were founded in the late summer of 1630, Roger Clap wrote, "Before they could build at Boston, they lived … in tents and wigwams at Charlestown; their meeting-place being abroad under a tree, where I have heard Mr. Wilson and Mr. Phillips preach many a good sermon."

Intersection of modern Dunster and Mt. Auburn, where the Cambridge meetinghouse stood. The brick building is the site of the former meetinghouse. Google Maps street view, Oct. 2017.

By 1637, the other buildings in New Town were, by ordinance, set back from the street, and to avoid chimney and roof fires, had wood or tile roofs instead of thatch. Being less than seven years old, the village would have had a very open, clean look, compared to the ancient, higgledy-piggeldy towns and cities the colonists left behind in England.

Anne had two small children and numerous older children who could were cared for by other family members, but it's not easy to stay focused on your trial defense (she wasn't allowed an attorney) when there are domestic issues to decide. She was mistress of a large home where she and William probably kept semi-permanent guests (as we see later, in Rhode Island), and mistress of a farm at Mt. Wollaston. She didn't milk goats and make cheese, but she managed the businesses and the domestic arrangements for the servants and laborers.

Before the trial began, Anne had attended the traumatic miscarriage of Mary Dyer's "monster," and the miscarriage of the middle-aged Margaret Winthrop's last pregnancy. She had relatives, friends and patients, and her husband's business associates in addition to the 80 or more people who came to her home for Bible studies and lectures twice a week. She was much esteemed in Boston.

But during her trials, she was on her own, thanks to Gov. Winthrop stacking the General Court with his own supporters and refusing to seat Boston supporters of Anne Hutchinson's.

Instead of only the single annual election in May, Winthrop dissolved the legislature (court assistants) elected in May, and called another election in November 1637. Boston's representatives were reduced from three to two deputies when Winthrop disqualified one of them for supporting the Wheelwright Remonstrance, and fully two-thirds of the deputies from other towns were newly elected to office. Mind you, the new deputies, what we would call legislators, were elected specifically to agree with the hard line agenda of Winthrop and the colonial theocracy. They knew that if they wanted to keep their office (and their freeman status), they needed to follow the governor's wishes.

Former Gov. Henry Vane, Anne's most vocal supporter, had returned to London. Furthermore, in the newly seated court held before Anne's trial began, Winthrop disfranchised, fined, and imprisoned men who had supported Rev. Wheelwright and Mistress Hutchinson over the past year, or insulted Gov. Winthrop at his May reelection. The ministers of the colony, even her mentor John Cotton, were very clearly arrayed against her.

You couldn't call it a kangaroo court (violating recognized standards of justice) because there was no law that you couldn't stack the jury. There were inquisitors, prosecutors, justices, and jurymen, each man wearing the same hat for those roles. There were 49 men with a negative prejudice against Mistress Hutchinson, and her only defenses were her home school education, logic, quick wit, and years of biblical study.

The outcome of Anne's trial was a foregone conclusion: Winthrop would triumph. He was in control. No more Mr. Lenient.

Chapter 14

Anne's Crime: Speaking While Female

Speaking, as a crime, is a gross generality. Mistress Hutchinson was tried first for sedition (conduct or speech inciting people to rebel against the authority of a state or monarch), then for heresy (belief or opinion contrary to orthodox religious doctrine). Rebellion against the state, rebellion against religion.

Social order in the Puritan colony depended upon an orthodoxy of Puritan (and therefore Calvinist) thought and behavior. As mentioned previously, the hierarchical pyramid had God at the top, then the church-state authorities of ministers and magistrates, followed by the church body, married men of community status and financial means, men who were fathers, married women who were mothers and mistresses of female servants (male servants answered to the master), and children.

A woman's place was subordinate to her father or male guardian in early life, and her custody and property was transferred to her husband when she married. Girls were taught by example what their place was in society, and learned to manage a household so that by age 13, they were as responsible as women for sharing household tasks such as churning, spinning, and weaving. Especially in Puritan households, where they were often taught to read well enough to understand their Bibles, women were expected to educate boys enough to have the skills to enter grammar school, and educate girls enough to read and keep accounts to manage the household and family farm.

If a wife was widowed, she needed to remarry as soon as possible to keep her children financially supported and their inheritance protected. Widows who had successful farms, a measure of wealth, or brewing businesses were sometimes accused of witchcraft. The ensuing mayhem saw her financial security confiscated or destroyed as she languished in prison. Sometimes, as we see often in genealogical research, a widow with seven or more children would marry a widower with a large family, including infants and teenagers, so the household (and labor to keep it running) might be 25 people.

*Drawing of a merchant class woman
by Wenceslaus Hollar*

Yes, women had a say in who they married, and they weren't forced to marry, but once they were married, there was almost no divorce in the event of domestic violence or alcoholism. Infidelity (especially on the woman's part) was divorce-worthy, but the adulterer was whipped.

Women were trained to be silent in public, particularly in church services. It was plain as daylight that the apostle Paul had written:

> Let the woman learn in silence with all subjection. I permit not a woman to teach, neither to usurp authority over the man, but to be in silence. For Adam was first formed, then Eve.
> 1 Timothy 2:11-13, *1599 Geneva Bible.*

There it was: "to be in silence with all subjection," and no teaching. The order of creation was man first, woman following. Man hears and interprets revelations from God; woman receives teaching of man.

At Anne's trial for sedition, she was astute enough in legal matters to understand that she had not violated a written law. John Winthrop, presiding on the bench and surrounded by the 49 members of his handpicked court, hoped to elicit a confession from Anne that she had violated both church and state principles by rebelling against her betters.

Winthrop opened the trial. "Mrs. Hutchinson, you are called here as one of those that have troubled the peace of the commonwealth and the churches here; you are known to be a woman that hath had a great share in the promoting and divulging of those opinions that are causes of this trouble. Therefore we have thought good to send for you to understand how things are, that if you be in an erroneous way we may reduce you that so you may become a profitable member here among us, otherwise if you be obstinate in your course that then the court may take such course that you may trouble us no further."

Anne's trial verdicts were a foregone conclusion, and we can be reasonably sure she knew that. Any verdict in theocratic Massachusetts would be based solely on the magistrates' and ministers' biases and preformed opinions. Everyone took strong positions on the religious controversy. No one was impartial. The foundation of court theory and practice today is that investigations must be impartial, that prosecutors and defenders follow procedures to ensure justice to the potentially innocent defendant, and that the jury isn't stacked or tampered with. But that was several hundred years down the road.

Winthrop's opening blast was to ask if she was in agreement with the men who had signed the Wheelwright Remonstrance the previous spring. Winthrop's court had just disfranchised, disarmed, fined, or put in freezing prison the signers (and supporters of Mistress Hutchinson) until they apologized.

She answered, "I am called here to answer before you but I hear no things laid to my charge." Of course she hadn't signed the Remonstrance. But she'd also not publicly spoken her opinion of it. She saw the trap and refused to set foot in it.

The leaders of the Bay Colony set the very same trap for Baptists and Quakers in the 1650s, as if they hadn't learned a thing from Anne Hutchinson. William Dyer, the Rhode Island attorney general from 1650-1652, recognized that the Bay Colony was quick to arrest and accuse, and then create a law to fit the "crime." He told them that they didn't have a law, from the Bible or their government, on which to charge Quakers. He wrote a letter that got his wife Mary, in prison for civil disobedience over the treatment of Quakers, released and saved from her first date with the gallows. He wrote,

> ...behold my wife without law and against Law is imprisoned and punished and so highly condemned [to death] for saying the light is the Rule! It is not your light within your rule by which you make and act such lawes for ye have no rule of Gods word in the Bible to make a law titled Quakers nor have you any order from the Supreme State of England to make such laws... your fundamental laws is that no person shall be imprisoned or molested but upon the breach of a law, yet behold my wife without law and against law is imprisoned and punished.

In a 2015 article in the *New York Times* entitled "Speaking While Female," Sheryl Sandberg and Adam Grant wrote:

> ...when a woman speaks in a professional setting, she is walking a tightrope. Either she's barely heard or she's judged as too aggressive. When a man says virtually the same thing, heads nod in appreciation for his fine idea.

Anne Hutchinson was clearly too aggressive and too uppity for her time. She had broken no laws and her accusers had no proof of her defiance of orthodox religion. In fact, she had her own scripture proof-texts to counter the Silent Women text: she referred to the letter to Titus, about older, experienced women teaching younger women.

Gov. Winthrop sneered that he had more arguments than Anne did and retorted in Hutchinson's sedition trial, "We do not mean to discourse with those of your sex."

Convicted of speaking while female.

Winthrop, at the end of Mistress Hutchinson's second trial, for heresy, said when she asked why they'd excommunicated and banished her, "Say no more, the court knows wherefore and is satisfied."

Speaking while female.

Chapter 15

The Frozen Man of Weymouth

Snow jumping, Buffalo, New York, 2014. Reuters photo, altered.

Boston's Mayor Marty Walsh said in 2015 that people shouldn't be jumping out of windows or off roofs to land in snow drifts, because it's dangerous. http://huff.to/1vTjauX

He's not the first Massachusetts official to describe the behavior. Governor John Winthrop wrote of it in his *Journal* (a public history of the colony, not a private diary) in February 1638 (New Style calendar).

There was serious trouble in the Puritan/Congregational churches of the colony, not only from the Wheelwright-Hutchinson Antinomian controversy drawing off many prominent members of the church and community, but strife from within the approved churches: the clash of salvation by God's grace versus the "covenant of works," that is, proving your love for God by strict adherence to Old Testament laws. The churches had stopped approving memberships, which meant the men couldn't be freemen voters, but worse, as non-members, they couldn't take Communion or be saved for heaven if they died by disease, accident, or age. So non-member men and women were deeply perturbed. No matter how they behaved or what they believed, if they didn't have the approval of the Elect (the ministers and members), they were probably going to hell.

In the extremely harsh winter of January-February-March 1638, Anne Hutchinson was on house arrest in Roxbury between her heresy and excommunication trials, and her adherents were on a real estate trip to scout and purchase Rhode Island, and make a start on surveying and marking land allotments.

Back in Boston and Salem, the 25,000-35,000 new emigrants of the Great Migration were existing on short rations and short tempers, and crowded living quarters.

One nor'easter after another battered the colony that winter. Probably also a polar vortex or two, if you consider that the Boston Harbor froze over several times.

And then a man who couldn't bear the stress of not knowing if he was saved or not, leaped out into a snow bank.

Winthrop wrote on Feb. 7:

A man of Weymouth (but not [a member] of the church) fell into some trouble of mind, and in the night cried out, "Art thou come, Lord Jesus?" and with that leaped out of his bed in his shirt, and, breaking from his wife, leaped out at a high window into the snow, and ran about seven miles off, and being traced in the snow, was found dead next morning. They might perceive, that he had kneeled down to prayer in divers places.

The man didn't jump out the window because he was having a bad dream. For some reason, he had not been admitted to church membership, and without it, he couldn't be saved. He had no assurance of heaven and he literally went over the edge, in the horror that he'd be condemned to hell.

Leaping into a snow bank, dressed only in a nightshirt and stocking feet, in darkness and deep snow: it's a wonder the man made seven miles, across the isthmus to Roxbury, and still kept ahead of the search party. As the James Taylor song goes, "Lord, have mercy on the Frozen Man."

Another man who once feared for his soul was Captain Roger Clap of Dorchester. He had come to Massachusetts Bay in 1630, two months before the Winthrop Fleet landed, but their ship's captain, instead of navigating the ship through unfamiliar waters to Charlestown, dumped the passengers, their cargo and domestic stock at Dorchester. It was after planting time. The next winter, hundreds of people in the greater Boston area died of illness, cold, and hunger. But Roger Clap hung in there, still praising God.

Good old Roger wrote of the succession of miracles God wrought in bringing him to Massachusetts, even though they'd suffered and nearly starved their first year. He exemplified the twentieth-century bromide, "If life hands you lemons, make lemonade."

> *It was God* that did draw me by his Providence out of my Father's Family, and weaned me from it by degrees; *It was God* put it into my Heart to incline to Live abroad; and *it was God* that made my Father willing. *God by his Providence* brought me near [Rev.] Mr. Warham, and inclined my Heart to his Ministry: *God by his Providence* moved the Heart of my [employer] Master Mossiour to ask me whether I would go to New-England: *It was God* by his Providence that made me willing to leave my dear Father, and dear Brethren and Sisters, my dear Friends and Country: *It was God* that made my Father willing on the first Motion I made in Person, to let me go: *It was God* that sent Mr. Maverick that pious Minister to me, who was unknown to him, to seek me out that I might come hither. So *God brought me* out of Plymouth [England] the 20th of March in the Year 1629-30, and landed me in Health at Nantasket [Dorchester] on the 30th of May, 1630, I being then about the Age of Twenty one Years. *Blessed be God* that brought me Here!
> (Italics mine.)

Unlike the Weymouth man, Captain Clap was admitted to the Dorchester church a few months after landing, and perhaps because of his ebullient disposition, he was well thought of.

In his *Memoirs*, Clap was full of praise for the pioneering ministers and government authorities of Massachusetts Bay Colony. He named names, including Winthrop, Cotton, Wilson, Weld, and many others whose names appear as Anne Hutchinson's accusers.

But when it came to most church members, Clap noticed that they lived in terror because they had no assurance of their salvation, and racked their memories for one forgotten sin that might keep them out of heaven. Thinking that was the way of Christianity, he suffered with them until Rev. John Cotton preached on Revelation, presumably the part where the redeemed of the Lord overcome sin and are taken to heaven. Roger gained hope that the prophecies showed God's people winning in the end, and that a small stream of godly sorrow (at their sins) was better than a flood of great horror. Still, the bottom line was that few would be saved, and most would be lost.

And then the light truly broke through for Roger: that

(A) If Jesus came into the world to save sinners, and

(B) Roger was a sinner, then

(C) Why couldn't he be saved?

"Why not me?" he asked. And instead of trying to obey the harsh laws out of fear of hell, he could honor his beloved Savior Jesus with his obedience, which was not a dread existence, but a life of grateful service.

He wrote: "If my Heart do not deceive me, I do prize him above Kingdoms: I desire him more than Life, and to be made more and more like him in Holiness and Righteousness all the Days of my Life."

In his *Memoir*, Roger Clap mentioned the Antinomian Controversy. Even though Clap found a true love of Christ in his Puritan church of Dorchester, and you might suspect that he'd fall in with the grace theology of the Antinomians, he had hard feelings for the Hutchinson group, and later on, the Quakers. Like his ministers and fellow church members, he thought that grace and forgiveness meant that one thanked God by keeping the Old Testament laws to the best of their abilities, and by this, an obedient society could attain a New Jerusalem and expedite the second coming of Christ.

The Antinomians, however, had this concept of "free" grace that could not be free, according to orthodox theology, because grace, like freedom, isn't free. Someone (Jesus) had had to pay a heavy price for it.

This is what Clap said about the controversy with the Wheelwright-Hutchinson faction, without naming names:

But this glorious Work of God towards his People here was soon maligned by Satan; and he cast into the minds of some corrupt Persons, very erroneous Opinions, which did breed great Disturbance in the Churches. And he [Satan] puffed up his Instruments with horrible Pride, insomuch that they would oppose the Truth of God delivered Publicly: and some times, yea most times they would do it by way of Query, as if they desired to be informed: but they did indeed accuse our godly Ministers of not preaching Gospel, saying they were Legal Preachers, but themselves were for free Grace, and

Ministers did Preach a Covenant of Works; which was a false Aspersion on them. The Truth was, they would willingly have lived in Sin, and encouraged others so to do, etc. And yet think to be saved by Christ, because his Grace is free; forgetting (it seems) that those whom Christ doth save from Hell, he also freely of his Grace doth save from Sin; for he came to save his People from their Sins, to give Repentance and Remission of Sins.

Clap described the home meetings of Anne Hutchinson, and her accusations that most ministers preached a Covenant of Works (having to earn salvation with good works) instead of the Covenant of Grace (faith alone in the gift – grace – of Christ's saving power) she said Rev. Cotton preached.

But Cotton would turn his back on Hutchinson, his friend of 20 years, in the early autumn of 1637, when he was pushed to conform to the orthodoxy of New England Puritanism.

A polar vortex had blown down on the City Upon a Hill.

Chapter 16

Anne's Incarceration

A nne was convicted of sedition, or undermining the authority of the Massachusetts theocracy and encouraging others to rebel, though the General Court didn't say specifically *which* laws she had broken. The court summary said, "Mrs. Hutchinson, the wife of Mr. William Hutchinson, being convented for traducing the ministers and their ministry in the country, she declared voluntarily her revelations for her ground, and that she should be delivered and the Court ruined, with their posterity, and thereupon was banished, and in the meanwhile was committed to Mr. Joseph Weld (of Roxbury) until the Court shall dispose of her."

Joseph Weld, born ca1599, who brought his wife Elizabeth and four of his five children to Boston in 1633-35, was a wealthy man, the richest man in New England. He came from the textile town of Sudbury, Suffolk, England, whose River Stour runs to the east and connected the town to the Flemish and Dutch textile trade. The Welds would have been very familiar with the Bayning family, also cloth merchants, who were joint founders of the East India Company. Paul Bayning was created Viscount Bayning of Sudbury in 1628, about five to seven years before the Welds emigrated to New England. The Welds and Baynings also would have known Boston's senior pastor, John Wilson, who ministered there as an adult, and whose father had come from Sudbury.

The fifteenth- and sixteenth-century Sudbury neighborhood where his family lived remained standing until the 1960s, when it was pulled down to build a garage.

Weld's immediate ancestors had lived in Sudbury for four generations, and though Joseph wasn't the eldest child who would inherit a double portion of his father's estate (there were nine children, and he was sixth), he still made a fortune in the cloth trade. Joseph sired twelve children by two wives, and my ancestor was his youngest child, eleven months old when Joseph died from "a sore on his tongue," which might have been an oral cancer.

He left a £10,000 sterling estate, which in 2018 would be worth about £1,243,000 or $1,634,421.

It's probably due to Joseph Weld and his brothers Edmund and Thomas that Roxbury's county was called Suffolk County.

Joseph was a man of several talents: he was by trade a mercer or cloth merchant (similar to William Hutchinson), a farmer, a military man, and a real estate tycoon. He had a license to draw wine, but gave it up. He was a freeman and a deputy to the General Court (which made him one of Anne Hutchinson's judges). He co-founded the Ancient and Honorable Artillery Company and was one of the first donors to Harvard College.

Joseph Weld took part in the Pequot War of 1636-37, when the military men of Plymouth Colony, along with Gov. John Endecott of Salem and Capt. John Underhill, slaughtered the Indians, the old, the women and children, until their blood ran into grisly pools. Some Pequot women and children were taken to be slaves in Boston, but they tended to run away to nearby tribes, so when they were caught, they were transported to Providence Island, a Caribbean island off Nicaragua, and exchanged for African slaves or tobacco. Puritans didn't like the idea of selling slaves – they preferred to call them servants, and trade them rather than sell them.

Weld's reward for participating in the Pequot War garnered him 278 acres in Roxbury, a very rich compensation for his services. Joseph's father had put his wealth into land holdings, and it appears that Joseph did the same in Massachusetts.

Weld had several other family members living in the Roxbury area. Probably the most famous of them was his brother, Rev. Thomas Weld. Thomas was the author of the vitriolic foreword to Gov. Winthrop's book on the Antinomian Controversy, and his vivid description of Mary Dyer's "monster" stillbirth is our main source of information on the fetus, from which doctors deduce that it was anencephalic (no brain except a brainstem) and had spina bifida. In the 1640s, Rev. Weld was an agent for the Bay colony interests in England, and he sent English orphans or poor children of the parishes as "servants" (remember: slaves) to Boston and other American ports. He also seems to have been unscrupulous about financial affairs, having created a fraudulent Narragansett Patent that claimed title to the new colony of Rhode Island and Providence Plantations as a part of Massachusetts (see later chapter in this book). Winthrop recalled Thomas Weld to Boston, which terminated Weld's service, but he probably knew he'd be punished there for his lies and fraud (though not for the white slavery), so he managed to get a call to minister in the north of England.

Now you have a picture of the sort of people and the place where Anne Hutchinson was committed to house arrest for the extremely harsh winter of 1637-38. Weld's home was in the Jamaica Plain area of Roxbury, and the Boston-Roxbury road, now called Washington Street, runs through what would have been his land. It was about two to two-and-a-half miles from the Hutchinson home in central Boston, to Weld's home, but keep in mind that this was one of the harshest winters known to the area, when the bay and marshes froze over hard enough to walk on. At that time, the Shawmut Peninsula was almost an island, with the isthmus called Boston Neck as its connection to the mainland. To get in and out of Boston by land, one had to take that Roxbury road onto the isthmus, and pass the gallows hill and burial pit before entering the fortified gate to the town.

Anne wasn't sent to the prison upon her conviction: she was a high-status woman and her husband was a respected man, but living with Joseph Weld's household could not have been pleasant. It wasn't meant to be a country club, and she didn't have her freedom. Further, Weld was known to be a strict ultra-Puritan without an Antinomian or Familist bone in his body. They didn't attend Boston First Church with Rev. Cotton's talk of a Covenant of Grace. Their church was made of sterner stuff. His brother Thomas was not only an inquisitor at Anne's trials, but the first minister of Roxbury's First Church of Christ. Those Weld boys were not to be messed with. Tough as nails.

Did she have a room of her own? Looking at Joseph's family, there are seven children and his first wife in the house, perhaps some of Joseph's or Elizabeth's siblings, plus servants. Anne was used to that size crowd at her own home, where she had her toddler Zuriel, small children, and young adults. If the Welds wanted the prisoner separated from their children, perhaps Anne had a room. But without central heating, the practice of most households was for siblings, or siblings plus parents, to share a bed for warmth. Perhaps Anne slept with female servants or older members of the family.

Anne may have been able to have visits from her children if they could make it through the snow and ice, but conjugal visits from her husband look very doubtful. He was ordered to defray the Welds' costs for keeping her. (Imagine having to pay your wife's room and board to the richest man in the colony, and a competitor for cloth business. Money was scarce for decades, so perhaps he paid in livestock, wampum, or imported cloth.)

An anecdote in Joseph Weld's genealogy information says that Anne "remarked that she could not have been treated with more respect and kindness had she been a guest in his home." If that's true, it might be to the credit of Joseph's first wife Elizabeth, who had borne eight children before she died in October 1638. Her last baby was born in July 1636, and her other surviving children were spaced two to four years apart, so it's possible that Elizabeth was pregnant during Anne's incarceration, but died a few months later at age 38.

Anne was reported to be ill during that winter, which may have been brought on by stress, viruses like colds or fevers, or menopause. But it could not have been pregnancy, as you'll see in a later chapter.

Mistress Hutchinson was subjected to frequent visits from her accusers, who argued theological points every few days, trying to trap her or convince her of her heresy. The ministers John Eliot (later called the Apostle to the Indians), Thomas Weld, Thomas Shepard, and Hugh Peter came to visit, not only to preach to her and tempt her to recant, but to use her answers against her at her church trial to be held in March.

I wonder if Anne had revelations about any of them, or if she could see the type of scoundrels that Rev. Thomas Weld and Rev. Hugh Peter would be within the next five years. (See Appendix for life sketch of Hugh Peter.)

Gov. Winthrop wrote in his *Journal* during this time,

Mistris Hutchinson being banished and confined, till the season of the year might be fit, and safe for her departure; she thought it now needless to conceal herself any longer, neither would Satan lose the opportunity of making choice of so fit an instrument, so long as any hope remained to attain his mischievous end in darkening the saving truth of the Lord Jesus, and disturbing the peace of his Churches. Therefore she began now to discover all her mind to such as came to her, so that her opinions came abroad and began to take place among her old disciples, and now some of them raised up questions about the immortality of the soul, about the resurrection, about the morality of the Sabbath, and divers others, which the Elders finding to begin to appear in some of their Churches, they took much pains (both in public and private) to suppress; the root of all was found to be in Mistris Hutchinson; whereupon they resorted to her many times, labouring to convince her, but in vain; yet they resorted to her still, to the end they might either reclaim her from her errours, or that they might bear witness against them if occasion were: For in a meeting of the Magistrates and Elders, about suppressing these new sprung errours, the Elders of Boston had declared their readiness to deal with Mistris Hutchinson in a Church way, if they had sufficient testimony: for though she had maintained some of them sometimes before them, yet they thought it not so orderly to come in as witnesses; whereupon other of the Elders, and others collecting which they had heard from her own mouth at several times ... sent them to the Church of Boston, whereupon the Church (with leave of the Magistrates, because she was a prisoner) sent for her to appear upon a Lecture day, being the fifteenth of the first month [15 March 1638], and though she were at her own house in the Town, yet she came not into the Assembly till the Sermon and Prayer were ended, (pretending bodily infirmity).

If you knew the church body, including visitors there for the spectacle, were hostile toward you and expected to revile you after the midweek lecture where attendance was mandatory, perhaps you would wait until after the two-hour sermon and prayer were finished, to come to the meetinghouse.

Imagine the headache, or the stomach tied in knots because of stress. Bodily infirmity, indeed. No need to fake it.

Chapter 17

The Silence of Winter

During Anne's winter incarceration, she stayed with the Weld family in Roxbury, while her family and friends were packing and preparing to move out of Massachusetts Bay Colony territory. There were only two realistic possibilities: north to New Hampshire, or south to the Narragansett Bay.

The severe winter raged on, with nor'easters pounding New England, and threatening to injure or kill those exposed to the elements by travel. Anne wasn't feeling well, whether from the cold, the depression of being held captive and subjected to the constant challenges of her inquisitors, the onset of menopause, or another physical malady. At her Boston home, where she was not allowed, she had a baby learning to walk and eat and talk without his mother. When her second trial began, she petitioned for the right to stay in Boston at the home of her former mentor, Pastor John Cotton, and his wife and young children. It would be easier to walk to the meetinghouse for trial, and Cotton would be able to monitor her and perhaps have one more chance to win her recantation.

Cotton was no longer her friend. He'd given her up last fall at the church synod.

Governor Winthrop wrote that the church elders of Boston found her obstinate, and propounded (sounds rather forceful!) that an admonition be given to Anne's supporters. The entire church body consented, except for Anne's son Edward and her son-in-law Francis. As they defended her, they also came under admonition, or official scolding, one of the disciplines of the church.

Dr. C. Matthew McMahon, a minister who contributes to the website *A Puritan's Mind*, wrote about the true church versus a false one, "Such marks are bound up in the classic Reformed formulation of the pure preaching of the Word of God as sound doctrine, with its lawful administration of the sacraments, and the exercise of censure and discipline pressing a holiness of life and obedience to the Word preached and taught." http://www.apuritansmind.com/pastors-study/the-three-marks-of-the-true-church-by-dr-c-matthew-mcmahon/

Though Dr. McMahon's words are written in the twenty-first century, he's a purist Puritan – he advocates a change of heart and behavior to go back to the Reformed gospel message they'd known when the Separatist movement was fresh and zealous for the fundamentals of the Bible, and keeping safe from heresy, even if it meant censure and discipline.

Winthrop wrote in his historical journal that Cotton was tasked with admonishing Anne's son and son-in-law, then Anne, and then the women of Boston who had shown interest in Anne's home studies or were in danger of believing Anne's heresy.

To the women of First Church who had known Anne as midwife, friend, neighbor, spiritual adviser, or leader of a new movement, Rev. Cotton said, "I admonish you in the Lord to take heed that you receive nothing for truth which hath not the stamp of the word of God... let not the good you have received from her in your spiritual estates make you to receive all for good that comes from her. For...she is but a woman."

Winthrop wrote:

Mr. Cotton gave the admonition, and first to her sons, laying it sadly upon them, that they would give such way to their natural affection, as for preserving her honour, they should make a breach upon the honour of Christ, and upon their Covenant with the Church, and withal tear the very bowels of their soul, by hardening her in her sin: In this admonition to her, first, he remembered her of the good way she was in at her first coming, in helping to discover to divers, the false bottom they stood upon, in trusting to legal works without Christ; then he showed her, how by falling into these gross and fundamental errors, she had lost the honour of her former service, and done more wrong to Christ and his Church, then formerly she had done good, and so laid her sin to her conscience with much zeal and solemnity. He admonished her also of the height of spirit, then he spake to the sisters of the Church, and advised them to take heed of her opinions, and to withhold all countenance and respects from her, lest they should harden her in her sin: so she was dismissed and appointed to appear again that day sevennight.

*The scold's bridle or "branks" was a medieval English device for silencing
shrewish women. It had a spiked bit that went into the mouth and punctured the
tongue if the prisoner attempted to speak. Its effect was to make of the sharp
speaker a "dumb animal." The bridle was not used in America until New
Haven Colony tied a large key into the mouth of a Quaker missionary in the
1650s. Use of the device was known for several hundred years before Winthrop,
Cotton, and Wilson had authority over Anne Hutchinson, but surely her high
status as a wealthy wife of a respected man would have saved her from application
of the cage for her head.*

To Anne, his follower and friend of two decades, Rev.
Cotton applied accusations that her meetings with both sexes
attending were a "filthy coming-together of men and women."
Further, the minister charged, "Your opinions fret like gangrene and
spread like leprosy, and will eat out the very bowels of religion."

Anne was dismissed. Not only in being "sent to her room."
Rev. Cotton and the church of Boston publicly dismissed her as
sinful, a heretic, a terminal disease on their godly society, and
someone to be shunned. She was excommunicated. She was put
down.

Like her father, and like most of Massachusetts' Puritan
preachers who had fled Old England, Anne Marbury Hutchinson was
silenced.

Anne's March 1638 trial lasted about three weeks. One of the
charges against her was the mixed meetings of men and women,
which Governor Winthrop called "a thing not tolerable nor comely
in the sight of God nor fitting for your sex, and notwithstanding that
was cried down you have continued the same. Therefore we have
thought good to send for you to understand how things are, that if

you be in an erroneous way we may reduce you that so you may become a profitable member here among us."

"That we may reduce you."

Had Anne set herself above the men of the colony, specifically the theocratic rulers? Or was that Winthrop's perception? Did Mistress Hutchinson break the fifth Commandment to honor her ecclesiastical "fathers," and the government selected by the autocratic Winthrop? She had defended her beliefs and actions before a court of ministers and elders of the church, some who had training in the law, and she had done it without an attorney of her own. How could this woman who hadn't attended university answer their tricky legal language and the traps they laid for her during her incarceration? Had the long-ago training she received from her father's story of his trials laid a foundation for Anne's current courtroom battle?

Her Bible scholarship and her logic frustrated the men who were trying her, and they saw her as getting above her station as a mere woman in God's hierarchy of power. The social structure of religious government over father-husband-master left the mistress of the house several rungs down the ladder of authority. Anne Hutchinson had taught men and was not submissive, in violation of 1 Timothy chapter 2.

And as Rev. Cotton had charged, the mixed crowd in the Hutchinson parlor was "filthy." In the twenty-first century, even in the most fundamental or conservative of communities, it's difficult to enter that mindset. But it was reality and tradition to the people of England and the colonists of New England. Anne was opening a new world, and many were scandalized and terrified with change.

One effect of "reducing" Anne Hutchinson would be keeping all the women of the colonies in place. Another was reaffirming to the men that they must crack down on insubordination in the family, and that they should remember their place in the social order: above women, but below the level of the ministers and the founders of the new colony. Lastly, it reminded them that in the biblical model of church governance and membership, excommunication was to be a temporary measure. In the case of Mrs. Temperance Sweete selling alcohol and allowing carousing in her home, she was scolded, excommunicated for a month, then restored.

Church members submitted to the "laws of Christ" and to oversight of their fellow members. The church as a body desired to be purified from the world and sanctified holy to the Lord.

The point of coming under church discipline was not to cast out the wicked, but to remove them from fellowship and possible contamination of other members for a time. They were to examine their behavior, and they could be visited by their ministers and elders. Then, if they were properly penitent, they could be brought back into full membership privileges, allowed to take Communion, and if they were men, to vote. If they lost their membership, they were still required to attend services and pay tithes to the church and fines to the government, and they couldn't vote.

Being a member of the church was a serious matter. It showed that you might be one of the Elect, the people predestined to salvation who showed their salvation by doing good works. After a short life on earth, they were concerned about the soul's eternity in heaven and not in hell.

Even the ministers were not immune to censure or admonishment. In 1637, Rev. John Wilson, senior pastor of Boston First Church, had been in England for three-quarters of a year and had recently returned to Boston. Perhaps feeling like he hadn't been missed and Cotton had taken over with his talk of a Covenant of Grace, he stirred up negativity against the very popular Rev. Cotton, the teacher of the same church. When Cotton and his faction got their hackles up and demanded censure of Wilson, Cotton graciously turned the situation to one of church unity. And Rev. Wilson was restored as a "profitable member" among them.

Having studied the public and the personal writings of Gov. John Winthrop, we can't treat him as a villain in the Hutchinson and Dyer stories. He was no two-dimensional cartoon. He was well loved by his family and respected among his peers and the people of Massachusetts. He had *gravitas* – a dignity rooted in his birth, his work and sacrifice for the colony in extreme conditions – that he desired, achieved, and deserved. So when he spoke of restoring Mistress Hutchinson (after an extended period of shame and discomfort) to the church, I believe he was sincere. He even tried to get the Hutchinsons back to First Church in 1640 (see later chapter) before he finally turned on Anne when he wrote his book about the controversy. In Winthrop's mind, he had to "reduce" Anne before she could be a profitable member of the community. In our minds, he abused his power. But in theirs, it was his right to correct an errant woman for her own good, and for the good of the community.

Did Winthrop say his piece with a haughty lift of his chin or eyebrows? Did he speak with a sob in his voice for effect? What about the physical appearance of the court inquisitors Dudley, Weld, Shepard, and Peter? In the spectator benches of the meetinghouse, what did Mary Dyer do – did she dig her fingernails into the heels of her hands?

How did Mistress Hutchinson take such a statement after five months in a hostile house?

A few years later, when Anne was dead, Winthrop wrote in his *Short Story*,

> See the Impudent boldness of a Proud Dame, that makes havoc of all that stand in the way of her ambitious spirit; … she vented her Impatience with so fierce Speech and Countenance, as one would hardly have guessed her to have been an Antitype of Daniel, but rather of the Lions after they were let loose.

Was she fierce of speech and countenance, or was she not the "little woman" she was expected to be? Perhaps she stood there, very still, with measured breathing, determined not to be reduced or made profitable to those who were looking for a spark of anger and insubordination, or a tightening of the lips, or a red flush of Anne's face.

"I bless the Lord," she said. "He hath let me see which was the clear ministry and which the wrong."

"How do you know that was the spirit?" asked Mr. Nowell.

"How did Abraham know that it was God that bid him offer his son, being a breach of the sixth commandment?" she replied.

"By an immediate voice," Thomas Dudley said.

"So to me by an immediate revelation," she responded.

"How, an immediate revelation?" the court scoffed.

"By the voice of his spirit to my soul," she answered.

But God wouldn't speak to a creature so far down the social ladder. So Mistress Hutchinson must be delusional or lying. God would speak to a man who was a member of the Elect, those pre-destined for salvation. But he would be silent to a woman. He would not give power and control, or reveal secret knowledge to a woman.

Men and women had different roles in the hierarchy that was Puritan society. Men gave permission to women to work and speak, and they decided the license she was given if they were away. Men-husbands-fathers could decide how the woman-wife-daughter-relative-servant they controlled represented them in the town, in church, and in the privacy of the family.

"You have power over my body but the Lord Jesus hath power over my body and soul," said Anne Hutchinson to John Winthrop, the governor and patriarch of Massachusetts Bay Colony. She would not accept that her female body was a cage or prison in which her spirit could be incarcerated or displayed as a captive. Because under the sovereign God, there was no preference for Jew or Gentile, man or woman, slave or free. That made all women, and Anne Hutchinson in that moment, the equal of her accusers and judges.

The court did not see the light, give Anne a hug, and lay hands on her shoulders and head in an ordination blessing, asking for God's will to be done in her ministry. Instead, they gasped in revulsion at her heresy.

"Assure yourselves thus much," said Mistress Hutchinson, "you do as much as in you lies to put the Lord Jesus Christ from you, and if you go on in this course you begin, you will bring a curse upon you and your posterity, and the mouth of the Lord hath spoken it."

John Cotton gave a long admonition to Anne, her sons, and her female supporters, to keep away from her. Her sons and son-in-law, by speaking at the trials on her behalf, had hardened her heart and nourished her unsound opinions, and had hindered the proceedings of the church against her. "Instead of loving and natural children, you have proved vipers, to eat through the very bowels of your mother... Desist from such practice." He admonished her sons to show her her wrong ways and reduce her from it.

To the sisters of the congregation who had been "too much seduced and led aside by her," Rev. Cotton said:

"You see she is but a Woman & many unsound and dangerous Principles are held by her, therefore whatsoever good you have received own it & keeps it carefully, but if you have drunk in with this good any Evil or Poison, make speed to vomit it up again & to repent of it."

To Anne herself, Cotton gave the longest speech of all, which said that all her good works had been nullified by the evil her opinions wrought. His speech can be summarized in these points:

- Dishonor brought to God by unsound tenets
- Evil of her opinions
- Souls she misled
- Conveyed the poison of unsound principles
- Razed the very foundation of religion to the ground, to destroy the faith
- Committed "filthy sin of the Community of Women, and all promiscuous coming together of men and women"
- Hadn't been unfaithful to her husband, "yet that will follow upon it."
- More dangerous evils and filthy uncleanness and other sins will follow
- God had left her to herself, and it was just to abase her and leave her to her desperate fall
- Even if she held her dangerous opinions sincerely, "yet if you do but make a question of them, and propound them as a doubt for satisfaction," others would think there was something in it.
- Her opinions "fretted like a gangrene, and spread like a leprosy, and infected far and near," and would "eat out the very bowels of religion"

Cotton said before the crowd pack in the meetinghouse:
"Therefore that I may draw to an End; I do Admonish you, & also charge you in the Name of Christ Jesus, in whose place I stand, & in the Name of the Church who hath put me upon this service; that you would sadly consider the just hand of God against you, the great hurt you have done to the Churches, the great Dishonor you have brought to Jesus Christ & the Evil that you have done to many a poor soul… & so the Lord carry home to your soul what I have spoken to you in his name."

Finally, John Wilson pronounced the judgment of the court.
"Forasmuch as you, Mistress Hutchinson, have highly transgressed & offended, & forasmuch as you have so many ways troubled the Church with your Errors & have drawn away many a poor soul, & have upheld your Revelations; & forasmuch as you have made a Lie, &c. Therefore in the name of our Lord Jesus Christ & in the name of the Church I do not only pronounce you worthy to be cast out, but I do cast you out

& in the name of Christ I do deliver you up to Satan, that you may learn no more to blaspheme, to seduce & to lie, & I do account you from this time forth to be a Heathen and a Publican and so to be held of all the Brethren & Sisters of this Congregation, & of others. Therefore I command you in the name of Christ Jesus & of this Church as a Leper to withdraw yourself out of the Congregation; that as formerly you have despised & condemned the Holy Ordinances of God, & turned your back on them, so you may now have no part in them nor benefit by them."

They went there, using the name and authority of Christ to blast Anne to perdition. Not a whiff of Christ's compassion, mercy, or grace. No resemblance to the biblical model of disfellowship.

In Massachusetts Bay Colony, Anne Hutchinson was silenced. Every accusation was a dagger to her heart, as it was meant to be.

For a leader, part of their ability to lead comes from *public perception* of their experience, their self-control and mastery of emotions in the face of getting the job done. A religious leader, particularly, must project faith and confidence in the "product," which is the gospel of salvation for the lost and dying. Their behavior and words are microscopically scrutinized. It's even more critical for a female leader to be the image of moral correctness to attract and keep her followers.

Her own children had been told to shun her. Her followers were on notice that they had been poisoned with Hutchinson gangrene and leprosy.

It's one thing to know intellectually that accusations are false, and another to feel emotionally that one has been wounded unto death, *in the name of Jesus Christ.*

But now, the ministers, elders, inquisitors, and elected representatives of the colony had stripped Anne Hutchinson almost to the bone. She was reduced to a seducer, a whore and liar, a blasphemer, an infectious leper. She was banished to the wilderness, the abode of the devil, far beyond the holy City Upon a Hill.

All she had left was to straighten her shoulders and put on the face of a lioness as she turned her back and walked down the center aisle where decent Christians would no longer look her in the eye.

Chapter 18

He Heals the Broken-hearted and Binds Up Their Wounds

Psalm 147:3

hen Anne had been cast into outer darkness – *in the name of Jesus Christ* – by Cotton, her former friend and mentor of 25 years, and delivered up to Satan – *in the name of Jesus Christ* – by Wilson, and she turned to leave the meetinghouse, a young woman stood up, pushed through the crowd, walked to Anne's side, and took her hand as they turned their backs on theocratic government.

She was Mary Barrett Dyer, 27 years old, lovely, prosperous, and educated. She and Anne were "much given to revelations," and Winthrop wrote that Anne and Mary were "chief fomenters" in the colony.

But at this moment, Mary Dyer was the only person present among hundreds of accusers and spectators, with the heart and spirit to bravely support the convicted heretic. Mary was the only person to show Christian compassion to a crushed heart.

Without words, she put Anne before her own certain censure, and did what Jesus would have done: come alongside with comfort and support in the time of greatest sorrow and need, with the right hand of fellowship. The fellowship that had been so cruelly snatched away was restored in that simple act.

It takes courage, loyalty, and love to support a person with life-threatening injuries to their soul, a person surrounded by enemies.

There are times in our lives when we need to feel or hear "I love you. I'm with you. I won't forsake you. Take my arm and we'll go through the fire together."

It was fire, indeed. Someone in the crowd outside asked who that young woman was, and another person said it was Mary Dyer, the mother of a "monster."

Mary, too, was outed as a heretic.

Chapter 19

What the Men of Massachusetts Said About Anne

Anne Hutchinson was a Jezebel. The biblical Jezebel, of the ninth century BC, was a Phoenician queen of Israel who oppressed and killed Yahweh's prophets, and led the people of ancient Israel in the worship of Baal and Astarte. Jezebel is remembered for her connection with the sex and fertility cults, for her makeup, wig, and jewelry, but especially for seducing Israel to leave Yahweh and follow Baal and Astarte. Anne was considered to be a seducer of God's people who led them into a false religion.

Once or twice a week, Mistress Hutchinson had most of the Boston women and many of its leading men in her home, a dangerous faction for the ministers and governing officials of the colony. She'd had the young Governor Henry Vane, and a member of the Winthrop Fleet, William Coddington, and many influential or up-and-coming tradesmen, merchants, and even magistrates on her side.

Her husband called her "A dear saint and servant of God."

But what did other men have to say about her?

Rev. Thomas Weld: "Some being tainted conveyed the infection to others ... Some of the magistrates, some gentlemen, some scholars and men of learning, some burgesses of our General Court, some of our captains and soldiers, some chief men in towns, and some eminent for religion, parts, and wit." He also wrote that "the custom was for her scholars to propound questions and she (gravely sitting in the chair) did make answers thereupon." [The chair was the throne of the head of family, and others sat on benches. Weld was saying that Anne was usurping the place of the God-ordained man of the family.]

Rev. John Cotton: "I sent some sisters of the Church [spies?] on purpose to her repetitions so that I might know the truth. But when she discerned any such present, no speech fell from her that could be excepted against."

Cotton also wrote that "She did much good to our town, in women's meeting and as childbirth travails, wherein she was not only skillful and helpful, but readily fell into good discourse with the women." It's possible that Anne had delivered Cotton's second child, Sarah, being a near neighbor.

Cotton wrote, also, that Anne was "one well beloved and all the faithful embrace her conference and bless God for her fruitful discourses. "

During Anne's trial, Cotton was pushed to testify as to Anne Hutchinson's revelations being miraculous communications, or if Hutchinson was discerning God's will through meditating on the Psalms. He was reluctant to make that judgment, but finally said, "That she may have some special providence of God to help her is a thing that I cannot bear witness against."

Cotton admonished Anne at her second trial about "and all promiscuous and filthy coming together of men and women, without distinction or relation of marriage, and though I have not heard, neither do I think, that you have been unfaithful to your husband in his marriage covenant, yet that will follow upon it. Your opinions fret like a gangrene, and spread like a leprosy, and infect far and near, and will eat out the very bowels of religion."

Gov. John Winthrop: "The pretense was to repeat [Cotton's] sermons, but when that was done, she would comment … and she would be sure to make it serve her turn."

He said directly to Anne, "Your opinions being known to be different from the word of God may seduce many simple souls that resort unto you."

He also wrote that "This American Jezebel kept her strength and reputation, even among the people of God, till the hand of Civil Justice laid hold on her."

Further, Anne was "A woman of a haughty and fierce carriage, of a nimble wit and active spirit, and a very voluble tongue, more bold than a man, though in understanding and judgment inferior to many women."

"But blessed be the Lord, the snare is broken, and we are delivered from this woman, an instrument of Satan so fitted and trained to his service for poisoning the Churches here planted, as no story records the like of a woman, since that mentioned in the Revelation [chapter 17]."

Governor Henry Vane said, "Come along with me, I'll bring you to a woman that preaches better gospel then any of your black-coats that have been at the 'Ninneversity,' a woman of another kind of spirit, who hath had many Revelations of things to come."

The ministers of the theological synod held in September 1637: "One woman (in a prophetical way, by resolving questions of doctrine, and expounding scripture) took upon her the whole exercise, was agreed to be disorderly, and without rule."

Thomas Leverett, ruling elder of the Boston church, called Anne "Haughty Jezebel," and a "railer" and "reviler."

Rev. Zechariah Symmes: "Have a care of Mistress Anne Hutchinson, who is come, so she says, to sit down at Brother Cotton's feet. It seems clear that she is come instead to broach heresies here among us. In the great cabin [on the ship *Griffin*] where we were together, she stirred up everyone against our preaching. She seemed to agree with Brother Lothrop and myself, yet there was a secret opposition to the things we delivered."

Capt. Roger Clap of Dorchester said about the controversy with the Wheelwright-Hutchinson faction, without naming names:

But this glorious Work of God towards his People here was soon maligned by Satan; and he cast into the minds of *some corrupt Persons, very erroneous Opinions, which did breed great Disturbance in the Churches.* And he [Satan] puffed up his Instruments [Anne Hutchinson and followers] with horrible Pride, insomuch that they would oppose the Truth of God delivered Publicly: and some times, yea most times they would do it by way of Query, as if they desired to be informed: but they did indeed accuse our godly Ministers of not preaching Gospel, saying they were Legal Preachers, but themselves were for free Grace, and Ministers did Preach a Covenant of Works; which was a false Aspersion on them. The Truth was, they would willingly have lived in Sin, and encouraged others so to do, etc. And yet think to be saved by Christ, because his Grace is free; forgetting (it seems) that those whom Christ doth save from Hell, he also freely of his Grace doth save from Sin; for he came to save his People from their Sins, to give Repentance and Remission of Sins.

Rev. Thomas Shepard of New Town (Cambridge): "She is a most dangerous Spirit, and likely with her fluent Tongue and forwardness in Expressions to seduce and draw away many, Especially simple Women of her own sex."

Richard Scott, Anne's brother-in-law by her youngest sister Katherine, defended Anne faintly at her heresy trial on March 22, 1638: "I desire to propound this one scruple, well keeps me that I cannot so freely in my spirit give way to excommunication whither it was not better to give her a little time to consider of the things that is advised against her, because she is not yet convinced of her Lie and so things is with her in Distraction, and she cannot recollect her thoughts." Richard was removed from the trial anyway, because his testimony was believed to be biased by his relationship.

Rev. Thomas Hooker of Hartford: "She is cast out as unsavory salt, that she may not continue a pest to the place."

Deputy-Gov. Thomas Dudley at the second trial: "Mistress Hutchinson's Repentance is only for Opinions held since her Imprisonment, but before her Imprisonment she was in a good Condition, & held no Error, but did a great deal of Good to many. Now I know no Harm that Mrs. Hutchinson hath done since her Confinement, therefore I think her Repentance will be worse than her Errors, for if by this means she shall get a party to herself, & what can any Heretic in the World desire."

Rev. John Wilson, minister of Boston First Church of Christ, said, "Consider whether we shall be faithful to Jesus Christ or whether it can stand to suffer such an one any longer amongst us; if the blind lead the blind, whither shall we go. Consider how we can or whether we may longer suffer her to go on still in seducing to seduce, & in deceiving to deceive, & in lying to lie, & in condemning Authority & Magistracy, still to condemn. Therefore we should sin against God if we should not put away from us so Evil a Woman, guilty of such foul Evils."

Chapter 20

Why the Pilgrim Governor Wanted to Know About the Dyer "Monster"

STRANGE NEVVES
ut of *Kent*, of a Monſtrous and misſhapen
Child, borne in *Olde Sandwitch*, vpon the 10. of *Iulie*
laſt, the like (for ſtrangenes) hath ne-
uer beene ſeene.

Drawing depicts an anencephalic
child born in England, but not
Mary Dyer's child.

It had no head, nor any sign or proportion thereof, there only appeared as it were two faces, the one visibly to be seen, directly placed in the breast, where it had a nose, and a mouth, and two holes for two eyes, but no eyes, all which seemed ugly, and most horrible to be seen, and much offensive to human nature to be looked upon, the other face was not perfectly to be seen, but retained a proportion of flesh in a great round lump, like unto a face quite disfigured, and this was all of that which could be discerned. The face, mouth, eyes, nose, and breast, being thus framed together like a deformed piece of flesh, resembled no proportion of nature, but seemed as it were a chaos of confusion, a mixture of things without any description...

In October 1637, Mary Dyer gave birth to a premature, stillborn girl, which, according to descriptions, was anencephalic (lacking more than a brainstem) and probably had spina bifida (neural tube defects). This was the first anencephalic baby ever reported in America.

Back in their native England, gravely-deformed babies or fetuses were called "monsters" or "monstrous births," and were commonly known to be heaven-sent proof of heresy or monstrous religious or political beliefs of the mother.

If the deformed child (say, born without arms) survived birth and infancy, and if the parents didn't abandon it from fear of being judged heretics, it could become a freakish monster to be shown, for an admission fee, to audiences in London or Norwich. It was an object of derision, not a human, in medieval and Early Modern thought. The monstrous child showed God's wrath at human sin, and was a brutish form of entertainment. A town's court, warden, or minister would pay for a display to prove the necessity of moral behavior. They instilled fear by showing proof of what happens to heretics or immoral parents.

Mary's unnamed daughter's birth deformities and burial place were kept a secret among a handful of people. But in March 1638, at Anne Hutchinson's heresy trial and conviction in Boston, Massachusetts, Anne was excommunicated and sentenced to leave the church and colony. Anne's and Mary's husbands were not at the trial, because they were preparing their newly-purchased land in Pocasset, on Rhode Island, for their impending move. When Anne was told to depart the meetinghouse, Mary stood up, took Anne's hand, and they walked out together. As they left the building, someone in the crowd mentioned that Mary was the mother of a monster.

Governor John Winthrop, in his zeal to further prosecute Anne and her supporters, ordered the exhumation and examination of this monster, Mary Dyer's baby, which had lain in the frozen ground for five months while Boston experienced a severely cold winter, and Anne was under house arrest in Roxbury.

The poor mite's remains were disinterred, and more than one hundred men gawked at the corpse before it was reburied. How did Winthrop learn how the labor and delivery, and the secret burial of the fetus came about? He used a classic interrogation technique still in use today: he *lied*, saying to Midwife Hawkins that Anne had revealed the story, and then the story came out; he did the same to Anne, saying that Hawkins had spilled the details. Between them, the story came out.

*A holograph of William Bradford's letter to John Winthrop
regarding Mary Dyer's stillborn baby.*
Massachusetts Historical Society

Then Rev. Cotton was questioned as to his role in keeping the secret and burying the fetus. The lurid, horrifying, putrefying details were teased out one by one.

Mary Dyer had been delivered when unconscious, and had nearly died from the complicated birth. She was probably shielded from most of the story – which she heard now, trumpeted in public. No one recorded her reaction or feelings, so perhaps she, like Anne, kept her game face on.

Governor Winthrop wrote a description in his history journal, and within about four years, the description of the monstrous features went viral in England, by way of several publications. One of those was a short book about Anne Hutchinson's theology, written by John Winthrop, with a foreword by Rev. Thomas Weld, which brought down hellfire and brimstone on both Mary and Anne.

But on April 11, 1638, in the first month after the revelation of Anne's trial and Mary's monster, the governor of Plymouth Colony, William Bradford, wrote a letter to his friend and colleague, John Winthrop. Most of the letter was about colonial boundaries and the islands in the Narragansett Bay, which Plymouth insisted were part of their original royal patent, but generously released to the Indians who "owned" it since time immemorial – who then sold it to the Hutchinson party being routed from Boston! Still, Bradford felt, it would be better to have English settlers, even if heretics, in the Narragansett Bay territory, than to have unfriendly Indian neighbors in the area. And there began a dispute that would last into the 1650s, when the Rhode Island charter and boundary was confirmed by the English Commonwealth government.

Illustration from a 1568 English book about monstrous births,
The Forme and Shape of a Monstrous Child

The first part of the Bradford letter asked for juicy details of Mary Dyer's baby. Like Winthrop, Bradford kept a historical journal (not a personal diary) meant for publication someday. Much of his work was used in William Brewster's book, *Mourt's Relation*, but today we know the Bradford original as *Of Plymouth Plantation*. Bradford, like Winthrop, used the court cases and interesting stories as moral lessons. For instance, Bradford remarked about the Pequot Indian massacre that his forces perpetrated in 1637: "It was a fearful sight to see them frying in the fire, with streams of blood quenching it; the smell was horrible, but the victory seemed a sweet sacrifice, and they gave praise to God." And he described the June 1, 1638 New England earthquake as the Lord's displeasure at a group splintering from New Plymouth and proposing to plant a new community.

So Bradford's request for information on Mary Dyer's monster was a request for evidence of God's displeasure with the heretics of Boston and then Rhode Island. In the end, though, he chose not to use whatever information he received. Other writers did not hesitate to reveal lurid details, in England and America. As you see in Bradford's letter, he'd already heard "many various reports," in the month since the baby's exhumation, so it was a major topic of the time.

Here follows part of Governor Bradford's letter to Governor Winthrop about Mary Dyer's monster and how the Hutchinsonians had bought and settled Aquidneck Island, which I've edited for twenty-first-century ease of reading:

Beloved Sir:

I thank you for your letter touching Mrs Huchinson. I heard since of a monstrous, & prodigious birth [Mary's miscarriage] which she should discover amongst you; as also that she should retract her confession of acknowledgment of those errors, before she went away; of which I have heard many various reports. If your leisure would permit, I should be much beholden unto you, to certify me in a word or two, of the truth & form of that monster &c.

… Thus commending you, & your affairs to the Lord; with my love remembered to your self, & the rest of my worthy friends with you, I take leave & rest

April. 11. 1638

Your unworthy friend

William Bradford

What was Gov. Winthrop's reply? He doesn't seem to have answered about the monstrous birth. He was taken extremely ill on about the first of May, and feared for his life for several weeks, so he may not have written a reply letter. According to the Massachusetts Historical Society, Winthrop made notes on Bradford's letter about colonial boundaries.

Chapter 21

How Anne Hutchinson's Theology Shaped Mary Dyer, the Quaker Martyr

This article was written for the September 2016
'Plain Language,' the annual publication of the
National Society of Descendants of Early Quakers

There are several points at which the lives of Anne Marbury Hutchinson and Mary Barrett Dyer touched. In one instance, the touch was literal. At the end of Anne's second trial, Mary took Anne's hand and they walked out of the meetinghouse together. Someone in the crowd outside asked who was publicly supporting a woman who had been convicted of heresy and excommunicated, and the whisper about Mary's stillbirth a few months before became a roar.

Before Anne's first heresy trial in October 1637, Mary had borne a seven-months-gestation female fetus with spina bifida and anencephaly (no brain, only a brainstem), and Anne was one of the midwives attending. Only two or three women, and the popular minister John Cotton, knew of the "monster" birth; they only knew that Mary had miscarried, which was a common event in their time. Cotton buried the tiny bundle in accordance with English law, probably on the common grazing land near the Dyers' house, deep enough that neither "hogg nor dogg" could dig it up.

As I researched my historical novels and nonfiction book on William and Mary Dyer, it was immediately apparent that I'd need to understand the relationship between Anne and Mary and their husbands, both named William. I believe the relationship between the Hutchinsons and Dyers began in England, when they lived about 25 and 16 miles, respectively, from John Cotton's church in Boston, Lincolnshire. William Hutchinson was a cloth merchant, and the young William Dyer was a haberdasher dealing in leather goods, so it's possible that their trades intersected in Boston and London. Further, Anne's youngest sister, Katherine Marbury Scott, was close in age to William and Mary, and they knew each other well over several decades; and Anne's granddaughter married the eldest son of the Dyers.

Having grown up in a fundamentalist denomination, I was curious about the word Antinomian, which by definition means "against the Law." My church said that Antinomianism was wrong because the Law of God stands forever, unchanged, and we're answerable for our actions and thoughts in the final judgment. But how are we to explain the New Testament epistles that say that the Law was nailed to the Cross and annulled, and the New Covenant said that God himself would write the new law on our hearts (what we'd call a conscience), not tablets of stone, and mercy and grace trumped judgment. That launched my quest to know more about Anne Hutchinson and her beliefs.

I've known for many years that one of my direct ancestors was Mary Barrett Dyer, the Quaker woman who was hanged for defying the Boston theocracy in 1660. I visited Boston and New England on a business trip in 1998, when a history professor told me a different story than the standard tale of the mean Puritans attacking and executing innocent Quakers. He explained that Quakers could have left the colony for safety in Rhode Island, but they chose to stay or even *return* to Massachusetts or Connecticut in defiance of being silenced or exiled. What? That was never in the encyclopedia articles!

That's exactly what happened, as I learned from seventeenth-century court records. Quakers were fined, stripped nude to the waist and whipped (leaving scars for life), tortured, dragged behind carts, had goods and animals confiscated, and they were imprisoned during winters in the Little Ice Age without fire or light. They could have avoided almost all of that, but they believed that the "fire and the hammer" in their hearts commanded them to confront authority, so they went to Boston, Plymouth, New Haven, and Salem, and got in the face of the theocratic government. Despite the cost to their health and lives, the biblical promise of eternal life was well worth the sacrifice. After all, we're only walking this world for a brief time, whereas heaven is forever.

What were some other points of contact between Anne and Mary?

When Anne conducted Bible studies in her Boston home between 1634 and 1637, the group was composed of women at first. As a midwife, she held a position of authority, and was probably licensed by the Church of England to baptize infants if it looked like they wouldn't survive long enough for a priest to do it. Labor and delivery were great social events that could last a day or two, with perhaps ten or twenty women of all ages, plus their babies and small children, telling stories, sewing, sharing their best dishes, and giving gifts. It was an extended baby shower. And there was time for the elder women to teach spiritual and behavioral principles to the younger. A birthing often brought death for mother and infant, so salvation was much on their minds. The middle-aged Anne Hutchinson surely made use of this venue to share her teachings, and Mary, twenty years younger, quickly became one of Anne's students, for in 1637, Gov. John Winthrop noted in his history that they were the "chief fomenting women" in Boston.

The two Williams, meantime, were signing the Wheelwright Remonstrance, involved in the European-American-Caribbean shipping business, and supporting Gov. Henry Vane instead of John Winthrop. In government, Hutchinson was a magistrate, and Dyer was a clerk and a member of a surveying and building commission, which was part of his leadership training in his London guild. The men who had signed the remonstrance were investigating buying land in New Hampshire or Rhode Island to form their own society away from the oppressive theocracy of Boston or Plymouth. Rev. Wheelwright went to New Hampshire, but almost all of the other "Hutchinsonians" decided on Rhode Island.

After Anne was convicted at her first trial in October 1637, she was kept under house arrest at the home of Joseph Weld of Roxbury. As a high-status woman, Anne would not have to do time in the prison, but she was in a pressure cooker, for Weld and his brothers were extremely strict, legalistic Puritans. She had to receive numerous three-man interrogations by ministers during that harsh winter when one polar vortex after another piled up snow and froze the bay as far as some of the islands. At one point, she recanted. But in her second trial which took place in the first three weeks of March 1638, she angrily prophesied against the colonial leaders – and she was busted. I don't believe it was as much about theology as it was "teaching" and arguing with the chauvinist men. So she was convicted, told to be out of Massachusetts Bay by the end of March, and excommunicated.

Anne was released from custody and began to prepare for a move to New Hampshire with Rev. Wheelwright. Where were her husband and William Dyer and the other men of her party? They were in Plymouth and Providence, buying Rhode Island from the Indian sachems. But over the course of a few hours, Anne changed her mind and decided to walk to Providence. Walk. Through three feet of snow on a rough wagon road through potentially dangerous Indian territory.

She and her followers (the husbands probably got back to Boston in time for the move) walked out of Boston on a Lecture Day when there were hundreds of visitors in town. At the Passover's full moon. Anne the Antinomian was walking away from the spiritual slavery to the Law and Boston authority, just as Moses led the Hebrews away from slavery and Egypt's pharaonic regime.

Two months later, near the time of Pentecost, Anne was leading a prayer meeting in Pocasset, which would be renamed Portsmouth, Rhode Island. The largest earthquake ever to shake New England struck at that time, and Anne said that it was the Holy Spirit visiting them. Mary Dyer and the other Antinomians were there when, three weeks later, there was a blood moon eclipse. The red moon and the earthquake were two strong signs of the soon-coming Christ. But Anne wasn't feeling well, the last six weeks. She'd resumed marital relations with her husband when they left Boston, and she was pregnant with hydatidiform moles. She delivered the mass of gelatinous globules sometime in late June, because the information came out immediately in early-July sermons in Boston. They called it a monster birth, God's punishment and proof positive of Anne's many heresies.

The news of Mary's and Anne's monsters was passed between ships at sea, and became tabloid news in England. It was a story that didn't die. John Winthrop wrote a book about the Antinomian Controversy and Rev. Thomas Weld wrote a lurid introduction about the monster births. Another book mentioned it in the 1650s, and there was a widespread rumor that women who preached (like Quakers) or *listened* to female preachers, would give birth to monsters. Four decades later, a book charged that Gov. Henry Vane, who became an important government leader in England, had fathered the monsters. Anne and Mary were infamous for unavoidable tragedies of nature.

In early 1639, a group that included the Dyers founded the town of Newport at the southern end of the island, while the Hutchinsons continued in Portsmouth. Anne seems to have lost her teaching and leadership edge after the move to Rhode Island and her molar birth, but her husband continued as governor of the town for a time. He bought or leased land on Long Island and died in 1642.

Anne and her youngest children (the oldest were married and living elsewhere) and household servants moved to a Dutch farm at what is now Eastchester, Pelham Bay, the Bronx. The Dutch governor of New Netherland may have incited the Siwanoy Indians to harass or kill English colonists, or the Siwanoy may have thought they were attacking the Dutch, but they fell upon the farm in August 1643, and killed almost everyone, and took young Susanna Hutchinson hostage. The news made its way to Newport, where Mary Dyer was delivered of her fifth child, whom she named Mahershallalhashbaz (he was called Maher). The name from Isaiah 8:4 means, in Hebrew, "suddenly attacked, quickly taken" or "swift to plunder and quick to carry away." The name is surely a reference to the death of Anne Hutchinson and family and the abduction of Susanna, and reflects the Dyers' heartbreak at losing people dear to them.

During the 1640s, everything we know about the Dyers is about William's career in Rhode Island government. He and Mary had three more children, the last born in 1650. Early in 1652, Mary went to England, as many other men and women did at the end of the English Civil Wars. However, once there, the Anglo-Dutch War heated up, and it wasn't safe to return to New England until about 1654. But she didn't sail to America until about January 1657. During that time, she was convinced of the Quaker beliefs. The ship she took from Bristol attempted to reach Boston during February 1657, but resorted to sailing all the way to Barbados to wait out the severe winter storms. They stayed with Friends there for several weeks, and one of the Friends wrote to Margaret Fell that he'd met one Mary Dyer.

I've found no evidence that Mary preached a message, particularly where men could hear, because if she had, she'd have been whipped like Anne's sister, Katherine Scott, who was a wealthy Baptist before she was a Quaker. Mary was imprisoned several times, but the records don't mention whipping. She was married to the colonies' first attorney general and the first commander-in-chief-upon-the-seas, and she was well-known for her education, beauty, and conversational ability. Perhaps those attributes literally saved her hide. But I suspect that she was never a preacher to men, and she was a high-status woman, so whipping and scarring her was never on the table. Mary may have followed Anne's example of teaching at baby birthings, and I wrote that into my books.

From her sole surviving letter to the General Court of Boston in 1659, it appears to me that Mary was extremely knowledgeable about both testaments of the Bible, particularly the book of Hebrews, which speaks of the substance of faith, the new covenant of God's will revealed to individuals without any mediator (like a minister or church) except Christ, and the description of how the witnesses and martyrs of the faith stayed loyal and faithful to a God they couldn't touch or see, but who was more real than they could discern with the senses.

It's not easy to unravel Anne Hutchinson's theology, twisted as it might have been by the ultra-Puritanical reporters at her trial and dialect that's changed over 400 years, but I believe Anne followed the words of Romans, Galatians, and Hebrews, where the apostle clearly said that the old law of Sinai had been nailed to the Cross, making it null and void. Ergo, Anti-nomian, against the whole Law. But you can't stop there. Nature abhors a vacuum. So what takes the place of the Law? A God-given conscience and a new law of love, justice, compassion, and mercy for others. And instead of God being dispensed by ministers or kept in a church building, he is alive in the hearts of mankind who accept his wooing. That was too warm-fuzzy for the stern Calvinists. But the concept that God loves us and *wants* to save us, I believe, is what attracted Mary Dyer to the Quaker beliefs. I learned as an author that one can never say too many times that God is personal and he loves you.

That's what she died for, too. It wasn't about mean Puritans and innocent Quakers and Baptists (the Baptists were sorely persecuted, too). It was Mary and other Friends committing what we call civil disobedience, knowing it could result in their deaths. They saw that the "mean Puritans" (really only a handful of men, since many had come to pity the Quakers) would continue their bloodlust and persecution unless there was some extraordinary event. Mary was merely visiting Friends in prison each time she was arrested. But with her deliberate disobedience to her banishment orders, she forced them to decide – take her life as they'd threatened, or discontinue their reign of terror on the Quakers and Baptists.

From Mary's last sentences as she stood on the gallows outside the gate to Boston, I think she was already entering the gates of Paradise, where all is Light and Love.

Immediately after her death, her letter to the court was copied and taken to England, where a Quaker minister used it to form a protest letter to the newly-restored king. The king responded with a diplomatic but pointed letter to stop the persecution and refer any capital case to him in England. Boston had to back down.

Mary's husband, William Dyer, was instrumental in the creation of the Rhode Island charter of liberties granted by King Charles II in 1663. They were granted the freedom to believe and act according to conscience, and Rhode Island, already a pioneer in religious liberty, became a safe haven for Baptists, Quakers, Catholics, Jews, Muslims, and those with no religious belief. That document was one of the templates of the US Constitution's First Amendment: freedom to speak, freedom to protest, freedom to assemble in peace, and religious liberty to act without government establishment or interference.

Religious liberty has been in danger ever since, and the struggle continues today, both nationally and at the state legislative level. Groups wrap their brand of religion in the flag, and try to discriminate against those of other beliefs, or no beliefs. I like what an ancestor, the Welsh minister Nathaniel Jenkins, had to say in 1720, when he stood up in the New Jersey assembly after they came up with legislation to punish those who held a different view of God than they did. "Although I believe these doctrines as firmly as the warmest advocate of the bill, yet *I would never consent to oppose those who rejected them with law or with any other weapon than argument.*"

If not for Anne Hutchinson's teachings and influence, Mary Dyer's sacrifice, and William Dyer's persistence in following through, we might have a very different sense of freedom today.

When the United States' founders convened to create the Constitution and Bill of Rights, they were only three to five generations removed – 130 years – from Mary's death. They remembered and they knew by experience what happens whenever religion and government marry in any society and any historical period: oppression and death. And they chose freedom and life.

Chapter 22

The Passover Exodus from Massachusetts

Anne Hutchinson, at her second trial before the Massachusetts Bay Colony theocratic government, was excommunicated from the Puritan First Church of Boston on 22 March 1638. She left her six-month house arrest, heresy conviction, and excommunication behind as she and some of her followers stalked out of Boston with the Passover.

One can imagine a female version of Charlton Heston's Moses in his striped red Hebrew mantle, striding out to heroic music, in front of the Children of Israel on their exodus from Egypt.

Charlton Heston as Moses, The Ten Commandments, 1956.

The first trial venue had been moved to New Town (Cambridge) to get away from Anne's many supporters in Boston. The second trial, in March 1638, was held in Boston at the First Church of Christ meetinghouse, when many of the men of the Hutchinson Party were away, having purchased Aquidneck/Rhode Island and begun surveying house lots and setting up wigwams and huts as temporary shelter for when the women and children would join them.

This was one of the coldest winters ever to strike New England. One nor'easter blizzard after another, and a complete freeze of Boston Harbor, struck the colony. On one hand, people didn't need a ferry to cross the ice of the Charles River; on the other hand, who could walk through the deep snows? (As I write this chapter, on 30 March 2015, there is more snow forecast this week for Boston, which has already measured more than nine feet of snow in 2015.)

This was no one-day trial, either, as you might gather from previous accounts in books and internet. Rev. Thomas Weld, brother of her jailer and one of the inquisitors, wrote in his preface to John Winthrop's book *Short Story of the Rise, Reign and Ruin of the Antinomians*,

> The first week we spent in confuting the loose opinions that we gathered up in the Country... The other fortnight [two weeks] we spent in a plane syllogistical dispute... In the forenoons wee framed our arguments, and in the afternoons produced them in public, and next day the Adversary [specifically Anne Hutchinson, but also a term for the devil] gave in their answers, and produced also their arguments on the same questions; then we answered them and replied also upon them the next day. These disputes are not mentioned at all in the following Discourse, happily, because of the swelling of the book [the book would be too long and costly to publish].

The trial ran three weeks, and for everyone from magistrates to defendant to the general community, it was a foregone conclusion that Anne Hutchinson would be convicted of heresy.

On March 15, Anne was summoned again to trial on Lecture Day, the midweek church service in their community where attendance was required, and the day when criminals were put in stocks, whipped, or executed by hanging. (Mary Dyer was hanged on a Lecture Day.) Anne had a high enough status, as a wealthy and educated woman whose husband had been a magistrate, that she was in little or no danger of corporal or capital punishment.

Instead of coming on time, she arrived after the long prayer and longer sermon. John Winthrop said she was "pretending bodily infirmity." Other authors have suggested that Anne was five months pregnant with her molar pregnancy, but that's impossible, as you'll see in this book's chapter on Anne's "monster." She may have been ditching the religious service that day, but she had been confined to a hostile home for five months, she was middle-aged and perhaps tired

of the stress of the trial, her supportive and loving husband was out
of town, and it was insanely cold and snowy, so she may have been
ill.

March 1638, Julian calendar

Sun	Mon	Tue	Wed	Thu	Fri	Sat
				1	2	3
4	5	6	7	8	9	10
11	12	13	14	15	16	17
18	19	20	21	22	23	24
25	26	27	28	Full Moon	30	31

April 1638, Julian calendar

Sun	Mon	Tue	Wed	Thu	Fri	Sat
1	2	3	4	5	6	7
8	9	10	11	12	13	14
15	16	17	18	19	20	21
22	23	24	25	26	27	28
29	30	31	1	2	3	4

*All dates in this article are according to the Julian Calendar used in the
seventeenth century, not the Gregorian Calendar we use now, so if you plot it on a
modern calendar, the days of the week are about 10 days different.
Most regular lecture days were held on Thursdays, and Sabbath church
services were on Sunday. Court was not in session on Sunday, but that
would not have stopped the ministers preaching against Anne and her followers. It
certainly didn't stop Rev. John Wilson and John Cotton.*

Anne Hutchinson walked out the door at the end of the trial,
and Mary Dyer took her hand in support. And that's when the mud
hit the fan. Gov. Winthrop learned that Mary had miscarried a
deformed fetus five months before, and that Rev. Cotton had buried
it secretly, at night. During Anne's trial, Winthrop ordered the
exhumation of the poor little bundle, and at least 100 men (those
who were trying Anne, no doubt) "examined" it. Winthrop and Weld
used that observation to describe Mary's "monster" in Winthrop's
book.

Record of the Colony of the Massachusetts in New England:
About Mrs. Hutchinson. It is ordered, that she shall be gone
by the last of this month; & if she be not gone before, she is

to be sent away by the counsel, without delay, by the first opportunity; & for the charges of keeping time for Mistress Hutchinson [house arrest at the home of Joseph Weld in Roxbury], order is to bee given by the counsel (if it be not satisfied) to levy it by distress of her husbands goods.

The Court desired that the 12th day of the 2nd month, called April, being a day of humility should be kept in the several churches, to entreat the help of God in the weighty matters which are in hand, & to divert any evil plots which may be intended, & to prepare the way of friends which we hope may be upon coming to us [emigrating from England].

On March 22, the day Anne was convicted, according to John Winthrop's *Journal,* he

...sent a warrant to Mrs. Hutchinson to depart this jurisdiction before the last of this month, according to the order of the court, and for that end set her at liberty from her former constraint [house arrest at Roxbury], so as she was not to go forth of her own house till her departure; and upon the 28th she went by water to farm at the Mount [Wollaston, where the Hutchinsons owned a farm], where she was to take water [a ship], with Mr. Wheelwright's wife and family, to go to Pascataquack [Dover, New Hampshire, where Rev. Wheelwright had gone into exile]; but she changed her mind, and went by land to Providence, and so to the island in the Narragansett Bay, which her husband and the rest of that sect had purchased of the Indians, and prepared with all speed to remove unto. For the court had ordered, that, except they were gone with their families by such a time, they should be summoned to the general court, etc.

Winthrop wrote in his *Journal* after learning, perhaps through a letter from William Hutchinson or Dr. John Clarke, about the Rhode Island experience:

On the first of June 1638, there was an earthquake which continued about four minutes and left the earth in an unquiet condition for twenty days afterwards. Mrs. Hutchinson and some of her adherents happened to be at prayer when the earthquake was at Aquiday [Portsmouth, Rhode Island], etc., and the house being shaken thereby, they were persuaded, (and boasted of it,) that the Holy Ghost did shake it in coming down upon them, as he did upon the apostles.

When the major earthquake hit New England, Anne Hutchinson thought that the shaking was the latter rain of the Holy Spirit (Proverbs 16:15), which many Christians call Pentecost, 50 days after Easter. Pentecost was the commemoration of when the earth shook and tongues of flame rested over the assembled Christians in a Jerusalem upper room after the first Easter (Christ's resurrection). In that experience, they received supernatural gifts of languages, healing, teaching, and other tools to grow the church.

Pentecost, by Gustav Doré

Historians have never connected the Easter and Pentecost dates to the Hutchinson story because Puritans did not celebrate those holidays – ever. They considered religious holidays to be pagan in origin, promoted by the papists they hated, and not scripturally mandated. When Puritans gained the upper hand in the English Civil Wars of the 1640s, they officially abolished celebration of Christmas, Easter, Whitsun (Pentecost), and all other traditional Catholic and Anglican holidays. Other sects of the era – Presbyterians, Reformed, Quakers, Baptists, and Anabaptists – also spurned church holidays.

However, Anne was aware of the date of Pentecost, or she wouldn't have exclaimed that the severe earthquake was the Holy Spirit coming down on them – at the time of Pentecost. And if she knew Pentecost, she knew the date of Easter. Easter falls on the first Sunday after the first full moon of the vernal equinox. The night of the full moon is Passover, which she also knew. "And on that very day the Lord brought the people of Israel out of the land of Egypt." Exodus 12:51.

Anne and her family and followers left Boston at Passover, the end of March. Rather than sailing around Cape Cod to Narragansett Bay, the Massachusetts exiles walked in the freezing, hostile wilderness. They left Boston, Charlestown, Cambridge, and Roxbury like the ancient Israelites left the bondage of Egypt, shaking off their shackles and slavery to the law. This exodus from Boston was made as a strong statement to John Winthrop and the rest of the theocratic magistrates.

If the Hutchinsonians left on March 29, the Passover with the full moon, it was also Lecture Day, when hundreds more people were in town to witness it! It would have been plain in Winthrop's eyes, surely, but the fact never made it into his books. (Winthrop himself likened Massachusetts' crop failures, insect invasions, and severe weather to the plagues of Egypt. A month after Anne's departure, Winthrop fell deathly ill, perhaps from the severe stress of the Hutchinson trial and losing scores of the colony's leading businessmen to exile.)

When Anne and her followers walked all the way from Massachusetts Bay to Providence (45-60 miles), they left during what we call Holy Week, the week between Palm Sunday and Easter. (Easter was on April 4 that year.) When the Hutchinsonians, including that "fomenter" Mary Dyer and her husband William and 27-month-old son Samuel, struck out through the forest and hills, it was still a frozen wilderness, having just received heavy snow. The snow lay three feet deep in some places, and they were on foot because horses were expensive and rare. They may have had an ox to pull a sled, but it's unlikely. They would have spent at least two nights and possibly six on the Pequot Path before they reached the small village of Providence, and then moved on to the north end of Aquidneck Island, where they founded the town that would be renamed Portsmouth, Rhode Island.

Snowy forest, late March 2015.
Photo courtesy of Jo Ann Butler, author of the Rebel Puritan novels.

When, before her hanging in 1660, Mary Dyer walked from Providence to Boston to defy the theocracy and call attention to the "bloody law" of religious persecution, she used the same road she'd walked out on. She knew exactly what she was doing: going back into the persecution and prison of Egypt. In her letter to the Massachusetts Bay general court, she wrote two references to the Hebrew Exodus:

"Its not my owne life I seek for (I chuse rather to suffer with the people of god then to injoy the pleasures of egypt)" ... and "the lord wil overturne you and your law by his righteous Judgments and plagues poured justly on you."

Chapter 23

From Reverend Teacher
to Reverend Teacher

John Cotton and Samuel Stone had surely known each other already when they both boarded the ship *Griffin* in the summer of 1633. They were both alumni of Cambridge University. Both were teachers in the Boston and New Town/Cambridge churches, respectively, which means that they preached less on Sundays, and more on Thursday lecture days, and were deeply involved with ongoing theological research and interpretation of scripture.

> In early New England a fully organized church had as officers a pastor, a teacher, and at least one ruling elder, and one deacon. The deacon was the treasurer, and the ruling elder the trustee and censor of morals. The pastor was the administrative head of the church, who was expected to inspire its life and activities; the teacher was the educational and doctrinal leader. This office of teacher was undoubtedly the distinctive feature of the New England system. ... The teacher may be described as a kind of theological professor whose sphere of work was exclusively a church.
> Vergil V. Phelps, *The Harvard Theological Review*, Vol. 4, No. 3 (Jul., 1911), p. 388.

Samuel Stone, born in 1602 and married to Hope Fletcher, the mother of his first five children, had earned his master's degree at Cambridge University in England, and was the Teacher of the New Town-Cambridge church from 1633 to 1636, when he and Rev. Thomas Hooker set out for Connecticut to found Hartford, which was named after Stone's birthplace in Hertford, England.

Five days after Anne Hutchinson's heresy conviction and excommunication, Rev. Cotton wrote a letter to Rev. Stone, which is the first known comment he made after the controversy. This was March 27, 1638. The Hutchinsonians had probably not left Boston yet.

After personal greetings, Cotton answered Stone's counsel of "becoming wise and fearful of myself, as not to vent new things without sufficient arguments," and confessed that he had agonized about his own spiritual estate and those who depended on him for instruction.

He said that God had brought him low, to humility in the eyes of the brethren ministers, and to a knowledge of his own sins and

> the Iniquities of sundry members of our Church, who... had harbored & secretly disseminated such Erroneous & dangerous Opinions, as (like a Gangrene) would have corrupted & destroyed Faith & Religion had they not been timely discovered, & disclaimed both by our own & other Churches. Mrs. Hutchinson (of whom you speak) though she publicly Revoked the Errors, yet affirming her Judgment was never otherwise, though her Expressions were contrary, she was Excommunicated by our whole Church *Nemine Contradicente* [unanimously]. Some others of our members that joined with her in the Opinions, were gone away before, to seek other Plantations elsewhere, as Presaging the Censure which otherwise was likely to overtake them. I had signified to our Brethren (the Elders) before the Conference, That if such Errors could be proved to be held by her, or any other of our members, God forbid, we should Neglect to bear witness against them according to God. But that which could not then be proved by 2 witnesses hath been since proved by many, to more general satisfaction of us all. ... Your very loving brother in Christ.
> J. C."

In the letter, Rev. Cotton likened the Hutchinsonians to Achan of the Israelite conquest of Canaan. Achan stole war booty dedicated to God, a rebellious act which brought God's wrath on the entire nation, and they were defeated at the battle of Ai. Achan's sin was revealed and he and his family and animals were stoned to death and then burned to cleanse their influence from the nation and restore their submission to God. The desolate place north of Jericho was called the Valley of Achor. It means "extreme trouble." The story gives us a glimpse of what Rev. Cotton thought of the Hutchinsonians.

Rev. Stone's wife "smoaked out her days in the darkness of melancholy" (depression) and died in 1640 in Hartford, according to Rev. Hooker. Samuel Stone remarried, had more children, became sole pastor of the Hartford church when Hooker died, and then he died in 1663, having been a scourge to Quakers and "witches" during his later years at Hartford. Among his belongings at his death were unpublished manuscripts of a catechism and a confutation of (wait for it!) Antinomianism.

Stone's table gravestone is carved with a poem that my mother rubbed with pastels on paper in 1976 and I keep rolled up in a tube. It reads,

An Epitaph on Mr. Samuel Stone,
Deceased ye 61 years of his
Age July 20, 1663
New Englands Glory & her radiant crowne,
Was he who now in softest bed of downe
Til glorious resurrection morne appeare
Doth safely, sweetely, sleepe in Jesus here,
In natures solid art, and reasoning well
'Tis knowne, beyond compare, he did excell
Errors corrupt, by sinnewous dispute,
He did oppugne, and clearly them confute:
Above all things He Christ His Lord Preferd,
Hartford; Thy richest jewel's here interred.

"Errors corrupt, by sinuous dispute, he did oppugn [fight against] and clearly them confute." Now we know what that epitaph means in context. Stone fought heretics: Anne Hutchinson and Antinomians, Quakers, and (falsely accused) witches.

The Cotton-Stone letter is excerpted from
The Correspondence of John Cotton. Sargent Bush, Jr., editor. The University of North Carolina Press, 2001.

Chapter 24

How the Hutchinsonians
Chose Rhode Island - By Love

In 1652, when he was a colonial agent in London, Dr. John Clarke described how he and others in the search committee, knowing that they faced censure and exile from Massachusetts in 1637-38, found the land they'd buy from Native Americans.

He had moved to Boston from London and landed in the Wheelwright-Hutchinson firestorm in 1637. He said he and others were requested to seek out a place where they could move out of colonial control. Initially, he went to the north (as Rev. Wheelwright had done) "by reason of the suffocating heat of the Summer before," but the "Winter following proved so cold, that we were forced in the Spring to make towards the South." Apparently, New England's climate is not for sissies!

Clarke said that they sought the Lord for direction. When their vessel was passing a large and dangerous Cape [Cape Cod with its shoals],

> ...we would cross over by land, having Long Iland and Delaware Bay in our eye for the place of our residence; so to a town called Providence we came, which was begun by one Mr. Roger Williams (who for matter of conscience had not long before been exiled from the former jurisdiction [Salem, Massachusetts]) by whom we were courteously and lovingly received, and with whom we advised about our design; he readily presented two places before us in the same Narragansett Bay, the one upon the main called Sowams [between Bristol and Barrington], the other called then Acquedneck, now Rode-Iland.

They wondered if the land at Sowams belonged to a colonial patent, and Williams suggested that they had time to inquire about its availability at Plymouth while they waited for their ship to come about.

Plymouth officials told them that Sowams belonged to Plymouth Colony and was practically the flower of their garden, but

Aquidneck Island, south of the Bristol peninsula, might be available for sale from the Narragansett Indians.

> They all with a cheerfull countenance made us this answer, it was in their thoughts to have advised us thereto, and if the provident hand of God should pitch us thereon they should look upon us as free, and as loving neighbours and friends should be assistant unto us upon the main, &c. So we humbly thanked them, and returned with that answer: So it pleased the Lord, by moving the hearts of the natives, even the chiefest thereof, to pitch us thereon, and by other occurrences of providence, which are too large here to relate: So that having bought them off to their full satisfaction, we have possessed the place ever since; and notwithstanding the different understandings and consciences amongst us, without interruption we agree to maintain civil Justice and judgment, neither are there such outrages committed amongst us as in other parts of the Country are frequently seen.

Long Island and Delaware Bay – that's very surprising. Long Island was under the control of the English New Haven Colony and of the Dutch West Indies Company of New Netherland. Of course, after only three years in Portsmouth, the Hutchinsons pulled up stakes and moved to the Dutch-controlled area that is now East Haven, in the Bronx.

But that they considered moving as far as Delaware Bay and rejecting it for suffocating heat is interesting. About 40 years later, Baptists from Ipswich and Salem, Massachusetts, fleeing severe abuse from Puritans, moved first to Swansea, Massachusetts, then Newport, Rhode Island, and ultimately to Shiloh, New Jersey, on the Delaware Bay. One of the relatives who stayed behind in Ipswich was hanged as a witch in 1692.

Back in the snowy spring of 1638, the search committee met with the sachems of Aquidneck, Canonicus and Miantonomo, and agreed to purchase most of the islands of the Narragansett Bay. Though they paid 40 fathoms of wampum (legal tender to both Native Americans and English colonists), Rev. Roger Williams recalled in 1658,

> It was not price nor money that could have purchased Rhode Island. Rhode Island was obtained by love; by the love and favour which that honorable gentleman Sir Henry Vane and

myself had with that great sachem Miantinomu, about the league [treaty] which I procured between the Massachusetts English, &c. and the Narragansetts in the Pequod war. ... Sir Henry Vane hath been so great an instrument in the hand of God for procuring of this island from the barbarians, as also for procuring and confirming of the charter, so it may by all due thankful acknowledgment to be remembered and recorded of us and ours which reap and enjoy the sweet fruits of so great benefits and such unheard of liberties amongst us.

Chapter 25

Founding Mother of Religious Liberty

Accan ording to this 1638 map of Portsmouth, Rhode Island, the land by Sanford's Cove marked "D" is the William Hutchinson allotment. The land marked "L" is the next plot over, and it belonged to William and Mary Dyer.

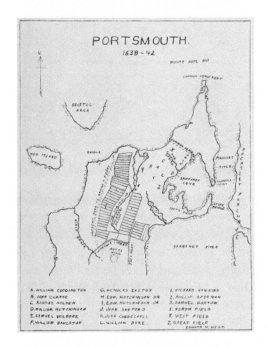

The Fall River Expressway, Route 24, if superimposed on the old map, runs directly over the properties of the founders of the town, among them Nicholas Easton, Randall Holden, William Coddington, and the Hutchinsons and Dyers.

Technically, the men of the Massachusetts Bay Colony who signed the Wheelwright Remonstrance and followed the Covenant of Grace were the negotiators, along with Roger Williams, for the purchase of Aquidneck Island. Anne was in two trials and house arrest during the record-cold winter of 1637-38. But because she was the outspoken leader of perhaps 80 families, she has been cast as the founder of Portsmouth.

The town was initially named Pocasset, the Native American name for widening water. Several rivers run from Massachusetts south into the Narragansett Bay. But within a year, the new colony had changed its name to Portsmouth, in the tradition of naming New England towns after English towns.

The men of the scouting party who bought the island created a document called the Portsmouth Compact. The paragraph at the top appears to be in William Dyer's handwriting. You may think that Dyer's penmanship is a mess, but it's actually quite legible and florid.

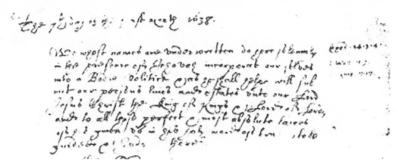

The 7th Day of the First Month, 1638. [March 7, 1638]
We whose names are underwritten do hereby solemnly in the presence of Jehovah incorporate ourselves into a Bodie Politick and as He shall help, will submit our persons, lives and estates unto our Lord Jesus Christ, the King of Kings, and Lord of Lords, and to all those perfect and most absolute laws of His given in His Holy Word of truth, to be guided and judged thereby.
Exodus 24:3-4 [Jehoiada made a covenant between the Lord and the king and people, that they should be the Lord's people; also between the king and the people.]
1 Chronicles 11:3 [So all the elders of Israel came to the king at Hebron, and David made a covenant with them at Hebron before the Lord. And they anointed David king over Israel, according to the word of the Lord by Samuel.]
2 Kings 11:17 [Jehoiada made a covenant between the Lord and the king and people, that they should be the Lord's people; also between the king and the people.]

Twenty-three men signed the covenant.

The settlers created a democratic governing body, where the freemen of the town voted and held courts at regular times. In establishing their community, they wrote, "it was voted that none should be received as inhabitants, or freemen, to build or plant upon the island [then called Aquidneck] but such as should be received in by consent of the body and submit to the government that was, or should be, established." –From *A Short History of the Slocums, Slocumbs and Slocombs of America.*

They could not join the town and be apportioned land if they were citizens (freemen) of another colony. They had to submit to the government of this new town.

Though it was a small group of people there, they were committed to the idea of a non-religious, neutral government. As you see by the Compact, they were deeply religious men and women who had risked everything – their families, their businesses, their inheritance in their homeland – and set out for the hazards and uncertain future in the New World. They did it to be free to worship God with their lives, and they listened carefully to their consciences, knowing that that was one of the ways God communicated with them.

The Portsmouth group was closely connected to Rev. Roger Williams as he helped them buy their island, and who had been persecuted and banished by Massachusetts Bay Colony for his beliefs and teachings. He had been a very strict Puritan and had criticized the Boston churches for not breaking with the Church of England. After he escaped their intention to put him in prison, he spent time with the Native Americans in what is now northwestern Rhode Island. He founded Providence Plantations as a haven for "liberty of conscience," and other religious refugees joined him. Though he's known as the founder of the Baptists of North America, he wasn't Baptist for very long. He became a Seeker, which we might compare to a non-denominational or independent Christian.

The Portsmouth settlers initially followed the lead of Providence in restricting government to civil matters, and not religious infractions. But Anne's antinomianism ("against the law") seemed to point to the New Covenant, which said that God would write a new law on the heart, and that people would act on that conscience. She called for no magistracy at all, no tyrannical power resting in one or two men, but a pure democracy of equals – which would mean that the women who had supported Anne's teachings for even longer than the men, would have an equal say in what was right and wrong. This was contrary to the experience and history of all or nearly all of her supporters, even though they'd so recently experienced the tyranny of Massachusetts' theocratic magistracy.

By January of 1639, William Coddington, who had been a Boston magistrate and was one of the wealthiest investors in the new colony of Rhode Island, had broken with the Portsmouth group. Portsmouth had amended their compact to keep their governor to a one-year term (so that other men could rotate in), and that a citizens' commission could review the court decisions to reject or ratify according to their opinion, which diminished the power of the magistrates and officers.

Coddington and others left Portsmouth in the spring of 1639 to found a new town and port about 10 miles to the south: Newport. William Hutchinson was elected governor of the Portsmouth group at that time, while Coddington was elected governor of Newport, though he gave himself a double vote (and more land in compensation for his work) in their courts. Coddington, who remained friends with John Winthrop and was of a more theocratic bent than other Rhode Islanders, tried to set himself up as a governor for life a few years later, but was foiled by the creation of a new charter for Rhode Island.

The two towns reconciled in March 1641 and formed a single, democratic government. When William Hutchinson's term as governor ended, the family prepared to move out of Portsmouth.

Meanwhile, Roger Williams originated the phrase "wall of separation" between church and state. He said that magistrates should not punish infractions of the first table of the Ten Commandments, the laws about God's relationship to mankind that included worship, blasphemy and using God's name as authority, and keeping a Sabbath holy.

In 1644, he wrote a treatise on religious liberty, from which we can take these highlights:

First, that the blood of so many hundred thousand souls of Protestants and Papists, spilt in the wars of present and former ages, for their respective consciences, is not required nor accepted by Jesus Christ the Prince of Peace.

Secondly, pregnant scriptures and arguments are … against the doctrine of persecution for cause of conscience.

Thirdly, satisfactory answers are given to scriptures, and objections produced by Mr. [John] Calvin, [Theodore] Beza, Mr. Cotton, and the ministers of the New English churches and others former and later, tending to prove the doctrine of persecution for cause of conscience.

All civil states with their officers of justice in their respective constitutions and administrations are proved essentially civil, and therefore not judges, governors, or defenders of the spiritual or Christian state and worship.

It is the will and command of God that (since the coming of his Son the Lord Jesus) a permission of the most paganish, Jewish, Turkish [Muslim], or antichristian consciences [atheists] and worships, be granted to all men in all nations and countries; and they are only to be fought against with that sword which is only (in soul matters) able to conquer, to wit, the sword of God's Spirit, the Word of God.

God requireth not a uniformity of religion to be enacted and enforced in any civil state; which enforced uniformity (sooner or later) is the greatest occasion of civil war, ravishing of conscience, persecution of Christ Jesus in his servants, and of the hypocrisy and destruction of millions of souls.

The permission of other consciences and worships than a state professeth only can (according to God) procure a firm and lasting peace (good assurance being taken according to the wisdom of the civil state for uniformity of civil obedience from all forts).

Lastly, true civility and Christianity may both flourish in a state or kingdom, notwithstanding the permission of divers and contrary consciences, either of Jew or Gentile....

The Rhode Island founders in the settlements of Portsmouth, Newport, Warwick, and Providence fiercely believed, and knew by experience, that the mixture of government and religion always resulted in persecution and death.

It wasn't only the Puritan government of Boston, or the Anglican oppression of Puritans that they had experienced. They saw the last 200 years of Inquisition in the Catholic countries of Europe. They knew the conflicts between the Catholics and Presbyterians of Scotland, and the Reformed Protestants on the Continent. They knew that hundreds of men and women who weren't witches had been burned as witches in Germany. They saw – and feared – the Spanish and Portuguese conflicts in Europe and the Americas. They saw the 30 Years War raging between Catholic and Protestant armies in Italy, Germany, and France. If they'd studied history, they knew about the Crusades in the Holy Lands, and the massacre of Jews at

Clifford's Tower in York. Death for religious reasons was everywhere.

But it would not be so in their new colony of Rhode Island. In their new society, the first of its kind in the world to allow religious liberty, the religious bodies, whether organized churches or informal fellowships, were separate from the courts and magistrates.

And whereas John Winthrop, Thomas Dudley, Rev. Cotton and Wilson, and many others disdained democracy as "the meanest and worst of all forms of government," most Rhode Islanders embraced it. They would nominate candidates for their assembly and officers, magistrates, and elect them for one-year terms.

If not for Roger Williams' teachings and influence, the expulsion of Anne Hutchinson and scores of families from Massachusetts Bay, and the pioneering work of forming a democratic government, there might not have been a new colony formed with a firm intention of respecting liberty of conscience, and separating ecclesiastical and civil powers.

If Roger Williams was the father of religious liberty in America, Anne was its mother.

Chapter 26

Mistress Hutchinson,
Mother of Civil Rights

Someone on Aquidneck Island stayed in contact with Rev. John Cotton, during the months of April or May 1638. Historians are not sure who Cotton wrote to in his June 4 response, but those mentioned in the letter were William Hutchinson, John Clarke, John Coggeshall, and William Baulston, so they are eliminated. The addressee could have been William Coddington, William Aspinwall, or others, but Cotton wrote to "Beloved brother."

When writing of Anne Hutchinson, he uses the pronoun "hir" but not her name. He uses other proper names, for both men and for Jane Hawkins and Mary Dyer. But for Anne – he won't write her name. This may be because Anne had been excommunicated, and consequently shunned.

Excommunication and shunning are not the same thing, but shunning can be a result of the apostolic counsel in 1 Corinthians 5. Paul wrote that in the case of disfellowship (for fornication, coveting, idol worship, or being a "railer," drunkard, or extortioner, none of which fit Anne Hutchinson), that members of the church should not eat with them at the same table. That doesn't mean regular meals, but taking Communion. However, the counsel to put them out of the church is to protect those still in the church, and uphold standards of beliefs and behavior for the safety of all believers.

A 2007 orthodox Puritan online forum discussed the finer points of shunning and excommunication. Some of the comments were that shunning was manipulative and mean-spirited; others said that excommunication was meant to "drive an excommunicated person to despair" over their sin and create a longing to return to the arms of their church. The two actions are different. The shunning is not the desirable outcome, but in reality, it is often the result of excommunication if the offender is unrepentant.

In Cotton's 1638 letter, he mentions answering two previous letters. One of them compared Cotton to the prophet and strong man, Samson, who was sent by God "for a time of storming against the Philistines to foil many of them with the Jawbone of an Ass." Cotton didn't like that comparison and rebuked the writer for his impudence. "Whom you may mean by Philistines, I may haply guess: but in my guessing so I shall wrong both them & you," he wrote.

It's rather easy to be impudent in our time, and guess that the Philistines were the key figures in Mistress Hutchinson's trials: accusers and judges John Winthrop, Thomas Dudley, John Wilson, Hugh Peter, Thomas Shepard, and Thomas Weld, among others.

The writer(s) had queried Boston's favorite teacher about the Covenants of Works and Grace, and he responded,

"I thank God, I know not wherein I have Condescended in that which is evil, Corrupt or unsound. In any Unsafe tenets of them that Difference of Judgment, & Profession is still the same, as it was ... I wish you a better Spirit of Discerning, then to Infer such a Conclusion upon such. ...The Doctrine of the Covenant of Grace hath been more grossly, & fundamentally opposed by some of our Brethren of the Island [Aquidneck], & others of their mind. ... unless the Foundation of the Covenant of Grace, as it is in Truth, be truly & soundly established amongst you, I know not, how you can build up either Church, or Commonwealth, but as an house without a Foundation. I hear of some Rents & Breaches amongst you, & wonder not at it."

Then Rev. Cotton answers the charge that he had betrayed Anne Hutchinson in her sedition and heresy trials. He wrote,

"Her Acknowledgement in the Church I did never call or Publicise. I sought a just Retractation of sundry dangerous Errors ... I deny any particular Invectives against her, or any other, so far as she remaineth steadfastly in the Doctrine professed by her in her Retractation; I deny also any such Purpose of mine of Coming to the Island, though she, & goodwife Hawkins parted from me."

By "coming to the Island," Rev. Cotton might be referring to the previous summer, 1637, when he and his house guest, Gov. Henry Vane, may have considered starting a plantation (a new town) on Aquidneck. (Cotton wrote in 1648 that if he had thought of leaving Boston, it would *not* be for Rhode Island. "I neither wrote nor spake, nor sent to Mr. [Roger] Williams for any such errand. If ever I had removed, I intended Quinipiack [New Haven], and not

Aquethnick." Since he wouldn't accuse Rev. Williams of lying, he implied the discrepancy in reports was politics.)

But Harry Vane suddenly left Boston and returned to London in early August 1637, before the early autumn theology synod, before the trials of Anne Hutchinson, before Mary Dyer's "monster" miscarriage, and before the disfranchisement of the Wheelwright and Hutchinson followers. He claimed that he had affairs to settle in England, and declared his "serious resolution to return to us again." He never returned, but he was a valuable ally to New England, the other American colonies, and territories in the Caribbean.

Cotton was much beloved in Boston and other towns, but did he consider creating his own church community? He had been senior minister at St. Botolph's in Lincolnshire for years, but in the new Boston, he was the Teacher, the Number Two man. A few years later, Cotton wanted to go back to England to participate in a theology synod, and was denied by Winthrop and the court assistants. Winthrop's *Journal* hints that he and his government couldn't allow Cotton the freedom to be his own master. They both loved him – and needed Cotton and his thousands of adherents if the new Boston was to become the New Jerusalem, the City Upon a Hill.

The letter continues.

> Your 5th [query], I cannot understand, That I should tell Sergeant Boston [William Baulston] said to me. They had those things from her [Mistress Hutchinson], & that she would [illegible word] to satisfy them. Nor can I well interpret your 6th what I meant, when in speech with her husband [William Hutchinson], I joined her & Mr Coxall [John Coggeshall], Mrs. [Mary] Dyer &c. in Judgment together, & yet proposed to them, I conceive a great deal of Difference between them. Possibly, I might speak of them {as sometimes} of one mind & Judgment in sundry things: but if she stand to her Retractation there is I doubt not a broad difference of Judgment between them.

He spoke then of midwife Jane Hawkins, who was connected with Anne Hutchinson and Mary Dyer, saying that he'd heard complaints of her and that her judgments were unsound, but had not had occasion to seek the truth of the matter. "I fear she might doe much hurt in corrupting the Judgments of young women," he wrote.

His last paragraph asks the Aquidneck Island man to continue to correspond with him, and warns that:

> for your sake, you should stand out against them too much in point of Civil Liberties or Rights. As God hath given more Ability to discern the Danger of their tenets, so God requireth of you, to take more pains in employing of your talents to Recover them (if it be the will of God) into the church. ... I pray you commend from me, together with my love, to Mr. [John] Clarke and his wife and yours. Yourself with the rest of our Brethren & Sisters, I heartily wish (as God helpeth me) all true Good unto, in the Lord, Especially the light of his Truth, & Grace & Peace in the Fellowship, & Acknowledgement of Christ Jesus God & Man. In whom I rest
>
> Your Compassionate Brother.
>
> I pray you let me hear, if you had the like Earthquake, as we had the last 6th day being the 1st of 4th [Friday, June 1, 1638].

Civil liberties and rights were always foremost in the minds of the people who founded the towns of Portsmouth and Newport. It's what drove them to sign the Wheelwright Remonstrance a year earlier, and what made them stand up for and follow Anne Hutchinson, against the wrath of Massachusetts Bay Colony, where they had hoped to make permanent homes. Even in the 1663 charter, or constitution, of the Rhode Island colony, they mentioned that they had risked everything to create a "livelie experiment."

The charter stated that the founders:

> did transport themselves out of this kingdom of England into America, but also, since their arrival there, after their first settlement amongst our other subjects in those parts, Nor the avoiding of discord, and those manic evils which were likely to ensue upon some of those our subjects not being able to bear, in these remote parties [Massachusetts, Connecticut, Plymouth, and New Haven colonies], their different apprehensions in religious concernments, and in pursuance of the aforesaid ends, did once again leave their desirable stations and habitations, and with excessive labour and travel, hazard and charge, did transplant themselves into the midst of the Indian natives [Narragansett Bay]...

They asked for and received rights to free travel, religious liberty, separation of church and state, a democratically elected government, and other liberties that were later enshrined in the United States Constitution's Bill of Rights.

That spirit of freedom in the pioneering, founding families of Rhode Island was stirred up by the rebel minister Roger Williams of Providence, and Anne, the leader of the movement called the Hutchinsonians.

Mistress Hutchinson lost her proper name and became a pronoun among the Puritan churches of New England, but she was the founding mother of civil rights in America and eventually many other countries.

Cotton letter excerpted from
The Correspondence of John Cotton. Sargent Bush, Jr., editor. The University of North Carolina Press, 2001.

Chapter 27

Hutchinson's Monstrous Birth:
"Strange Newes from the Isle of Rogues"

Anne Hutchinson statue in Boston.

In books, transatlantic letters, and journals, Mary Dyer's 1637 "monstrous birth" story was kept alive for decades, not just because it was an unusual deformation and the people of Boston had nothing else horribly fascinating to gossip about. The premature stillbirth of an anencephalic fetus with spina bifida was the first recorded in the American colonies.

But the monsters of Mary Dyer and her mentor and friend, Anne Hutchinson, were spoken of as a pair. Mary's travail took place in October 1637 in Boston, and Anne's probably in June 1638 in Portsmouth, Rhode Island.

Deformed babies, dead or alive, and malformed fetuses were called monsters for several centuries, and seen as evidence of the mother's heresy, sexual immorality, or that she had left her proper place in subjection to her husband and ministers. The monstrous birth was punishment from God.

There were several ways a woman could be cursed with a monstrous birth. Having sex during her menstrual period contaminated the man's "seed." Or she might have imagined or seen a terrible and traumatic incident or hideous creature when she conceived. It might have been God choosing to exercise his sovereign power as a moral lesson to society in general. Or God demonstrated his wrath at a promiscuous, immoral, or heretical woman – and at her community.

"If there was something in the atmosphere that made early modern England particularly susceptible to monsters it was more likely to be found in the miasma of political conflict, religious anxiety, and cultural tension than in the water, the diet, or the air." Cressy, David. *Agnes Bowker's Cat: Travesties and Transgressions in Tudor and Stuart England.* Oxford University Press, 2000.

In a 1613 book by Puritan minister Robert Hill, is a prayer for women in travail. A snippet of the wordy beseechment was "Give unto this woman, thy Handmaid, neither a monstrous, a maimed, or a deadbirth: but as thou hast blessed the conception of this infant, so let thy blessing be upon it, that eftsoon it may be brought with perfection into the world."

Mercury, a.k.a. quicksilver, was often used as a medication for various ills, and drinking vessels and lead or pewter dishware poisoned those who used them regularly – particularly pregnant women. Mercury or lead poisoning might have been the cause of Mary's fetus deformations in her first weeks of pregnancy.

Anne's monster, which is now known to be hydatidiform moles, or a molar pregnancy, was probably due to her age, 47, as women over 40 years of age are five to ten times more likely to develop the condition. Modern thought is that the moles are precancerous cells.

Anne had been imprisoned at the home of Joseph Weld of Roxbury, Mass., between November 1637 and her heresy trial in March 1638, when she was released to prepare to move out of Massachusetts Bay Colony by the end of April. *She could not have been pregnant* during her house arrest, or she would have borne the "monster" during that period; nor was she allowed conjugal visits during the time in Weld's house.

Molar pregnancies that continue past three months are usually fatal to the woman, because they implant in the uterine wall and become malignant cancers.

When Anne appeared to be ill during her trial in March 1638, it may have been menopausal symptoms or even a fever. She might not have had access to her medicinal herbs.

So she conceived in April, probably, when she and William reunited. She had borne 15 babies that survived infancy by then, the youngest being two years old.

Anne, her family, and scores of other families, including the Dyers, made their exodus from Boston on foot, and walked 45-60 miles through fresh, deep snow to the tiny town of Providence. Shortly after that, they set up a camp in Pocasset/Portsmouth, Rhode Island, and began to build their town.

On June 1, 1638, when they'd only been there a few weeks, they experienced the largest New England earthquake ever reported. By its description of damages and length of time shaking, seismologists today think it might have registered 6.5 to 7.0 on the Richter scale.

At the time of the quake, on a mid-afternoon with nice weather, Anne and her followers were praying. The shaking went on for about four minutes, and in other ports there were ships that leaned over as the water probably built into a tsunami. With the sandy soil and marshes around the Sanford Cove, there also might have been soil liquefaction, where water is forced up in bubbles and spreads a thin layer of floodwater over the area.

Probably soon after the earthquake, while they were still experiencing aftershocks, Anne, an experienced midwife, began feeling weak, and consulted the young doctor in their company because she feared for either her or her baby's life.

Molar pregnancies can last three months or less before they spontaneously abort (as in Anne's case) or are removed by surgical procedure. A hydatidiform mole is an abnormal growth of placental tissue, or it could be from a non-viable fertilized egg. It develops as a cluster of water-filled sacs, and it's not a baby or fetus. Complications can include anemia, toxemia of pregnancy, heart failure, hemorrhage, and sepsis. If the moles invade the uterine wall, they can lead to deadly thromboses and even cancer. It seems from the description of Anne's case, that she was very lucky or very blessed not to have suffered the latter. Moles can mimic a full-term pregnancy, though today they are diagnosed at or before three months, then removed.

The women most likely to have delivered Anne's moles would be midwife Jane Hawkins, Mary Dyer, and Anne's sister Katherine Marbury Scott. Doctors did not deliver babies at that time.

*****

Even Dr. Clarke had never heard of such a delivery as Anne Hutchinson's. Once he'd examined her and was sure that her womb was clear and she'd recover, he went home to study and record the pathology. Reverend Doctor John Clarke was the same age as William Dyer: twenty-nine. He'd emigrated to Boston in 1637, immediately joined the Hutchinson side in the Antinomian controversy, and traveled to Portsmouth with them when all were banished. He'd received his doctorate in theology at Oxford, but his subsequent training in the Netherlands might have included medicine. But he may not have been a physician at all.

William Hutchinson wrote a letter to his friend and pastor of more than twenty years, Rev. John Cotton, telling him the news of their new settlement, that he'd been elected assistant governor of Portsmouth, and that Anne's pregnancy had ended in grief.

In his next sermon at Boston First Church, in early July, Rev. Cotton preached about the monstrous birth, proclaiming that it signified Anne's error in "denying inherent righteousness but that all Christ was in us, and nothing of *our* faith, love, *et cetera.*"

Rev. Cotton protested that goodness could not be human nature because it could only be imparted to a faithful believer by the grace of Christ, and the evidence of Christ in one's heart was one's faithfulness to and love for the laws of Moses. In modern terms, he might say that one is saved by God's gift of mercy, but the human part was to keep the biblical laws to prove to God that we've accepted the gift. If we were to die with even one unconfessed sin, we couldn't be saved.

Anne Hutchinson, the heretic, said that the necessity of law-keeping had been abolished at the cross. Her heresy had been confirmed by Almighty God with this monstrous birth.

Governor John Winthrop, hearing of Anne's miscarriage, seized upon the opportunity to write to John Clarke, to ask if the story was true.

Dr. Clarke wrote in reply:

Mrs. Hutchinson, six weeks before her delivery, perceived her body to be greatly distempered, and her spirits failing, and in that regard doubtful of life, she sent to me, etc., and not long after (in a heavy discharge from the womb) it was brought to light, and I was called to see it, where I beheld, first unwashed, (and afterwards in warm water,) several lumps, every one of them greatly confused, and if you consider each of them according to the representation of the whole, they were altogether without form; but if they were considered in respect of the parts of each lump of flesh, then there was a representation of innumerable distinct bodies in the form of a globe, not much unlike the swims of some fish, so confusedly knit together by so many several strings, (which I conceive were the beginning of veins and nerves,) so that it was impossible either to number the small round pieces in every lump, much less to discern from whence every string did fetch its original, they were so snarled one within another. The small globes I likewise opened, and perceived the matter of them (setting aside the membrane in which it was involved,) to be partly wind [air] and partly water.

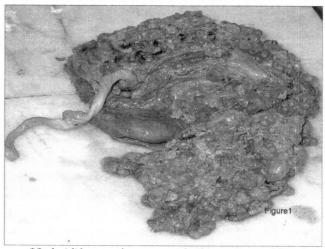

Hydatidiform molar mass with placenta, resembling the description by Dr. Clarke. When the mass with placenta affects the uterus, a hysterectomy may be required, and death is a possibility.

Of these several lumps there were about twenty-six, according to the relation of those, who more narrowly searched into the number of them. I took notice of six or seven of some bigness; the rest were small; but all as I have declared, except one or two, which differed much from the rest both in matter and form; and the whole [afterbirth] was like the lobe of the liver, being similar everywhere like itself. When I had opened it, the matter seemed to be blood congealed.

This was not enough for John Winthrop, who wasn't after the gory pathology report, but a moral reason for Anne's miscarriage. And Clarke's report seemed to be at variance with Cotton's sermon. Winthrop later spoke to Dr. Clarke, who confirmed and summarized his report. Cotton corrected himself in the pulpit, saying he'd gotten his information from William Hutchinson.

Winthrop recorded his impressions.

Thus it hath pleased the Lord to have compassion of his poor churches here, and to discover this great imposter, an instrument of Satan so fitted and trained to his service for interrupting the passage of the Kingdom in this part of the world, and poisoning the Churches here planted, as no story records the like of a woman, since that mentioned in the Revelation...

The "woman" of Revelation Winthrop mentions was not the woman of chapter 12, who represents the true believers of the church of God. No, he meant the evil woman of Revelation 17:4-6, who represented a false religion,

And the woman was arrayed in purple and scarlet, and gilded with gold, and precious stones, and pearls, and had a cup of gold in her hand full of abomination, and filthiness of her fornication.

And in her forehead was a name written, A mystery, that great Babylon that mother of whoredoms, and abominations of the earth.

And I saw the woman drunken with the blood of Saints, and with the blood of the Martyrs of JESUS: and when I saw her, I wondered with great marvel.

What a spiteful accusation!

As a result of the letters, the private meetings and public sermons to discuss Anne's obvious divine punishment, the news of the monstrous births, including Mary's miscarriage, spread over all of New England, and tales were told across the Atlantic as well. Anne's teachings and prophetic authority, which brought so many to Rhode Island, lost so much respect that dissension grew among her followers. William Hutchinson had been made judge or governor of Portsmouth, but a split had formed. The Portsmouth group had initially contracted with one another to form a new theocracy, which Anne called "magistracy."

Some of the Pocasset founders, led by William Coddington, prepared to begin a new town, Newport, on the south side of the island, where there was a deeper harbor and better land for development.

*****

In the months after Anne's molar pregnancy, or monster birth, her authority and ministry suffered, perhaps because she was ill and recovering. Or because once the Antinomians were out of reach of the Boston magistrates and ministers, her message lost some urgency. Or it could be that the people of Pocasset still held the superstitious beliefs of their parents and grandparents that monsters were the proof of a woman's heresy.

In 1645, eight years after Mary Dyer bore a stillborn daughter labeled a monster, and after Anne miscarried a molar pregnancy, her husband's brother-in-law, Rev. John Wheelwright, preached and published a pamphlet, *Mercurius Americanus*, that refuted Gov. Winthrop's 1644 book *Short Story of the Rise and Reign...* Wheelwright mentioned their misfortune as the fruit of their fancies.

> The next is Mxs. [Mistress] Dyer, the wife of Mr. Dyer aforenamed, she was devoted to Mrs. Hutchinsons fancies; this is she, who (he [Gov. Winthrop, the author] says) had the monster: whether the conceptions of her brain had influence upon the conceptions of her womb, or these of the womb upon those of the brain, I will not discuss. This discoverer [Rev. Thomas Weld, who wrote the introduction to the Winthrop book] inclines to the former, I think he might by a deeper search have reached the natural cause whilst he in his Method telling us her penalty, judges her for her errors immediately sentenced from heaven: in which passage, as in many other in his book, a spirit of censure and malice is pregnant.

Now, to improve his professional lot as being aligned with the powerful Rev. Cotton and the magistrates, Wheelwright changed his tune and said that Mary and Anne were deluded by fancies or fantasies (as women do).

By the 1650s, when scandalous women were speaking in public as sectarian preachers and missionaries, there was a caution that women who preached, or even who listened to women preachers, gave birth to monsters. This was a direct reference to Hutchinson and Dyer, who were famous on both sides of the Atlantic not for what they might have taught or spoken of, but because of their wombs.

In 1660, shortly after Mary's execution for civil disobedience, Rev. John Eliot, known as the apostle to the Indians, was still horrified at the dread judgment of God on Mary and Anne, saying,

> I now write... to answer that desire of Mr. [Richard] Baxter ... about the monster ... Mrs. Dyer (a great fomenting of those horrid opinions being the mother) ... There being none present but some women of her own stamp, it was hushed up and suddenly buried ... a most hideous creat[ure], a woman, a fish, a bird, & beast all woven together ... [I write] with prayers to the father of all mercy to look down upon us in these sad times, and support us under all our fears.

Actually, Rev. Eliot neglects to mention that his old colleague, Rev. Cotton, was the one who hushed up the monstrous birth, and buried the fetus according to English law.

Phyllis Mack wrote: "More clearly than evidence extracted under torture, these monstrous births 'proved' either that the women's very essences or imaginations had become depraved when they embraced heretical doctrines or that their true essences were evil from the beginning, but had been masked by their respectable social position and behavior." *Visionary Women: Ecstatic Prophecy in Seventeenth-Century England.*

Seventy-five years later, people were still talking about the pair of monsters born in New England, including the Richard Baxter that Rev. Eliot mentioned above.

> Sir Henry Vane had a set of Disciples, who first sprang under him in New-England, when he was Governor there, But their Notions were then raw and undigested, and their Party quickly confounded by God's Providence, as appears from Mr. Tho. Weld's Account [the preface to Winthrop's book].

One Mrs. Dyer, a Chief Person of the Sect, did first bring forth a Monster, which had the Parts of almost all Sorts of Living Creatures; some Parts like Man, but most ugly and misplac'd; and some like Beasts, Birds, and Fishes, having Horns, Fins and Claws: And at the Birth of it the Bed shook, and the Women were forced to leave the room. Mrs. Hutchinson, the chief Woman among them; and their Teacher, (to whose Exercises a Congregation of them used to assemble) brought forth about 30 Misshapen Births at once; and being banish'd into another Plantation, was kill'd there by the Indians.

Richard Baxter, Edmund Calamy (editor). *An Abridgement Of Mr. Baxter's History Of Young Sir Henry Vane, His Life And Times*, pp. 98, 99. 1713.

Mary Dyer and Anne Hutchinson were by no means the only English women to bear monsters, but they were and are the most famous of them.

Chapter 28

Boston Wants its Heretics Back

This chapter was published first in *Mary Dyer Illuminated,* the first volume of my double-biographical novel about Mary and William Dyer. It closely follows the account of three elders of the Boston First Church who were sent to try to get Anne Hutchinson and her followers to repent of their heresy, and reunite with the church. One might suspect that Gov. John Winthrop and his fellow leaders wanted to bring the heretics back into their spiritual and civil control, punish them (perhaps with the death penalty), and then annex the Rhode Island lands to Massachusetts Bay Colony.

*****

Newport, Rhode Island
May 1640

While their men attended general court in Newport, Mary and Anne worked together around the monthly washing. Servants carried the heavy water buckets to fill the cauldron in the yard, and a hired laundress labored over the steaming vats with a long paddle to agitate the harsh soap and textiles. All the bed linens, curtains, rags and towels, and clothing of family and laborers were scrounged for laundry day. When the much-abused textiles were hung to dry on a rope, or spread on bushes, it was apparent that mending would be necessary, and that's what kept them occupied.

Mary picked up a pair of Will's breeches and inspected them for wear. After vigorous washing, this pair was no longer fit for court business, so she patched the rips, strengthened the seams, and reserved them for a servant's use. She made a mental note to start Will's new pair on the morrow. Anne noticed the condition, and promised to have her son Edward, who had moved back to Boston and submitted to the church there, send some lengths of wool for new garments.

Will had been elected Recorder of the Rhode Island colony last year, and he received three shillings per day of work at two General Court sessions, and the four quarterly court days. Mary glowed just a bit to think that his work was valued at twice the rate of skilled laborers like masons or carpenters, and he was only beginning his career in government.

Anne placidly hemmed an overstitch. "William and I are planning to remove further afield from the reach of Mr. Winthrop. He's sent delegations to Pocasset – I mean Portsmouth, its new name – to exhort us, and particularly me, to recant our beliefs. They think that by exercising their covenant of works to us again and again, that we'll be worn down. William had words for the latest of those servants of Satan who came around in February."

Mary stopped breathing for a moment. "What did he say?"

"First, you shall know the circumstances of their coming. Three men, John Oliver, William Hibbins, and Captain Edward Gibbons, came through the forest on the same paths we used, though they would have had a more difficult journey in the deep snows. Arriving in their canoes, they slept overnight at John Coggeshall's house. They approached me as I worked in my garden. 'From whom do you come?' I asked, though I knew the answer, for I recognized them.

"'From the church of Christ at Boston, to convince you of truth,' said Captain Gibbons. I answered that I knew of no such church, neither would I admit that it is anything but the Whore and Strumpet of Boston, but no church of Christ."

Mary didn't know whether to laugh or be horrified.

Anne continued. "I refused to let them read their letter from Boston and denied that they came with authority, speaking the words of the Lord. 'There are lords many and gods many, but I acknowledge but one Lord. Which Lord do you mean?'

"'We came in the name of but one Lord, and that is God,' they said.

"I answered, 'Then so far we agree.'

"Again they replied, 'We have a message to you from the church of Christ in Boston.'

"'I know no church but one.' Besides, of course, they had excommunicated me, so I was not under their jurisdiction." Anne smirked at bettering the men.

"'In Scripture, the Holy Ghost calls them churches,' said they.

"'Christ had but one spouse,' said I. They replied that he had as many spouses as he did saints, but I would not acknowledge that group as any church of Christ. They gave me up as too quarrelsome, and went to my husband to urge him to force my conformity. To compel me to listen to their censorious letter."

Mary couldn't resist a chuckle at the Boston men's expense. "Your William would never do that!"

"When confronted by those vipers, he answered with words that warm my heart, Mary. I'll never forget them. He told those serpents, '*I am more nearly tied to my wife than to the church. I do think her to be a dear saint and servant of God.*'"

Anne let her hands rest idly in her lap, and looked out over the bay. "I confess that I've thought about what it would be like to go back to Boston and recant publicly and believe privately, instead of having to carve a home and life out of nothing. To have our children in school and choice apprenticeships, and to live in a warm and sturdy brick house in our declining years." She closed her eyes, slumped a little, and sighed. Then her back straightened and she picked up her mending.

"But that's vain and slothful thinking. The Lord has called us out to the wilderness like the woman in Revelation. I knew years ago that it would be a dark and dangerous journey, and even so, I was willing. William and the older children were willing. We are convinced that no matter what we suffer in this world, it will be as dung, compared to the glorious riches of being present with the Lord."

The women had been sitting near a large pine tree while they worked. Now the bay breeze sprang up and lifted the needles above them in a gentle sigh. The afternoon sun broke through the thin overcast and illuminated Anne's head and shoulders in a moment of light. Strands of silver-streaked hair that escaped from her cap caught the light for a moment, reminding Mary of embroidery thread.

"Next year, we hope to have a farm in New Netherland or Long Island, across the Sound. If my teaching is not wanted in Boston, I shall teach Indian women and children the covenant of grace without their ever having known of the covenant of works. And my children will grow up, uncorrupted by the law of sin and death, but instead, filled with the inward light of the Holy Ghost."

The women were quiet for a few moments, letting the thoughts settle in. Samuel was teaching Zuriel and Susanna a chant to remember the names of the Narragansett islands:

"Prudence, Patience, Hope, and Despair,
And little Hog Island right over there."

Then Mary spoke: "Anne, we've heard news about King Charles and the rumors of war in our homeland. The king has turned the Puritans like Oliver Cromwell against him, with not only his tax policies, but his insistence, along with Archbishop Laud, of religious conformity between England, Scotland, and Ireland.

"Forcing the Church of England's liturgy and use of the *Book of Common Prayer* were ill-received by the Scottish Kirk. So after two years of conflict, the King is even deeper in debt, with no tax revenue, and he's forced to recall Parliament after eleven years of ruling on his own."

Anne shook her head and sighed deeply. "The Lord speaks his judgments and kings and lords fall before him. Six years ago, and far away in Alford, I would have sung for joy at such news, before the Lord showed me his will. Now – "

Her voice trailed off to a whisper. "Now, it's too late for the king. He and Laud will never succeed. There will be bloody war across England, Scotland, and Ireland. Famine, plagues, exposure, and misery will kill more men, women, and innocent children than cannon and musket shot. Long before the war ends, the king and the bishop will lose their heads. And still, the war will rage. All for vainglorious power."

"Now, our struggles, Mary, as great as they've been or will be, are as nothing, compared with the surpassing greatness of knowing Christ in our hearts. He is the light of the world, and the light to our path. He will preserve us for his kingdom. Though we pass through the valley of the shadow of death, we fear no evil, for he is our refuge. The body they may kill, but our spirits are saved for eternity."

As she finished a seam and set down her needle and thread, Anne switched from prophet to midwife with no hesitation.

"While your babe is still a tiny seed, and you lie with your husband, fix your mind upon your husband's face, that the child will resemble him in looks and in vigor. You need to eat properly, to nourish the babe and give him a good start. You must eat plenty of hot and moist meats, and beets and dark greens, and you'll notice that your own moods will be calm and reasonable." The older woman laughed. "Will would enjoy a reasonable wife while you're breeding. Do him a favor."

Chapter 29

William Hutchinson's Response to a Woman's Plea for Justice

In June 1640, one James Sabire, who had been set in stocks in Portsmouth, Rhode Island, moved to Boston. There, he may have demanded a divorce from his pregnant wife Barbara, of the Boston magistrates. He charged Barbara with being an adulteress, and denying him his rights in the marriage bed.

Barbara Sabire wrote to the governor and assistants of Rhode Island, asking for a character reference and witness to her husband's abuse and her stellar behavior, probably hoping not to be set in stocks at Boston – or hanged as an adulteress! It appears that she sheltered in the home of William and Anne Hutchinson for nine months, perhaps during her pregnancy and delivery.

The letter below was written by William Hutchinson to John Winthrop, who had just been replaced in the governor's seat by Thomas Dudley.

Not only does the letter describe the horrible behavior of James Sabire, but between the lines, we can read what kind of relationships were expected of godly men toward their wives: honor, protection, providence, love, tenderness, loyalty.

It's interesting that Anne and William Hutchinson had 11 or 12 of their children living with them at the time, as well as the midwife Jane Hawkins and her husband and sons, and Barbara Sabire. Add to that William Hutchinson's sisters and maybe cousins, and who knows how many other people who needed a home, either temporary or permanent? It gives us a good sense of the Hutchinsons' hospitality and efficiency in ordering a home and business.

The letter can be read in the negative, of course, showing what actions were reprehensible to the leaders of Rhode Island's new colony, but read as a defense of Mrs. Sabire, she appears to be a virtuous woman faithful to her vows, who worked to support her family when her debauched husband refused.

I've put James Sabire's many offenses in bold print.

To the Worshipful & much respected friend John Winthrop Esquire at his house in Boston

Right worshipful,

We have lately received a letter from Barbara Sabire, the wife of James Sabire, now resident in Boston, with you, wherein we understand that he hath made complaint of her, if not false accusations laid against her, therefore we thought good to testify, being desired thereunto, what he confessed upon examination, before us whose names are here underwritten.

The ground of his examination was from some **false reports** he had raised up against his wife. We called them false because they proved so to be when they were inquired into, but not to trouble you with those:

1. A word or two of what he did confess, when the question was demanded of him, Did your wife deny unto you due benevolence, according to the rule of god or no? His answer was she did not, but she did and had given her body to him, this he confessed, & did clear her of that which now he condemns her for and this may evince it and prove it to be so.

2. He did here likewise report his wife was with child, which we understand he doth also deny unto your worships and that will also prove him to **speak falsely** if he shall say his wife did deny him marriage fellowship until he did come under your government:

3. This we must witness that his wife was not the ground or cause of his being set in the stocks, but for his **disturbance of the peace** of the place at unseasonable hours whereas people were in bed, and withal for his **cursing and swearing** and the like.

Again a word or two concerning his life when he was with us, It was **scandalous** and **offensive** to men, **sinful** before God; and towards his wife. Instead of putting honour upon her as the weaker vessel, he wanted [lacked] the natural affection of a reasonable creature, **we also found him idle** and indeed a very **drone sucking up the honey** of his wife's labour, he taking **no pains to provide for her**, but spending one month after another **without any labour at all,** it may be some found one day in a month he did something being put upon it, being threatened by the government here; and indeed had he not been relieved by his wife and her friends where she did keep, he might have starved. Besides he is given very much to **lying, drinking** strong waters [whiskey], and towards his wife **showing neither pity nor humanity**, for indeed **he could not keep from boys & servants** [sexual predation of both sexes], **secret passages betwixt him and his wife** [sexual demands she felt were immoral? rape?] about the marriage bed, and of those things there is more witnesses than us, and concerning her.

She lived with us about 3 quarters of a year, whose wife was unblameable before men for anything we know, being not able to charge her in her life & conversation but, beside her masters testimony, who best knows her is this, that she was a faithful, careful, & painful both servant & wife to his best observation, during the time with him.

Those things we being requested unto, we present unto your wise considerations hoping that by the mouth of 2 or 3 witnesses, the innocent will be acquitted, & the guilty rewarded according to his works; thus ceasing further to trouble you we take our leaves & rest.

Your worshipful Loving friends
William Hutchinson [assistant governor]
William Baulston [treasurer]
William Aspinwall [secretary]
John Sanford [constable]

Portsmouth, Rhode Island, the 29th of 4th 1640 [29 June 1640]

Letter from:
Chapin, Howard M. *Documentary History of Rhode Island, Vol. 2, Being the History of the Towns of Portsmouth and Newport to 1647 and the Court Records of Aquidneck.* Providence, Rhode Island: Preston and Rounds Co., 1919.

Chapter 30

Anne Hutchinson Guilty of Breach of Covenant Over Her Son

Francis Hutchinson, born in 1621 in Alford, Lincolnshire, was Anne's and William's sixth child. He was unmarried and living with his parents at age 17, when his mother was excommunicated from Boston's First Church of Christ. Two years after they were exiled from Boston, on July 9, 1640, he wrote to the Boston church whose teacher had been his parents' friend and mentor since before his birth, and requested to be removed from church membership. The letter was possibly written with the assistance of his parents, having been couched in scriptural terms as we see in the response. He asked to be "recommended to the word of Gods Grace, according to Acts 20.32," to be dismissed from his covenant with them, because he "being forced to attend upon your Parents there where you live," he could not "Attend upon the Duties of the Covenant."

It was read in a church meeting on the 19th of July.

Rev. John Cotton answered Francis' request on the sixth of August, calling Francis "Beloved brother in our Lord Jesus." Again, there was no specific mention of Anne Hutchinson's name.

Cotton said the church was unwilling to let Francis go "because they hear a good Report of your Constancy in the Truth, & Faith of the Gospel: yet in this motion they neither can, nor dare Assent unto you, as wanting warrant from Scripture-light. The Place which you quote doeth not suit with your Case."

Cotton said that they would not release Francis as a member unless it was to another Church of Christ (Puritan) – "any Orthodox, & Orderly Church." If there were elders preaching the word of God, or if Francis himself were older and gifted with speaking, they would recommend him from their fellowship to another, from one covenant to another.

Yet we dare not Recommend you from a Church to no Church, nor Dismiss you from our Covenant, till the Lord Dismiss you. Do not think the Lord dismisseth you by your Parents Authority, who call you to serve them in a place so far distant, that the Duties of Church Covenant cannot be performed between us & you. For first, your Parents deal sinfully, & bring upon themselves the guilt of your Breach of Covenant, if they detain you there needlessly; seeing the Covenant which you entered into with the Church, was undertaken with their Consent & Desire & therefore now it will stand in force before the Lord both against them & you, if you do break your Covenant.

The church said it was William's and Anne's sin, and that God would hold them accountable if the nineteen-year-old Francis were detained in Rhode Island. The church elders, referring to Cotton as their Teacher, also addressed a rumor or concern about Francis associating with his mother, an excommunicated and unrepentant sinner.

The Boston elders gave Francis a bit of grace when they allowed that he wasn't sinning by eating at the table with his own mother, though she was excommunicate.

One thing we thought good further to Acquaint you with, That our Teacher being thought by some to say, that you forbore sitting at Table with your mother, though others deny it, & others remember it not, nor he himself: yet to be sure, that no mistake might follow of it, He publicly professed before the face of the Church, That if he so spake, it was his forgetfulness, but verily thinketh it was either his own misplacing of his Intentions & words, or a mistake in the Hearers, who applied what He spake in general, to your particular case ... that with excommunicate persons no Religious Communion is to be held, nor any civil familiar Communion, as sitting at the Table. But yet He did put a Difference between other Brethren in Church-fellowship, & such as were joined in natural, or civil near Relations, as Parents & Children, Husband & wife &c. God did allow them that liberty, which He denied others. Upon his speech, the Offence that was conceived by some was removed: & we hope, neither doth any Offence rest upon you therefrom. To your Father & self, & others of our brethren we have written at large, to satisfy such Doubts, as we understand by our Messengers [Oliver, Gibbons, and Hibbins, the three men who had visited Portsmouth earlier in the year] have troubled them.

The Lord watch over you all for good, & keep you spotless, & blameless, faithful & fruitful to him to his heavenly kingdom in Christ Jesus,
In whom we rest, your loving Brethren,
J. Cotton, with the rest of the Elders in the Name of the Church.

Francis and his brother-in-law, William Collins, returned to Boston in 1641 and were arrested and imprisoned, with huge fines levied on them (see next chapter). One year after his request to be dropped, he was excommunicated by the First Church of Christ for "sundry Errors" including giving reviling speeches against the church and calling it a whore and strumpet.

Oh, that sounds exactly like his mother's words to the three messengers from Boston in May 1640. There was a slight difference between a whore (a prostitute or sexually promiscuous person) and a strumpet (a debauched adulterer). Both words were extremely incendiary.

Francis wasn't allowed to leave the church in 1640 but they excommunicated him in 1641. It's like your company's boss saying, "You can't quit, you're fired!"

The Cotton letter is excerpted from
The Correspondence of John Cotton. Sargent Bush, Jr., editor. The University of North Carolina Press, 2001.

Chapter 31

Why the Hutchinsons Had to Leave Rhode Island

Prudence Island

In the north-central waters of Narragansett Bay is Prudence Island. In the twenty-first century, it's shaped like two islands connected by an isthmus, but during the Little Ice Age when sea levels were lower, there may have been more dry land, with a wider isthmus.

From 1637, Prudence Island belonged to Roger Williams and John Winthrop. Williams owned the top part nearer Providence, and Winthrop owned the part that was across the channel from Pocasset, which the Hutchinsonian party would settle in 1638 and later call Portsmouth, Rhode Island.

Roger Williams to Gov. John Winthrop
The last of the week, I think the 28th of the 8th. [Oct. 28, 1637.]
Sir, – This bearer, Miantunnomu, resolving to go on his visit, I am bold to request a word of advice from you concerning a proposition made by Canonicus and himself to me some half year since. Canonicus gave an island in this bay to Mr. Oldham, by name Chibachuwese, upon condition as it would seem, that he would dwell there near unto them. The Lord (in whose hands all hearts are) turning their affections towards myself, they desired me to remove thither and dwell nearer to them. I have answered once and again, that for present I mind not to remove; but if I have it from them, I would give them satisfaction for it, and build a little house and put in some swine, as understanding the place to have store of fish and good feeding for swine. ... I spake of it now to this Sachem, and he tells me, that because of the store of fish, Canonicus desires that I would accept half, (it being spectacle-wise, and between a mile or two in circuit, as I guess,) and he would reserve the other ; but I think, if I go over, I shall obtain the whole. ... So, with respective salutes to your kind self and Mrs. Winthrop, I rest

Your worship's unfeigned, in all I may,
Roger Williams.

—*Letters of Roger Williams. 1632-1682. Now first collected*, Oct. 28 1637, (Providence: Printed for the Narragansett Club, 1874) pg. 70.

As you can see by my aerial photo, Winthrop's portion of Prudence Island is a short distance across Narragansett Bay from the northern part of Aquidneck Island, on which the Hutchinson party settled in the spring of 1638.

Winthrop's part of Prudence Island, tiny Dyer Island in the middle, and the west coast of Portsmouth in the foreground.

Having Winthrop's swine across the channel was no threat to Anne Hutchinson or the other members of the new town. But because the increasingly hostile Winthrop owned this chunk of land, and the Plymouth Colony, also antagonistic toward the Antinomians who had colonized formerly Native American land that Plymouth Colony claimed was part of their chartered territory, you see the danger.

Kidnap and heresy

The Hutchinsons and other Rhode Islanders who had been exiled from Massachusetts Bay Colony were being pressured to submit themselves to Boston or Plymouth, and be reconciled with the church by putting away their heresy.

The midwife Jane Hawkins, already associated with Anne, was being gossiped about as being a witch, though she wasn't charged and arrested for such. The First Church of Boston had sent their three-man delegation to attempt to bring the Hutchinsons back.

Meanwhile, Anne's brother-in-law, Rev. John Wheelwright, who had been banished from Massachusetts Bay and moved to the Province of New Hampshire, now had to move farther east to Maine because Massachusetts had annexed New Hampshire and extended their reach onto land Wheelwright owned, meaning that his banishment was also pushing him off his own land.

William Collins, a son-in-law who had married the fifteen-year-old Anne Hutchinson, and Francis Hutchinson, born in 1620, were arrested in 1641, and imprisoned in Boston.

> William Collins being found to be a seducer, & his practices proved such, he is fined one hundred pounds [in today's value, $24,380], & to be kept close prisoner till his fine be paid, & then he is banished, upon pain of death.
>
> Francis Hutchinson, for calling the church of Boston a whore, a strumpet, & other corrupt tenets, he is fined £50 [today's value, $12,190], & to be kept close prisoner till it be paid, & then he is banished, upon pain of death.
>
> Records of the Governor and Company of the Massachusetts Bay in New-England, September and December 1641.
>
> Eric W. Nye, Pounds Sterling to Dollars: Historical Conversion of Currency, accessed August 2018, http://www.uwyo.edu/numimage/currency.htm.

They refused to pay, and after their fines were reduced to £40 and £20 respectively (which they also didn't pay), they were released December 10 upon a bill by Thomas Dudley.

According to Samuel Gorton, Massachusetts Bay Colony intended to annex and take into their own authority all of Narragansett Bay, which of course is surrounded by Rhode Island and Providence Plantations.

If Boston pursued the Hutchinsons into Rhode Island and annexed and further banished the dissenters, might they not persecute the group who had supported her in 1638? Perhaps the Hutchinsons perceived themselves as a magnet for persecution, and left Portsmouth to take the heat off Rhode Island supporters.

Indeed, in the autumn of 1643, Massachusetts men invaded Shawomet (later Warwick), Rhode Island, abducted Samuel Gorton, Randall Holden, and others, and hauled them to Boston for trial. Ostensibly, they were to be charged with criminal trespass of Massachusetts land in defiance of the 1638 banishment orders. But while they sat in prison awaiting trial by the General Court, different charges were filed: *sedition and religious error.*

That's right: the same charges that convicted Anne Hutchinson in 1638. Winthrop and Dudley, Wilson, Cotton, and Shepard hadn't evolved at all in five years. In fact, Rev. Cotton was in favor, along with the Massachusetts Bay Colony magistrates, of the death penalty for the Rhode Island men, because he felt it important to "preserve New England's good name in England," where he thought that such theological views were unfavorable to his brand of Congregationalism. The court voted six for and three against the death penalty, and the men escaped hanging.

Gorton, Holden, and Greene were convicted and sentenced to banishment, with their Shawomet land confiscated. Kept in separate custody over the winter and forced to hard labor in irons, and forbidden to speak to anyone lest they spread theological error, they were released in March 1644, when they sailed out of New Amsterdam (Manhattan), and thence to Britain, to obtain a legal patent to their land.

The historian Henry Charles Lea wrote in his 1888 book, *A History of the Inquisition of the Middle Ages,*

> "There is no doubt that men of the kindliest tempers, the profoundest intelligence, the noblest aspirations, the purest zeal for righteousness, professing a religion founded on love and charity, were ruthless when heresy was concerned, and were ready to trample it out at the cost of any suffering. ... With such men it was not hope of gain or lust of blood or pride of opinion or wanton exercise of power, but sense of duty, and they but represented what was universal public opinion."

The Gorton-Holden harassment and abductions happened slightly after the Hutchinson events of 1643, but show the political climate. Mistress Hutchinson was vulnerable to capture, retrial – and execution.

Narragansett Patent

Rev. Thomas Weld, one of Anne's inquisitors and the brother of Anne's jailer, now in England with Rev. Hugh Peter as an agent of the Massachusetts Bay Colony, invented the fraudulent Narragansett Patent that said that the northern and northwestern reaches of Rhode Island and Providence Plantations were part of the Bay's 1629 patent. Between 1642 and 1645, Weld managed to get the support of eight members of Council on Foreign Plantations, though not all, to agree that the lands (legally sold to Rhode Islanders by Miantonomo, a Narragansett sachem), actually were part of the grant to

Massachusetts by the King. Weld should have presented his petition to Parliament, but lobbied council members individually. He failed to have the fraudulent document sealed and enrolled as required, and inserted a December 1644 date on it. But the date he chose was a Sunday, when Parliament was most certainly not in session.

Weld's fraudulent patent was spoken of as a threat in 1645, but it's unclear when the Massachusetts government learned that it was a lie. They recalled Weld, but knowing he would be punished, he found employment as a chaplain to Oliver Cromwell's army.

Much of the Narragansett affair happened during and after the months that Anne Hutchinson lived at Pelham Bay, New Netherland, but it does shed light on what might have been her fate if she'd stayed in volatile Rhode Island.

Long Island

William Hutchinson may have been ill or feeling near the end of his 54 years when he leased land on Long Island just before he died in 1642. (Or it's possible that he died in Rhode Island, and the Dutch-controlled Brooklyn land was fraudulently leased in his name by a Dutchman.)

There were English towns on the north coast of Long Island, administered by Massachusetts Bay Colony and New Haven Colony, but they had an uneasy relationship with the Dutch for many years.

With her husband William dead, he who had protected her from witchcraft charges and given her the high social status that kept her from prison or hanging in the Puritan colonies, Anne needed to find a home in a different jurisdiction.

New Haven was a Puritan colony. Their preacher was Rev. John Davenport, who had been a new arrival in Boston when he sat on the court that convicted Anne of heresy and banished her. He co-founded the New Haven Colony later that year, and was still their minister when the first Quaker missionaries arrived in 1656. (In the winter of 1657-58, he and his fellow theocrats tortured Humphrey Norton, a Quaker.) New Haven administered the English towns across the Sound on Long Island.

Therefore, the communities on the north shore of Long Island were not safe for Anne and her family.

New Netherland: Manhattan, Brooklyn, Queens, Bronx

Sometime in 1642, Anne and her younger family members and several supporters and servants had moved to what is known today as Eastchester, New York, and began to build a plantation. Pelham Bay and the Bronx are better-known names for the area.

The Dutch West India Company (WIC) owned Manhattan, parts of Long Island, and trading posts north along the Hudson River. Collectively, the lands were known as New Netherland. Back in the home country, there was a degree of religious liberty, where Catholics, Protestants, and Jews managed to live mostly harmoniously. But in America, the Dutch interests were governed by Willem Kieft, who was a strict Calvinist Dutch Reformed man much like the most conservative Puritans of New England. He was not elected by the residents of the colony: he was appointed by the WIC across the Atlantic.

Gov. Kieft's harsh policies with the local Native Americans had created antipathy on the parts of the English, Dutch, and the Lenape and Siwanoy tribes. The white settlers, including the mercenary Captain John Underhill who had been an Antinomian (and was married to a Dutch woman), had slaughtered natives a short time before, and natives were sick of the English cattle trampling and eating their corn and other crops. There were unscrupulous Dutch and Englishmen who had illegally traded alcohol, guns, powder, and shot for furs and food.

Further, Kieft was harsh in his religious beliefs. He was as tough as any Boston churchman when it came to nonconformists or heretics.

"Kieft's War" took place in February 1643, when European colonists ambushed two camps of native tribes, first in New Jersey, and then on Corlear's Hook on Manhattan, using the full moon reflecting off the snow to light their dark deeds.

A Dutch witness, David Pieterz de Vries, wrote of the slaughter of natives by the Dutch, "Infants were torn from their mother's breast and hacked to death in the presence of their parents, and the pieces thrown into the fire and in the water. Other sucklings, being bound to small boards, were cut, stuck and pierced, and miserably massacred in a manner to move a heart of stone. Some were thrown into the river, and when the fathers and mothers endeavored to save them the soldiers would not let them come on land but made both parents and children drown – children from five to six years of age, and also some old and decrepit persons."

The same night, the vicious killings continued on Manhattan. "Some who fled from this onslaught, and concealed themselves in the neighboring sedge, and when it was morning, came out to beg a piece of bread, and to be permitted to warm themselves, were murdered in cold blood and tossed into the fire or the water. Some came to our people in the country with their hands, and some with their legs cut off, and some holding their entrails in their arms, and others had such horrible cuts and gashes, that worse than they were could never happen."

The Dutch soldiers returned with severed heads and about 30 captives, who were probably sold into Caribbean slavery. The soldiers, like those who had massacred the Pequot Indians in 1636-37, believed they were doing good deeds pleasing to God, in vanquishing the enemies of Christ, and claiming their lands and properties as blessings from God, to be enjoyed and exploited.

Anne had lived harmoniously with the tribes near Boston, Portsmouth, and Providence, so she may have thought that the tribes of New Netherland would have a similar relationship with Dutch and English settlers.

But there, in the summer of 1643, Anne and the younger members of her family were slaughtered by Native Americans.

Chapter 32

They Cruelly Murthered Her

E dward Johnson, a pious Puritan of Massachusetts Bay, wrote a history of the colony. Of the leaders he approves, he names names. He purposely omits the names of those he considers to be heretics and lawbreakers, so as not to bring them to memory. This is his account of the Hutchinson massacre.

...Although the Lord be secret in all the dispensation of his providences, whether in judgment or mercy, yet much may be learn'd from all, as sometimes pointing with the finger to the lesson; as here these persons withdrawing from the Churches of Christ (wherein he walketh, and is to be found in his blessed Ordinances) to a first and second place, where they came to a very sad end; for thus it came to pass in the latter place, The Indians in those parts forewarned them of making their abode there; yet this could be no warming to them, but still they continued, being amongst a multitude of Indians, boasted they were become all one Indian; and indeed this woman, who had the chief rule of all the roast [roost], being very bold in her strange Revelations and mis-applications, tells them, though all nations and people were cut off round about them, yet should not they; till on a day certain Indians coming to her house, discoursing with them, they wished to tie up her dogs, for they much bit the man, not mistrusting the Indians guile, did so; the which no sooner done, but they cruelly murthered her, taking one of their daughters away with them, and another of them seeking to escape is caught, as she was getting over a hedge, and they drew her back again by the hair of the head to the stump of a tree, and there cut off her head with a hatchet; the other that dwelt by them [neighbors?] betook them to boat, and fled, to tell the sad news; the rest of their companions, who were rather hardened in their sinful way, and blasphemous opinions, than brought to any sight of their damnable Errors, as you shall after hear; yet was not this the first loud speaking hand of God against them; but before this the Lord had pointed directly to their sin by a very fearful Monster, that another of these women [Mary Dyer] had brought forth, they striving to bury it in oblivion [actually, Rev. Cotton buried it], but the Lord brought it to light, setting forth the view of their monstrous Errors in this prodigious birth.

Johnson, Edward. *Wonder Working Providence*, p. 186, 187

The Siwanoy chief, Wampage, and his men came to the Dutch homestead where Anne and her family were living and building a farm. The guard dogs must have been biting and barking at the strangers, and they were closed into the house. Then the Indians fell upon the Hutchinson group with hatchets. When their bloody work was done, they pulled the bodies and the hated livestock into the house and fired it.

The Hutchinson family who were killed that day were:
Anne Marbury Hutchinson, aged 52
Francis Hutchinson, aged 23
Anne Hutchinson Collins, aged 17, and husband William Collins, aged 19
Mary Hutchinson, aged 16
Katherine Hutchinson, aged 14
William II Hutchinson, aged 12
Zuriel Hutchinson, aged 7

In addition, there might have been servants and relatives, as well as supporters like Richard Maggson or Maxson.

The Siwanoy spared the nine-year-old child Susanna, named after her elder sister who had died of plague in 1630, who had been picking berries at the nearby Split Rock, and abducted her.

There's speculation that it happened August 20, 1643, and others think it was a month earlier. Edward Johnson said it was in September. The exact date is unknown.

Some writers have said that Susanna was held for nine years before she was returned to the custody of her brother Edward Hutchinson. But Gov. John Winthrop, who died in March 1649, wrote on 5 July 1646:

"A daughter of Mrs. Hutchinson was carried away by the Indians near the Dutch, when her mother and others were killed by them; and upon the peace concluded between the Dutch and the same Indians, she was returned to the Dutch governor [Kieft], who restored her to her friends [her brother

Edward] here. She was about eight [actually nine] years old, when she was taken, and continued with them about four [actually three] years, and she had forgot her own language, and all her friends, and was loath to have come from the Indians."

Split Rock, Eastchester, New York

There's a rumor that Susanna bore a child fathered by a Siwanoy during her long captivity and that a certain family descends from that Native American and royal English connection. You'd have to suspend belief in

1. The orderly passage of time (Winthrop dates the entry to July 1646, three years after her abduction),

2. In human biology (because Susanna was too young, ages nine to twelve, during her captivity to bear a baby when girls got their menstrual cycles at ages 12 to 17), and

3. In Boston social conventions (Susanna married the son of Boston's wealthy tavern keeper when she was 18, and she would not have been an acceptable catch after giving birth to a mixed-race child).

Winthrop would not have known of Susanna's redemption if it happened in 1652, as he had died in March 1649. If Susanna had "forgotten her language," perhaps she was reluctant to speak of her trauma to those who would grill her for details for their own entertainment, or sell her story to London penny broadsheets. It's possible that her older brother Edward, now a 33-year-old attorney in Boston, counseled his 12-year-old sister to be silent.

In today's terms, at Susanna's redemption, we might say she had survivor's guilt, Stockholm syndrome, or post-traumatic stress syndrome. Three years of living rough, in extreme hardship, not knowing if any of her family were aware she was alive, would be unimaginable. Yet the strength and spirit she'd inherited from her parents William and Anne, and even the hardships of being a captive, must have given her some resilience. When she was 18, only six years after her release, she married and later had children, and her descendants over the last 370 years are countless.

All Hutchinson descendants can claim a goodly heritage from Anne and William Hutchinson. As the Hutchinsons' Bible said, "The Lord is the portion of mine inheritance and of my cup: thou shalt maintain my lot. The lines [wherewith my portion is measured] are fallen unto me in pleasant places: yea, I have a fair heritage. I will praise the Lord, who hath given me counsel." Psalm 16:5-7, *1599 Geneva Bible*

Chapter 33

How Anne's Death Affected the Dyers

In the late summer of 1643, Mary Dyer's mentor and close friend, Anne Marbury Hutchinson and her youngest children were massacred by the Siwanoy Indians they'd come to evangelize. One daughter, nine-year-old Susanna, was abducted by the sachem, Wampage, and redeemed later in a negotiated settlement.

Massacre of Anne Hutchinson.

Source: Wikipedia

Mary Dyer heard about it soon after the tragic event, and the news may have brought on labor and childbirth. She named her newborn son "Maher-shallal-hash-baz," and called him Maher. (The other children had "normal" names like Samuel, William, Mary, Henry, and Charles.) Maher's name comes from Isaiah 8:4, and means, in Hebrew, "suddenly attacked, quickly taken" or "swift to plunder and quick to carry away."

An entry in *A Genealogical Dictionary of The First Settlers of New England, Before 1692, Volume #2 Dunen–Earl,* by James Savage, gives information on Maher's name.

"MAHERSHALLALHASHBAZ, s. of William. R. I. Hist. Coll. III. 252. The name is reverent. borrow. from Isaiah viii. 1. Some antiquary of R.I. ought to inform the world, how, in soft moments of relaxat. so formidab. a Hebrew prefix was abbrev. to a monosyl. by his mo. or sis. or br. It may have been Mar, or Buz, as either end was chos. for this discipline of affection; but to write it, as my friend and learned corresp. at Providence has, Mayhershall, is a wantonness of perversion that may seem his highest moral obliquity. *Prob. no other ch. on this side of the ocean has suffer. such infliction* tho. it has been long a tradit. that a fondness for Old Testam. names, in one instance, brot. Beelzebub into use."

According to New England court records, he was not called Mar or Buz, but Maher.

Mary Dyer named her son in a time of grief and despair over the deaths of Anne and the children, in a sudden and vicious attack where an innocent girl was carried away. Mary's question surely would have been, Why did God allow such a tragedy, when Anne was such a strong witness for him?

"Remember those earlier days after you had received the light when you stood your ground in a great contest in the face of suffering. Sometimes you were publicly exposed to insult and persecution; at other times you stood side by side with those who were so treated. You sympathized with those in prison and joyfully accepted the confiscation of your property, because you knew that you yourselves had better and lasting possessions. So do not throw away your confidence; it will be richly rewarded. You need to persevere so that when you have done the will of God, you will receive what he has promised." Hebrews 10:32-36.

What was the promise?

Long before Mary Dyer died on a gallows in 1660 for civil disobedience and in the cause of religious freedom, she had found the answer for herself. Mary knew what sustained Abraham, Job,

Moses, David, Solomon, and all the heroes of faith listed in Hebrews chapter 11. She understood that God is sovereign, and we are his trusting children.

And she knew the Bible promises were not of a mansion or riches in heaven, not of a bubble of safety and prosperity, but of intimacy with God, for all eternity. *Intimacy begun* in a garden where Adam and Eve walked with God and talked face to face. *Intimacy restored in part* by the incarnation of Jesus Christ, the temple veil to the Holy of Holies being torn to allow us access to God's mercy, and the miracle of the Holy Spirit speaking in human hearts. And *intimacy restored fully* by the reunion to be celebrated when Immanuel, God With Us, tenderly wipes away tears and takes believers into his heart forever.

Mary Barrett Dyer knew that although suffering in this life is terrible for both victims and the survivors who love them, that God brings us through it together with him, that one day we'll know why the pain was allowed, and that because of the surpassing glory of that day, we'll look back and consider our human suffering as a split-second of learning and growing deep in trust.

Mary was already experiencing the bliss of that intimacy while she was lying on a prison's dirt floor before her execution, when she wrote "he gloriously accompanied with his Presence, and Peace, and Love in me, in which I rested from my labour..."

Where was God? Inside her. All around her. Holding her in his arms. Welcoming her to eternity with him.

Chapter 34

How Anne's Death Was Seen in the Colonies

Governor Winthrop wrote in his book *Short Story* that the Massachusetts theocratic government feared Anne Hutchinson as a representative of the devil, and it was a necessity to rid themselves of her for self protection. She was banished to the wilderness, the abode of Satan. Did they wish her dead, but not by their hands?

He wrote:

So that the Court did clearly discern, where the Fountain was of all our Distempers ... gave just occasion to fear the danger we were in, seeing ... we had not to do with so simple a Devil, as managed that business ... but Satan seemed to have Commission now to use his utmost cunning to undermine the Kingdom of Christ here ... The Court saw now an inevitable necessity to rid her away, except we would be guilty, not only of our own ruin, but also of the Gospel: so in the end the Sentence of Banishment was pronounced against her.

*****

Randall Holden was one of the Rhode Island men abducted in 1643 by the Massachusetts Bay Colony. He wrote a long, angry letter to the General Court from his prison cell in Salem.

Holden, 41, Samuel Gorton, 51, John Green, 49, and other men had been supporters of Anne Hutchinson, and shortly after founding Pocasset/Portsmouth, had moved to lands they purchased in January 1643 from the sachem Miantonomo, at Shawomet, now called Warwick, Rhode Island. It was land falsely claimed by Massachusetts Bay Colony. Rev. Thomas Weld, an agent and envoy of the Bay now in London, created a fraudulent charter and presented it to important government figures for their signatures, as if they'd approved it in Parliament.

The Gorton party had been violently harassed with rocks thrown at women and children, and their valuable cattle shot with Indian arrows. While they tried to harvest their crops, they were summoned to Boston and given words of safe conduct. But when they'd ignored the summons because they weren't in Massachusetts' jurisdiction, they'd been violently abducted by a 40-man force, beaten, and imprisoned in several Massachusetts Bay towns, with iron fetters on their legs to prevent escape. They were not charged or tried on their possession of the disputed land, but on new charges of sedition and heretical religious beliefs – the same charges Anne Hutchinson had faced. They were saved from execution by three votes of the nine-man General Court.

Gorton, a fiery-tempered man in those years with good reason (though he later mellowed and was a credit to Rhode Island), was warned that if he should speak or write of his blasphemous and abominable heresies, he'd be condemned to death and executed. Holden, Greene, and the others were similarly threatened with death if they spoke to anyone but an officer of state or church. They were "silenced." After a winter at hard labor, they were banished upon pain of death, both from Massachusetts Bay and from their homes at Shawomet.

In the letter, Holden called Gov. Winthrop and the Court the "Idol General" and "Judas Iscariot's fellow confessor for hire," and he'd heard that Winthrop had said that either the Rhode Islanders (Holden, Gorton, and Greene, Robert Potter and Richard Waterman) would be subjected to him or removed to Boston, *"though it should cost blood."*

Holden knew that Gov. Winthrop had written, "The Court saw now *an inevitable necessity to rid her away, except we would be guilty, not only of our own ruin, but also of the Gospel:* so in the end the Sentence of Banishment was pronounced against her, and she was committed to the Marshal, till the Court should dispose of her."

Ridding the church and colony of Mistress Hutchinson by banishment was their *second choice*, so that they would not be guilty of their own ruin; it sounds like their first choice would have been blood.

Conspiracy theory – or fact?

At the end of Randall Holden's letter was a lengthy *Postscriptum* which spoke of the recent massacre of the Hutchinson family in Pelham Bay. Three hundred seventy-five years later, it looks like Holden is accusing Winthrop and the Bay authorities of knowing the danger of Anne moving to the Dutch farm in harm's way, and not properly warning her. Holden wrote:

> The Lord hath added one to our hands in the very conclusion of it, in that effusion of blood and horrible massacres now made at the Dutch plantation of our loving countrymen, women and children, which is nothing else but the complete figure, in a short epitome, of what we have writ, summed up in one entire act; and lest you should make it *a part of your justification, as you do all such like acts, provided they be not upon your own backs, concluding them to be greater sinners than yourselves;* we tell ye, nay, but except you repent, you shall likewise perish. *For we ask you who was the cause of Mrs. Hutchinson, her departure from amongst you?* was it voluntary? No; she changed her phrases according to the dictates of your tutors [Holden refers to the ministers Shepard, Weld, and Peter, Cotton and Wilson, who grilled Anne during her incarceration and wore her down to a partial recantation], and confessed her mistakes, that so she might give you content to abide amongst you; yet did you expose her, and cast her away. *No less are you the original of her removal from Aquethneck* [Aquidneck Island, a.k.a. Rhode Island]; for when she saw her children [William Collins and Francis] could not come down among you, no, not to confer with you in your own way of brotherhood, but be clapt up and detained by so long imprisonment; *rumours also being noised about, that the island should be brought under your government, which if it should, they were fearful of their lives,* or else to act against the plain verdict of their own consciences, *having had so great and apparent proof of your dealings before;* as also the island being at such divisions within itself, some earnestly desiring it should be delivered into your hands, professing their unity with you [William Coddington]; others denied it, professing their dissent and division from you; though for what, themselves know not, but only their abominable pride to exercise the like tyranny.

From these and such like workings, having their original in you, *she gathered unto herself, and took up this fiction, (with the rest of her friends) that the Dutch Plantation was the city of refuge...*

But you know very well, you could never rest, nor be at quiet, till you had put it under a bushel. ... Do not therefore beguile yourselves, in crying out against the errours of those so miserably fallen, for they are no other things which they hold, but the branches of the same root yourselves so stoutly stand upon.

... We say fill not up your talk as your manner is, *crying that she went out without ordinances* [Holy Communion, and without that ordinance, she would be lost to heaven], for God can raise up out of that stone which you have already rejected, (as children) so also ministers and ordinances unto Abraham. Nor can you charge them in that point, *for it was for protection or government they went;* and however hire in other respects, yet the price of a wife and safety of his own life adjoined, carried a minister along with them of the same rise and breeding, together with your own. *To add unto the blood so savagely and causelessly spilt, with which a company of such as you take pleasure to protect; for they are all of one spirit, if they have not hands in the same act.*

We say their death is causeless; for *we have heard them affirm, that they would never heave up a hand, no, nor move a tongue against any that persecuted or troubled them, but only endeavour to save themselves by flight,* not perceiving the nature and end of persecution; neither of that antichristian opposition and tyranny, the issue whereof declares itself in this so dreadful and lamentable asportation [the detachment, movement, or carrying away of property, considered an essential component of the crime of larceny].

Source: Letter of Randall Holden to the Massachusetts Bay Court, Collections of The Massachusetts Historical Society

Did Holden believe that the Bay government had treated with the Native Americans, to attack and kill the Hutchinsons? That would be one colossal conspiracy theory, but if that was his belief, we can see why he thought so, having experienced such a thing himself in 1643, and having seen that Boston commissioned the murder of

Miantonomo by the Mohegan Uncas at the same time as Anne's massacre. As you'll see in the next chapter, Samuel Groome may also have believed in Boston's conspiracy to murder Anne Hutchinson.

Holden's last statement, that Anne and her family didn't fight back against the Siwanoy attackers, is interesting. Holden says that he heard the Hutchinsons affirm that they wouldn't raise a hand or say a word against any that persecuted them, only that they would try to flee if they were in danger. And that's what they did, fleeing Rhode Island for Pelham Bay.

Yet Anne had known in Alford, Lincolnshire, ten years before, that she would face persecution – and that God would be with her.

"It was revealed to me that I should meet with affliction, yet I [God] am the same God that delivered Daniel out of the lion's den, and I will also deliver thee." Another revelation was that "though I must come to New England, yet I must not fear nor be dismayed."

Anne Hutchinson believed that she and her family were secure in the promise of eternal life. They did their best to secure their safety on this earth, but ultimately they were in God's care.

Holden, Greene, and Gorton went to England in 1644 to resolve their grievance and get a charter from the Earl of Warwick, a Puritan who was an overseer of colonies in the western hemisphere. The three Shawomet men had to sail for England from New Amsterdam (New York City) because of the animosity of Boston's authorities. They were successful in their quest, but the King was executed in 1649, which meant that Rhode Island needed a new charter in 1650-51, when William Dyer was the colony's attorney general, and Sir Henry Vane sat on the English Council of State.

Chapter 35

What Quakers Thought of Hutchinson's Death, and the Letter She Wrote to Elder Leverett

In 1676, the English Quaker, Samuel Groome, a merchant and trader (primarily with Virginia and Maryland), published a 64-page book that was a letter to Gov. Richard Bellingham of Boston. Bellingham, a magistrate, had been in on Anne Hutchinson's two trials in 1637 and 1638, and had been involved with Mary Dyer's imprisonments, banishments, and execution by hanging in 1660.

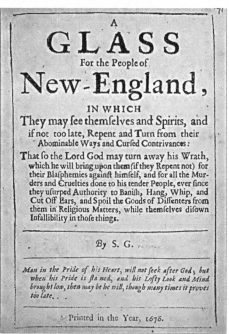

A

GLASS

For the People of

New-England,

IN WHICH

They may see themselves and Spirits, and if not too late, Repent and Turn from their Abominable Ways and Cursed Contrivances:

That so the Lord God may turn away his Wrath, which he will bring upon them (if they Repent not) for their Blasphemies against himself, and for all the Murders and Cruelties done to his tender People, ever since they usurped Authority to Banish, Hang, Whip, and Cut Off Ears, and Spoil the Goods of Dissenters from them in Religious Matters, while themselves disown Infallibility in those things.

By S. G.

Man in the Pride of his Heart, will not seek after God; but when his Pride is stained, and his Lofty Look and Mind brought low, then may be he will, though many times it proves too late.

Printed in the Year, 1676.

Groome's book which reproduces part of Anne's letter.

Groome wrote:

The next Piece of Wickedness I am to mind you of, is *your barbarous action committed against Ann Hutchinson, whom you first imprisoned, then banished and so exposed her to that desolate Condition, that she fell into the Hands of the Indians who murdered her* with her

Family except one Child, and after that made a notorious Lie on the destroyed Woman, the which one of their Priests put in Print – and another of that Tribe, Samuel Clark Priest of London, taking the Lie out of his Brother Weld his *Short Story [of the Rise, Reign and Ruin of the Antinomians]*, and must needs put it into his Book called, *God's Judgments against Heresie*, in which he also scandalized Mary Dyer and Midwife Hawkins, all which were known to be Women of honest Lives and Conversations, only protested against their false Church and Worships, for which they faltered in their Names and Estates, and some lost their Lives for their Testimony sake: For Mary Dyer they banished and hanged at Boston [June 1, 1660], for her Testimony against them, which she was moved of the Lord to bear amongst them.

But because you Professors have banished, and so been a means of destroying a Woman and her Family, as before, and have covered yourselves by saying, she held about Thirty Monstrous Heretical Opinions, but have not that I can find laid down so much as One of them, for Indifferent Persons to judge.

So I may do a little of that Work for you and others, by which it may be seen what the Ground of your Quarrel was and I will do it in short, and honestly, as *I found it in her Letter, to one Mr. Leverett as she writ him in her Answer to his,* 1st month [March] 1643,

It seems by that Letter which Leverett sent to Anne Hutchinson he termed her Haughty Jezebel, and said she was a Railer and Reviler, and such like Terms and Names, and yet in the same Letter asked her what was become of the Light she once shined in, in their Parts?

And now Anne Hutchinson, to that Letter Leverett's,

> *If it were the True Light, in which you say I did once Shine in, I am sure the Author thereof, and the Maintainer of it is God, and it shall break forth more and more unto the perfect Day, and when I was with you it discovered the best Light in your self to be Darkness, as your self confessed to me in your own Parlour.*

> *And whereas you say I speak great swelling Words of Vanity, that Scripture is fulfilled in your false Teachers, who follow the Way of Balaam and Bozer, And that Water holds*

out the Spirit, John 7.38, 39. And Christ Jesus came by this Water, or Spirit, Mat. 1.18. And hereby we shall know the Spirit of Antichrist, because he confesseth not that Jesus Christ is come in the Flesh. And as to that in Rev. 12, which you say must be meant of Constantine, and not of Christ, being brought forth in the Gentile Church, then the Woman that brought forth Constantine must be crowned with Twelve Stars.

But your Church standing in the City Order, by your own Confession must needs be one of the Cities of the Nations, which the Lord hath said should fall, Rev. 16.19. And if what you called Railing or Reviling, were a Truth of God, acted by him through me, then you have called the Spirit of God a Railer and Reviler.

And so far Anne Hutchinson, with much more in her Answer to Leverett's Letter of the 1st Month [March] 1643. After they had imprisoned her, and banished her.

So Reader if thou hast an understanding of what the Woman held forth, thou may soon conclude what the Thirty Heretical Opinions were, that so much enraged New-England Professors to imprison, banish, and so (in a Sense) murther her and her Family by the wicked Hands of the Indians.

But how shall these People hide their Wickedness from the simple-hearted, that they should not see their Wickedness, and cry out against their Cruelty? Well, I'll shew thee honest Inquirer, how they hide themselves and the Innocent Blood. The Woman [Anne Hutchinson] before mentioned having been imprisoned and there by the Priests and Professors pumpt and sifted to get something against her, laying their Snares to entrap her, and having so done take their Opportunity when her husband & Friends were absent, as it is told, and examined her in the forepart of the Day, and banished her in the after-part.

Notable quick Work! so she goes by Water with many others that perceived they must go to Pot next, and providentially fell with Rhoad Island and there they made a Cave or Caves, and in them lived until the cold Winter was past, in which time it was known to the Professors, where they were, that they had bought the Island of the Indians and the Professors began to stir and Endeavour to bring the

Island within the Compass of their Patent, so the poor molested Woman, it's like let in Fear, and thought she would go far enough from their Reach, so going Southward to seek a Place to settle upon, where she and her Family might live in Quietness, fell upon a Piece of Land that was in Controversie between the Dutch and the Natives, and *the Natives being in a Heat came upon them, and were the Executioners of what the New-England Priests, Magistrates and Church-Members were an Occasion of, through their wicked and cruel proceeding, in forcing them to flee from their Rage and Fury.*

And because I promised thee to tell thee honest Inquirer, how they hide and cover their Wickedness, I do it by rehearsing what Priest [Thomas] Weld & chief Actor in this matter, printed in his Book entitled Weld's Short Story (page 44.) as Samuel Clark, in his lying Book quotes his Brother Weld for his Author, of this and such like most Notorious Lies, of which he prints that, Ann Hutchinson, Mary Dyer and Midwife Hawkins, see Clark's Examples page 249 and they have been known to be honest Women, and such as were of good Report, and never accounted either Witches or such Persons, as these two Priests and Brethren in Wickedness would have People believe, that so their Wickedness might be undiscovered.

Now here Priest [Samuel] Clark he had writ and printed a most cursed Lie of Mary Dyer, whom they banished and afterward hanged at Boston, as also of Midwife Hawkins.

Saith he, About the same time, and in the same place One Anne Hutchinson, held about Thirty Monstrous & Heretical Opinions, whereof yet I have a Catalogue set down by the same Author, page 59, find growing big with Child and towards the Time of her Labour, at last brought forth Thirty Monstrous Births, or thereabouts, some bigger and some lesser, some of one Shape and some of another, few of any perfect Shape, none of human Shape: This Anne Hutchinson was first banished by the Magistrates of New-England into Rhoad Island for her Heresies, but not staying long there, she removed with all her Family, her Daughter and her Children into the Dutch Plantation to a Place called Hell-Gate, where the Indians fell upon them, and slew her and her Family, her

Daughter and her Daughter's Husband, with all their Children save only one that escaped.

So here is the Priests and Professors Cover, and they wipe their Mouths, and I warrant they would *by saying the Indians committed this Murder be thought clear of this Innocent Blood.*

So Reader thou mayest see the Rage and Envy of this professing Generation, for they banished, imprisoned this tenderly bred Woman in or towards Winter, and what with Fears and Tellings to and fro the Woman miscarried, upon which they grounded their abominable Untruth; many Witnesses might be produced to prove this, and to disprove their abominable frequently told Slanders, and also printed by Priests and New-England Professors, and their Confederates here in England.

I might insert that other Story which the same Lie makers made of Mary Dyer, and Midwife Hawkins, but it's not worth while, as to his Description of a horrid Monster, wherein their Lies were apparent to many sober People.

*****

Groome then goes on to castigate them for severely whipping Newport Baptist minister Obadiah Holmes.

It was common for Quakers to call ministers of the Church of England, or the Congregational (Puritan) churches of New England, "priests." Not pastor, minister, or reverend, but "priest." It was a derogatory term. Quakers, who preferred to be called Friends, believed that God spoke to their hearts and was the Inner Light, so they didn't need churches and priests to be their interpreter or intercessor. They had direct access to God because of his Holy Spirit.

That's a place where Anne Hutchinson's beliefs were similar to those of George Fox, the founder of the Quaker movement a few years after her death. But it was very different from the doctrine of Massachusetts Bay. She believed that God spoke to her and gave her revelations, which the Puritan magistrates and ministers said was only available to men. Mary Dyer and Anne Hutchinson were "much addicted to revelations," according to Winthrop. That was probably the biggest attraction to Quaker beliefs for Mary in the 1650s. And if Anne had lived, we can wonder if she would have embraced Quaker beliefs, or if she was prickly enough to keep her own ways. We might have an educated guess by looking at Anne's sister, Katherine Marbury Scott.

$$*****$$

Samuel Groome died in England in 1683. His line ceased when his son died, but there are Groome descendants through his brother.

https://archive.org/details/glassforpeopleof00sgsa

In the book

A glass for the people of New-England : in which they may see themselves and spirits, and if not too late, repent and turn away from their abominable ways and cursed contrivances that so the Lord God may turn away his wrath, which he will bring upon them (if they repent not) for their blasphemies against himself, and for all the murders and cruelties done to his tender people, ever since they usurped authority to banish, hang, whip, and cut off ears, and spoil the goods of dissenters from them in religious matters, while themselves disown infallibility in those things

by S. G. (Samuel Groome), -1683; Fox, George, 1624-1691. Queries by another hand for New-England priests and elders to answer; Tyso, John, -1700. Copy of a letter which was delivered into the hands of R. Bellingham, late governour of Boston in New-England, for him to read and consider

Chapter 36

Katherine Marbury Scott: the Quaker's Uppity-female Speech Scarred Her for Life

How Commonwealth England perceived Quakers in 1655:
Free-love familists, preachers of the Light, gluttons and drunkards, and disruptors
of services when men and women walked into Anglican services naked, saying they
were as pure as Adam and Eve before the Fall.

Katherine Marbury, the younger sibling of the famous Anne Marbury Hutchinson, was born between about 1609 and 1611 as one of a veritable tribe of children of Rev. Francis Marbury and Bridget Dryden Marbury. Not all of the children survived infancy or childhood. (The dates and numbers of children vary by genealogical records. One record had Katherine's birth date six years after her father's death.) Some records give Katherine's birthplace as Alford, Lincolnshire, but their family had moved to London by 1605, and her father died there in 1611. Perhaps her mother or one of her educated siblings taught Katherine to read and write. Many women could read, but few could write, and Katherine did write.

Katherine married Richard Scott in 1632 where her mother lived in Hertfordshire, about 28 miles northwest of London. In summer 1634, they set sail with Anne and William Hutchinson on the *Griffin*, moving their households and children to Boston to follow their minister, Rev. John Cotton, who had emigrated the year before. The Church of England was making life dangerous for dissenters like Cotton.

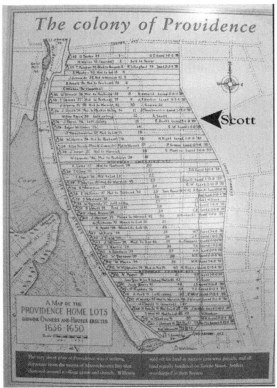

The Scotts owned two lots
behind Roger Williams' cove-side lots.

The Hutchinsons settled in Boston; the Scotts moved first to Ipswich, near Salem, where they would have been exposed to the teachings of Rev. Roger Williams. There, they also would have been well acquainted with Gov. John Endecott and John Winthrop, Jr. When Roger Williams fled to what would become Providence Plantations, Rhode Island, to escape Puritan persecution, the Scotts also moved. Richard wrote the Compact that Providence founders signed. Their house plot backed up to Roger Williams' property. And they, like other original settlers, had other parcels of farmland, pasture, woods, and marsh nearby, the better to make use of natural resources.

On January 16, 1638, Gov. John Winthrop wrote, "At Providence things grow still worse; for a sister of Mrs. Hutchinson, the wife of one Scott, being infected with Anabaptistry, and going last year to live in Providence, Mr. Williams was taken (or rather emboldened) by her to make open profession thereof, and accordingly was rebaptized by one Holyman, a poor man late of Salem." There is no other evidence that Katharine Scott had, or wished to have, any influence upon Roger Williams. They never agreed, and upon two occasions Roger Williams had her, with other wives of his neighbors, arrested, but he did not carry his suits to a conclusion before the Court. Source: Stephen F. Peckham, "Richard Scott and his Wife Catharine Marbury, and Some of Their Descendants," *New England Historical and Genealogical Register*, Vol. 60 (1906):170

From 1638 to 1642, Katherine and Richard didn't live far from her older sister. It was 28 miles by land, but it would have been a quick trip by water. Anne would have been welcome assistance as Katherine's first children were born. Katherine herself may have been a midwife, since it was their mother who trained her daughters to the profession.

In any case, Katherine's family was growing. She gave birth to five, seven or nine children (according to online genealogy sites), and seven survived to adulthood. *The Great Migration* names James, John, Mary, Joseph, Patience, Hannah and Deliverance.

Two of the girls, Mary Scott Holder, and Patience Scott Beere, are said by Quaker historians to have accompanied Quakers on speaking missions to Boston. Because of their youth, and possibly because of their cousin Edward Hutchinson's legal influence in Boston, they were confined at the jailer's home instead of in the prison, until their fees and fines were paid. Both girls, at age 11 and 16, accompanied Mary Dyer on her walks from Providence to Boston, knowing from their own and their mother's experience that they risked whippings, forced labor, or even death.

But I've jumped forward several years. Let's go back to the 1650s.

In 1650, Richard Scott's property taxes were second only to Benedict Arnold, which means that he was a wealthy man. His initial profession was shoemaker (his father was a London clothier), but he must have become wealthy by real estate transactions, farming, and perhaps sea trading. Though Katherine Marbury had aristocratic roots, her father was a clergyman and teacher, the father of many children, and died when she was a toddler. Katherine would not have brought money to the marriage. That tells us that Richard Scott must have worked hard, bought some indentured servants, and taken risks that paid off.

Richard may have sailed to England in 1654, and become a Quaker there. Most people think that he became a Quaker Friend, though, in 1656, when the first missionaries sailed to America and the Scotts provided hospitality to them in their home in Providence. Surely there must have been transatlantic correspondence for the Scotts, who were Baptists, to embrace such a change so early. The Scotts are considered to be the first Quaker converts in New England.

Among the first missionaries were Quakers from England and Barbados, and one of them, Christopher Holder, fell in love with the teenage Mary Scott, who was still too young to marry. Holder, John Rous, and John Copeland traveled New England to preach their faith, and to disrupt the Puritan services. When they were beaten nearly to death, or starved in prison and released, they came back to Providence and Newport, Rhode Island, for sanctuary and recuperation.

In June 1658, Katherine Scott wrote a protest letter to John Winthrop, Jr., governor at Hartford, Connecticut, about the Quaker persecution there. Unfortunately, Winthrop was away and didn't receive her letter for months.

KATHERINE SCOTT TO JOHN WINTHROP, JR.
For the hand of John Winthrop called Governor, at Harvard in New England, there deliver with trust.
Providence, this 17 June 1658
John Winthrop, – Think it not hard to be called so, seeing Jesus, our Savior and Governor, and all that were made honorable by him, that are recorded in Scripture, were called so. I have writ to thee before, but never heard whether they came to thy hand; my last, it may be, may trouble thee, concerning my son; but truly I had not propounded it to thee but to satisfy his mind, and to prevent his going where we did

more disaffect; but I hear no more of his mind that way. I hope his mind is taken up with the thing which is the most necessary, and first to seek his kingdom, &c. Therefore let you be burred in silence: but my later request I must revise, and that is only out of true love and pity to thee, that thou mayest be free, and not troubled, as I have heard thy father was, upon his death bed, at the banishment of my dear sister Hutchinson and others. I am sure they have a sad cup to drink, that are drunk with the blood of the saints.

O my friend, as thou lovest the prosperity of thy soul and the good of thy posterity, *take heed of having thy hand, or heart, or tongue lifted up against those persons that the wise yet foolish world in scorn calls Quakers: for they are the messengers of the Lord of Hosts,* which he hath in his large love and pity sent into these parts, to gather together his outcasts and the distressed of the children of Israel: and they shall accomplish the work, let the rage of men be never so great: *take heed of hindering of them,* for no weapon formed against them shall prosper. It is given to them not only to believe, but to suffer, &c., but woe to them by whom they suffer.

O my friend, try all things, and weigh it by the balance of the sanctuary: how can you try without hearing of them, for the ear tries words as the mouth tastes meat. I dare not but bear witness against the unjust and cruel laws of my countrymen in this land: for cursed are all they that cometh not out to help the Lord against the mighty; and all that are not with him are against him, &c. Woe be to men that gather and not by the Lord, & cover with a covering, and not with his Holy Spirit: which woe I desire thou mayest escape.
KATHERINE SCOTT

But finally in 1658, the Quaker missionaries' repeated disobedience in Massachusetts Bay Colony was too much for Gov. Endecott. He and the magistrates of the court sentenced the three Quaker men to have their right ears cropped as previously threatened.

The hearts of Boston residents were softening because of the severity of punishment of Quakers, who were other (possibly misguided but not heretical) Christians. They saw their neighbors fined, their stock or crops confiscated, and lives threatened, yet the Quaker numbers grew exponentially.

The court decided to execute judgment on the three Quaker men secretly, inside the prison and away from the public. They wanted to punish the Quakers and banish them without arousing sympathy. The method of ear amputation involved binding the prisoner's head to a post and then slicing off the ear, or sometimes the prisoner's head was locked in the pillory and his ears nailed to the board and later sliced off. It was not a common punishment, but three Puritans had been cropped in 1637 by Church of England officials. Perhaps Endecott thought this was a fitting revenge, 21 years later. William Dyer referred to that episode in a 1659 letter, so it was at the top of their minds, and exemplified cruelty.

Quaker historian George Bishop wrote,

And Katharine Scott, of the Town of Providence, in the Jurisdiction of Rhode Island (a Mother of many Children, one that had lived with her Husband, of Unblameable Conversation, and a Grave, Sober, Ancient Woman, and of good Breeding, as to the Outward, as Men account) coming to see the Execution of John Copeland, Christopher Holder, and John Rouse, all single young men, their ears cut off the 7th of the 7th month [7 Sept.] 1658, by order of John Endicott, Gov., whose ears you cut off, and saying upon their doing it privately, — That it was evident they were going to act the Works of Darkness, or else they would have brought them forth Publickly, and have declared their Offence, that others may hear and fear. — Ye committed her to Prison, and gave her Ten Cruel Stripes with a threefold corded knotted Whip, with that Cruelty in the Execution, as to others, on the second Day of the eighth Month [2 October], 1658. Tho' ye confessed, when ye had her before you, that for ought ye knew, she had been of an Unblameable Conversation; and tho' some of you knew her Father, and called him Mr. Marbury [Mister was a term of respect], and that she had been well-bred (as among Men) and had so lived, and that she was the Mother of many Children; yet ye whipped her for all that, and moreover told her — That ye were likely to have a Law to Hang her, if She came thither again — To which she answered, – *If God call us, Woe be to us, if we come not; and I question not, but he whom we love, which will make us not to count our*

Lives dear unto ourselves for the sake of his Name, — To which our Governor, John Endicott replied, – 'And we shall be as ready to take away your lives, as ye shall be to lay them down.'

The whip used for these cruel Executions is not of whip cord, as in England, but of dried guts, such as the Base [bass] of the Viols, and the three knots at the end, which many times the Hangman lays on with both his hands, and must needs be of most violent Torture and exercise of the Body.

Katherine knew that private punishments were against the law, because executions and whippings were meant as a warning to the public not to err. She publicly protested the wrongdoing of Gov. Endecott and his deputies on two points: that they were cruelly torturing the Quakers, and that they were going about it against their own laws. Her protest, made worse because a woman was accusing men, resulted in her being cast into the prison for a month, as well as being publicly exposed, nude to her waist, and whipped 10 stripes with the triple knots, which was a common punishment for lawbreakers.

Katherine was about 50 years old. She knew exactly what she was doing, and what the consequences would be. In twenty-first-century language, she was telling them, "Bring it on!"

The Massachusetts State Archive holds the original document, signed by Edward Hutchinson (Anne's son and Katherine's nephew), that says,

Petition submitted to the general court by Edward Hutchinson regarding the disposition of fees paid for the release of his aunt and three other Quakers from jail. General court order directing that the fees be taken by the jail keeper until further order. Consented to by the magistrates and deputies.

*****

Katherine and her daughters were released to Edward's custody, and sent home to Providence to recover. The three earless Quaker men were incarcerated until they could be hustled onto a ship (at their expense, which they refused to pay) and sent to England.

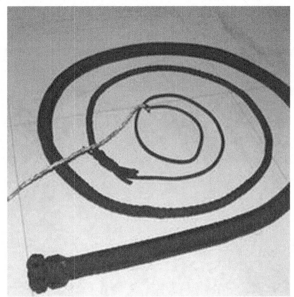

Whips left skin flayed, sometimes down to the bone, resulting in horrific scars.

The winter of 1658-59 was a quiet one in the Quaker-versus-Puritan conflict. Most of the original Quaker missionaries went to England or the West Indies to preach, or to heal from their wounds.

In May of 1659, several Quakers heard God's call for them to go to Boston and take a stand against the bloody laws that so persecuted their brothers and sisters. They left Newport to gather at the home of Richard and Katherine Scott. But as their boat came into the harbor and they transferred to a canoe, one of the women drowned in the sinking of the canoe. They found Sarah Gibbons' body at low tide the next day, and buried her in the Scotts' orchard. William Robinson, Marmaduke Stephenson, and 11-year-old Patience Scott went on to Boston, and Mary Dyer followed a few weeks later. That was the beginning of the end for William Robinson and Marmaduke Stephenson, and Mary Dyer was reprieved from the gallows in October 1659.

Katherine almost surely sailed from Newport, and not Boston, where she'd been banished on pain of death, to England with her daughter Mary Scott, in March or April 1660. She planned to see Mary safely married to the one-eared Christopher Holder in August 1660. (Mary had two children with Holder, and died in 1665.)

Katherine may have stayed with one of her siblings on her only visit to England since her 1634 emigration. But it was a quick turnaround. She returned to Providence in September-October 1660. Apparently, she became disenchanted with Quakers on that trip. Rev. Roger Williams said in a letter of September 8, 1660 to Governor John Winthrop Jr.: "What whipping at Boston could not do, conversation with friends in England and their arguments have in great measure drawn her [Katherine Scott] from the Quakers and wholly from their meetings."

Richard Scott of Providence died before July 1, 1679, at about age 73. He had remained a Quaker until he died. And Katherine must have returned to Quaker beliefs, because her death is noted in Quaker records. She was about 76 years old, and died in Newport on May 2, 1687. (*Rhode Island Vital Records* put her at 70 years, but that would place her birth six years after her father died – quite a feat.) Her daughter, Patience Scott Beere, lived in Newport, so Katherine may have been living with her daughter's family after Richard died.

In the book *Mary Dyer: For Such a Time as This*, I speculated (after several years of research and reading hundreds of books and articles) that the Scotts and Dyers were closely connected through the Hutchinson family. Mary journeyed to Boston with two Scott daughters, and she stopped at Providence between her winter at Shelter Island and her May 21, 1660 appearance in Boston. William Dyer's May 27, 1660 letter to the Massachusetts court used bitter words against the nameless people who had helped her on her final journey. (Katherine and Mary Scott were in England, so that would be Richard Scott.) And when the names were provided to John Clarke for the 1663 Rhode Island charter, Richard Scott's name, though a founder of Providence and an early Rhode Island settler, was conspicuously missing.

Chapter 37

Winthrop's Deathbed Reference

Gov. John Winthrop, who had been a friend to William Hutchinson and an enemy to Anne from 1637 to 1644, when his book on the Antinomian Controversy was published, lived with Margaret, his beloved wife of 30 years, until she died during an epidemic of yellow fever in 1647. She had been his third wife, and it seems that John just couldn't live without a mate.

Six months after Margaret Tyndal Winthrop rested in the Burying Ground at Tremont and School Streets, John married a young widow with a son. Martha Rainsborough Coytmore was already an acquaintance of the family, because her sister had married John's and Margaret's son, Stephen Winthrop.

John Winthrop had several bouts of an unexplained illness in 1648, and he was weak for more than a month in the autumn. His and Martha's baby son Joshua was christened in Boston's First Church in December. John succumbed to illness on March 26, 1649, leaving 31-year-old Martha a widow again. John's properties had already been deeded to his adult sons, but as widow of the high-status Winthrop, and mother of his baby, she would have been treated with respect, and had some sort of settlement. Martha's son by Mr. Coytmore died, and the baby Joshua Winthrop died by 1651. Martha married once more, and that man died in 1658. She had no suitors except a farmer who apparently wanted to marry her for her fortune. Martha took her own life in the autumn of 1660 by ingesting rats bane, which is arsenic trioxide.

While John Winthrop was ill in the winter or spring of 1649, his longtime colleague, friend, and adversary, former Gov. Thomas Dudley, visited him. Someone in the colony had been judged to be a heretic (what a surprise!) and Winthrop, as presiding governor, needed to sign the banishment order. But Winthrop refused, saying that "he had done too much of that work already."

Katherine Marbury Scott, as we have seen, had no doubt that Winthrop was referring to her sister Anne and her followers. Nine years after the governor's death, Katherine wrote to Winthrop's son, the governor of Connecticut, "... but my later request I must revise, and that is only out of true love and pity to thee, that thou mayest be free, and not troubled, as I have heard thy father was, upon his death bed, at the banishment of my dear sister Hutchinson and others. I am sure they have a sad cup to drink, that are drunk with the blood of the saints." (Katherine made no secret that she thought Winthrop was *not* enjoying the pleasures of heaven.)

The governor died on March 26, 1649, the first day of the new year, as they reckoned it on the Julian calendar, and was laid to rest in the Burying Ground with Margaret. Later, they were joined by son John Winthrop Jr., and his son and grandson. Other Winthrop descendants have been added to the vault.

Table cenotaph for Gov. John Winthrop's family. Once down the steps, the vault extends under the fence and sidewalk.

Governor Winthrop's tomb is not well kept. Bostonians and tourists walk over the vault on the sidewalk outside the fence, without knowing or thinking that such an illustrious man lies buried there with little mention. However, if you visit the Unitarian church that is the descendant of Boston First Church, there is a monumental statue of John Winthrop.

The metal plaque reads:
John Winthrop
First Governor of Massachusetts Bay Colony
One of the Founders of Boston
And of the First Church in Boston.
AD 1630

Chapter 38

Did Anne Bring Forth a Cockatrice?

*A cockatrice is a mythical two-legged dragon or
serpent-like creature with a cock's head.*

Governor Thomas Dudley was well-known for his integrity and strict, unbending, forceful personality. He considered Governor Winthrop to be too lenient. But in an era where many women were kept quiet, or were expected to be submissive to all men (not just their husbands), his wife Dorothy was educated enough to write, and his daughter, Anne Dudley Bradstreet, not only wrote but composed poetry. Like John Winthrop and John Cotton, he dismissed democratic principles in favor of oligarchy.

Dudley, who espoused the Puritan reform beliefs in the 1590s, had been the steward to the fourth Earl of Lincoln, Theophilus Clinton-Fiennes, for many years before he joined the Massachusetts Bay Company, signed the Cambridge document for the colony, and emigrated with the Winthrop Fleet in 1630.

Dudley and the Hutchinsons were probably acquainted when they both lived in Lincolnshire, though he would have attended the earl's church in Sempringham, pastored by Rev. Samuel Skelton, who in 1629 became the first minister of Salem's First Church. Rev. John Cotton, pastor of St. Botolph's Church in Old Boston, would have been a mutual friend.

Dudley was governor of the Massachusetts Bay Colony for four terms, a deputy governor thirteen times, and a magistrate for most of his life there. He and John Winthrop were also connected as fathers whose children married.

As you might imagine, he never approved of the Covenant of Grace that Anne Hutchinson embraced and spread to her followers. Rooting out heresy was a passion of Dudley's: he was the prime mover behind Roger Williams' prosecution and banishment in 1636, and that of Thomas Morton (the Maypole rebel), as well as Anne and her many followers. One of the labels attached to the Hutchinsonians was that they were libertines, defined as "a person without moral principles; who rejects accepted opinions in matters of religion; a freethinker."

After Thomas Dudley's death in July 1653, his poem was found with his belongings. You can see how heresy boils his blood even after many years.

> Dim eyes, deaf ears, cold stomach shew
> My dissolution is in view;
> Eleven times seven near lived have I,
> And now God calls, I willing die:
> My shuttle's shot, my race is run,
> My sun is set, my deed is done;
> My span is measured, tale is told,
> My flower is faded and grown old,
> My dream is vanished, shadow's fled,
> My soul with Christ, my body dead;
> Farewell dear wife, children, and friends,
> Hate heresy, make blessed ends;
> Bear poverty, live with good men,
> So shall we meet with joy again.
> **Let men of God in courts and churches watch,**
> **O'er such as do a toleration hatch;**
> **Lest that ill egg bring forth a cockatrice,**
> **To poison all with heresy and vice.**
> **If men be left, and otherwise combine,**
> **My epitaph's, I dy'd no libertine.**

That's not the epitaph you'll find at his tomb in Roxbury, though. Rev. Ezekiel Rogers wrote:

In books a Prodigal they say;
A table talker rich in sense;
And witty without wits pretense;
An able champion in debate;
Whose words lacked number but not weight;
Both Catholic and Christian too;
A soldier timely, tried and true;
Condemned to share the common doom;
Reposes here in Dudley's tomb.

Dudley family tomb in Roxbury, Massachusetts.

Chapter 39

Ordinary Heroes

Anne Hutchinson and her followers didn't invent civil democracy or achieve separation of church and state by making speeches, or by writing journals and white papers. They did it with their lives.

They were ordinary people: cloth merchants, midwives, ministers, seamstresses, brewers, farmers, mariners, shoemakers, teachers, haberdashers, servants. Mothers and fathers, elderly grandparents, infants and children, widows, orphans, unmarried women, soldiers, prosperous businessmen. People of faith, excommunicates, dissidents, saints, heretics.

Those who committed acts of heroism could not have realized it in their time, but hundreds of millions of people have benefited from their careful thoughts and deeds, and their brilliant "livelie experiment" in establishing a "civil bodie politick" (as opposed to a religious government) over the last 400 years.

No one, alone, accomplished a slate of civil and human rights. They did it together, by placing their livelihoods, the health and safety of their loved ones, and their very lives, on the altar of liberty and clear conscience. They shared resources during famines and harvests, and took tender care of the helpless. And they must have realized that establishing just laws and upholding rights is a never-ending process.

Instead of being bystanders to history, they made the most of what they had. They spoke up boldly when they knew they were right, and marched away from oppression with heads held high. They sold what they owned, traveled in tiny ships on the raging seas, bought new land (instead of conquering or stealing it), built homes and infrastructure, formed a government, founded towns that became cities, debated and wrote laws and a constitution and had it ratified properly in their home country. They weren't bystanders. They were participants.

They didn't become pioneers or heroes so we could raise statues or write books about them, but because they refused to be oppressed, and wanted freedom, peace, education, and prosperity for their children. Their liberty of conscience was never about wedding cakes or Christmas decorations, religious schools versus public schools, public prayer or proving biblical accuracy. These may seem like unimportant or isolated incidents to us, but some religio-political groups use them to move us toward a tightly controlled society that discriminates against those who believe differently. They are quite open about their goals.

Our ancestors knew firsthand what the blend of civil and ecclesiastical government felt like, in large and small ways. For them, the struggle was about blood. Ears sliced off. Chains. Hanging. Burning at the stake. Banishment. Bankrupting fines. Property confiscation. Being banished in a blizzard. Starving in a prison. Beatings.

"These were all commended for their faith, yet none of them received what had been promised, since God had planned something better for us so that only together with us would they be made perfect." Hebrews 11:39-40 New International Version.

We are the heirs of the heroism of Anne Hutchinson, Mary Dyer, Roger Williams, and countless others.

We also inherited the zeal and dedication of John Cotton and John Winthrop.

We will not be silenced.

"True heroism is remarkably sober, very undramatic. It is not the courage to surpass others at whatever cost, but the courage to serve others at whatever the cost." – Arthur Ashe, athlete and civil rights activist.

We must not, we dare not, be lazy about human and civil rights, or incremental encroachments on our liberty. The people in this book were not born heroes – they *became* heroes. We must remain vigilant, and we must be bold. We may not feel courageous now, but we can become so on the way while remembering that we are not alone, or isolated in a wilderness. We are in this together, and we owe our service to others because of the great gifts we were given by our founding fathers and mothers.

"From everyone who has been given much, much will be demanded; and from the one who has been entrusted with much, much more will be asked." Luke 12:48 New International Version.

APPENDIX

More Cultural Information
Relating to the Hutchinsons

Chapter 40

The Wheelwright Remonstrance
and its Shrapnel

S ome of the church of Boston, being of the opinion of Mrs. Hutchinson, had labored to have Mr. Wheelwright to be called to be a teacher there [at Boston, in addition to Teacher John Cotton]."

In November 1636, John Winthrop, deputy governor under Gov. Henry Vane, wrote in his *Journal* that:

> It was propounded the last Lord's day, and was moved again this day for resolution. One of the church stood up and said, he could not consent, etc. [This was almost certainly John Winthrop, writing in third person]. His reason was, because the church being well furnished already with able ministers, whose spirits they knew, and whose labors God had blessed in much love and sweet peace, he thought it not fit (no necessity urging) to put the welfare of the church to the least hazard, as he feared they should do, by calling in one [Wheelwright], whose spirit they knew not, and one who seemed to dissent in judgment and, instanced in two points, which he delivered in a late exercise there;

> 1. That a believer was more than a creature.

> 2. That the person of the Holy Ghost and a believer were united.

> Hereupon the governor [Vane] spake, that he marveled at this, seeing Mr. Cotton had lately approved his doctrine. To this Mr. Cotton answered, that he did not remember the first, and desired Mr. Wheelwright to explain his meaning. He denied not the points, but showed upon what occasion he delivered them.

> Whereupon, there being an endeavor to make a reconciliation, the first replied, and though he thought reverently of his godliness and abilities, so as he could be content to live under such a ministry; yet, seeing he was apt to raise doubtful disputation, he could not consent to choose him to that place. Whereupon the church gave way, that he might be called to a new church, to be gathered at Mount

Wollaston, and Braintree. [Winthrop carried the day because the church membership had to *unanimously* agree to a new minister.]

This is an excerpt from Rev. John Wheelwright's sermon at Boston First Church of Christ, January 1637. Now that we've seen the theocratic governing of the Bay colony, it's easy to pick out the incendiary devices Wheelwright lobbed. He used words like enemies, pagan, antichrist, condemnation of well-meaning law keepers of the church, and God's wrath sending fire on the earth.

In his own words, Rev. Wheelwright preached:

Objection: It may be objected that there will be little hope of victory for the servants of God, because the children of God are but few, and those that are enemies to the Lord and truth are many?

Answer: True, I must confess and acknowledge the saints of God are few, they are but of a little flock, and those that are enemies to the lord, not only Paganish, but Antichristian, and those that run under a covenant of works are very strong: but be not afraid, the battle is not yours but Gods.

Objection: It will be objected that diverse of those who are opposite to the ways of grace and free covenant of grace, they are wondrous holy people, therefore it should seem to be a very uncharitable thing in the servants of God to condemn such, as if so be they were enemies to the Lord and his truth, while they are so exceedingly holy and strict in their way.

Answer: Brethren, those under a covenant of works, the more holy they are, the greater enemies they are to Christ... It maketh no matter how seemingly holy men be, according to the Law; if they do not know the work of grace and ways of God, they are such as trust to their own righteousness, they shall die sayth the Lord...

Objection: This will cause a combustion in the Church and commonwealth, may be objected.

Answer: I must confess and acknowledge it will do so, but what then? did not Christ come to send fire upon the earth. . .

That was a firebomb to the New Jerusalem society they'd undertaken to build. Rev. Wheelwright's sermon lit an inferno that changed Massachusetts forever. It convicted Anne Hutchinson and more than a hundred others (that we know of).

*****

Winthrop commented in his book *A Short Story*:
Sedition doth properly signify a going aside to make a party [an opposition party]... Now in our present case, did not Mr. Wheelwright make sides when he proclaimed all to be under a Covenant of works, who did not follow him (step by step) in his description of the Covenant of Grace? did he not make himself a party on the other side, by often using these and the like words, We, us? Did he not labor to heat the minds of the people, and to make them fierce against those of that side, which he opposed... a mind inflamed with indignation (among some people), would have been *more apt to have drawn swords* [the Nov. 2, 1637 court order to disarm] by the authority of the examples he held forth for their encouragement...

On the ninth of March, the General Court of Massachusetts concluded that Wheelwright was guilty of contempt and sedition.

More than 60 men of the Massachusetts Bay Colony created a response to the trial and conviction of Rev. Wheelwright. The response was called a Remonstrance or Petition.

The Remonstrance

We, whose names are underwritten, have diligently observed this honored court's proceedings against our dear and reverend brother in Christ, Mr. Wheelwright, now under censure of the court for the truth of Christ. We do humbly beseech this honorable court to accept this remonstrance or petition of ours, in all due submission tendered to your worships.

For, first, whereas our beloved brother, Mr. Wheelwright, is **censured for contempt** by the greater part of this honored court, we desire your worships to consider the sincere intention of our brother to promote your end in the day of fast; for whereas we do perceive your principal intention the day of fast looked chiefly at the public peace of the churches, our reverend brother did, to his best strength, and as the Lord assisted him, labor to promote your end, and therefore endeavored to draw us nearer unto Christ, the head of our union, that so we might be established in peace, which we conceive to be the true way, sanctified of God, to obtain your end, and therefore deserves no such censure, as we conceive.

Secondly, whereas our dear brother is **censured of sedition**, we beseech your worships to consider, that either the person condemned must be culpable of some seditious fact, or his doctrine must be seditious, or must breed sedition in the hearts of his hearers, or else we know not upon what grounds he should be censured. Now, to the first, we have not heard any that have witnessed against our brother for any seditious fact. Secondly, neither was the doctrine itself, being no other but the very expressions of the Holy Ghost himself, and therefore cannot justly be branded with sedition. Thirdly, if you look at the effects of his doctrine upon the hearers, it hath not stirred up sedition in us, not so much as by accident; we have not drawn the sword, as sometimes Peter did, rashly, neither have we rescued our innocent brother, as sometimes the Israelites did Jonathan, and yet they did not seditiously. The covenant of free grace held forth by our brother hath taught us rather to become humble suppliants to your worships; and, if we should not prevail, we would rather with patience give our cheeks to the smiters. Since, therefore, the teacher, the doctrine and the hearers be most free from sedition, (as we conceive,) we humbly beseech you, in the name of the Lord Jesus Christ, your Judge and ours, and for the honor of this court and the proceedings thereof, that you will be pleased either to make it appear to us, and to all the world, to whom the knowledge of all these things will come, wherein the sedition lies, or else acquit our brother of such a censure.

Farther, we beseech you, remember the old method of Satan, the ancient enemy of free grace, in all ages of the churches, who hath raised up such calumnies against the faithful prophets of God. Elijah was called the troubler of Israel, 1 Kings, 18.17, 18. Amos was charged for conspiracy, Amos 7.10. Paul was counted a pestilent fellow, or mover of sedition, and a ringleader of a sect, Acts 24.5; and Christ himself, as well as Paul, was charged to be a teacher of new doctrine, Mark 1.27. Acts 17.19. Now, we beseech you, consider, whether that old Serpent work not after his old method, even in our days.

Farther, we beseech you, consider the danger of meddling against the prophets of God, Psalm 105.14, 15; for what ye do unto them the Lord Jesus takes as done unto himself. If you hurt any of his members, the head is very sensible of it; for so saith the Lord of Hosts, He that toucheth you toucheth the apple of mine eye, Zech. 2. 8. And better a millstone were hanged about our necks, and that we were cast into the sea, than that we should offend any of these little ones, which believe on him, Matt. 18.6.

And, lastly, we beseech you consider, how you should stand in relation to us, as nursing fathers, which gives us encouragement to promote our humble requests to you, or else we would say with the prophet, Isa. 22. 4, Look from me, that I may weep bitterly; Labour not to comfort me, &c.; or as Jer. 9. 2, Oh that I had in the wilderness a lodging place of a wayfaring man! – And thus have we made known our griefs and desires to your worships, and leave them upon record with the Lord and with you, knowing that, if we should receive repulse from you, with the Lord we shall find grace.

More than 60 men signed the Remonstrance.

The signers of Boston:

Capt John Underhill	Henry Elkins	Robert Hardinge
John Sanford	John Button	Richard Wayte
John Biggs	Hugh Gunnison	John Porter
Thomas Oliver	Zache Bosworth	Jacob Eliott
Richard Cooke	Robert Rice	James Pfenniman
Richard Gridley	William Wilson	Thomas Wardell
William Hutchinson	William Townsend	William Warden
Richard Fairbanke	Robert Hull	Thomas Watson
Edward Bates	William Pell	William Baulston
William Aspinwall	**Richard Hutchinson**	John Compton
Thomas Marshall	James Johnson	Mr. Parker
William Dinely	Thomas Savage	William Freeborn
Samuell Cole	John Davy	Henry Bull
Oliver Mellows	George Burden	John Walker
William Litherland	John Odlin	William Salter
William Dyre (Dyer)	[illegible]	Edward Bendall
Samuell Wilbore	**Edward Hutchinson**	Thomas Wheeler
Mathew Ivans	William Wilson	W Clarke
Edward Rainsford	Isaack Glosse	John Coggeshall
John Oliver	Richard Carder	

The signers of Salem, Newbury, Roxbury, Ipswich, Charlestown:

Mr. Scrugs	Mr. Nicholas Easton	Philip Sherman
Mr. Alfoot	Mr. Spencer	Mr. Foster
Mr. Cousins	Mr. Edward Denison	Samuel Sherman
Robert Moulton	Richard Morris,	Mr. George Bunker
Goodman King	Richard Bulgar	James Browne
Mr. Dwyer	William Denison	

In the March Remonstrance, the signers declared their peaceful intent, and mentioned they had "not drawn the sword" and had no intention of taking up arms, but in fact, would turn the other cheek in patience if their petition did not prevail.

On November 2, when Gov. Winthrop dissolved the government elected in May, the newly appointed deputies responded by disarming every signer, implying that the Bay government feared armed insurrection.

Judgment of the Court:

Whereas the opinions & revelations of John Wheelwright & Mrs. Hutchinson have seduced & led into dangerous errors many of the people here in New England, insomuch as there is just cause of suspicion that they, as others in Germany, in former times, may, upon some revelation, make some sudden eruption upon those that differ from them in judgment, for prevention whereof it is ordered, that all those whose names are underwritten shall (upon warning given or left at their dwelling houses) before the 30th day of this month of November, deliver in at Mr. Canes house, at Boston, all such guns, pistols, swords, powder, shot, & match as they shall be owners of, or have in their custody, upon pain of ten pound for every default to be made thereof; Which arms are to be kept by Mr. Cane till this Court shall take further order therein. Also, it is ordered, upon like penalty of £10, that **no man** who is to render his arms by this order shall buy or borrow any guns, swords, pistols, powder, shot, or match, until this Court shall take further order therein.

Reverend Wheelwright was disfranchised and banished from Massachusetts Bay Colony with two weeks' notice, in March 1637.

Anne Hutchinson was on notice not to hold conventicles. She continued as usual, though.

In November 1637, Coggeshall, Baulston, Aspinwall, Gridley, Marshall, Dyer, and most of the other signers were disfranchised and disarmed just ahead of Anne Hutchinson's sedition trial, making them ineligible as jurors.

Ralph Mousall, William Larnet, Ezechiell Richardson, Richard Sprague, Edward Carington, Thomas Edward, Benjamin Hubbard, William Baker, Edward Mellows, and William Frothingham changed their minds, "acknowledged their sin," and asked that their signatures be crossed off the Remonstrance.

Edward Hutchinson and William Dyer (who had just returned to town and learned of his wife Mary's tragic miscarriage) had, among others, apologized for signing the Remonstrance and received their weapons back, but they remained disfranchised, and began preparing to leave the colony in the spring.

Chapter 41

How Anne Marbury Learned to Write

This is the writing method taught before 1612, which Anne and her siblings learned. First they learned how to make a pen, then they copied the cursive or print letters and words, which were often moralistic proverbs.

A teacher named John Brinsley published a tutorial on how to teach grammar school subjects, including handwriting. This is part of chapter four of his book for young teachers.

1. The Scholar should be set to write, when he enters into his accidence [the part of grammar that deals with the inflections of words] so every day to spend an hour in writing, or very near.

2. There must be special care, that every one who is to write, have all necessaries belonging thereunto; as pen, ink, paper, ruler, plummet, ruling-pen, pen-knife, etc.

3. The like care must be, that their ink be thin, black, clear; which will not run abroad nor blot; their paper good; that is, such as is white, smooth, and which will bear ink, and also that it be made in a book. Their writing books would be kept fair, straight ruled, and each to have a blotting paper to keep their books from soiling, or marring under their hands.

4. Cause every one of them to make his own pen, other-wise the making and mending of pens will be a very great hindrance, both to the masters and to the scholars ...

The best manner of making the pen is thus:

1. Choose the quill of the best and strongest of the wing, which is somewhat harder, and will cleave.

2. Make it clean with the back of the pen-knife.

3. Cleave it straight up the back; first with a cleft made with your pen-knife, after with another quill put into it, rive it further by little and little, till you see the cleft to be very clean; so you may make your pen of the best of the quill, and where you see the cleft to be the cleanest and without teeth. ...

The speediest and surest way to learn to make the pen is this: When your scholar shall have a good pen fit for his hand, and well-fashioned; then to view and mark that well, and to try to make one in all things like unto it. A child may soon learn to make his pen; yet, few of age do know how to make their own pens well, although they have written long and very much, neither can any attain to write fair without that skill.

The pen is to be held close to the nib, the thumb and two forefingers almost closed together round the nib 'like unto a cat's foot, as some of the scriveners call it.' ... The copy-book should not be more than two inches in breadth, and is to contain four or six copies in a book, half Secretary [cursive style], half Roman [an italic (from Italy) style]. One line of the copy should contain small letters, and under that 'great' letters; and under both, a line or two of 'joining' hand containing all the letters in them.

For Secretary [hand], the copy may be: 'Exercise thyself much in God's book, with zealous and fervent prayers and requests.

– *How the Master may direct his Scholars to write very fair, 'though himself be no good penman.'* Chapter iv of the *Ludus Literarius Ludus literarius: or, the grammar schoole shewing how to proceede from the first entrance into learning, to the highest perfection required in the grammar schooles, with ease, certainty and delight both to masters and schollars; onely according to our common grammar, and ordinary classical authours: begun to be sought out at the desire of some worthy fauourers of learning, by searching the experiments of sundry most profitable schoolemasters and other learned, and confirmed by tryall: intended for the helping of the younger sort of teachers, and of all schollars* (1612), by John Brinsley, 1612.

The seventeenth-century teachers used several styles, depending on the documents to be written or transcribed, among them:

1. Secretary, a cursive style that evolved into English round-hand;

2. Italic or Roman, which looked like individual letters;

3. Mixed Secretary and Italic Cursive;
4. Court or Chancery, used by clerks who worked for attorneys, though they often used secretary hand.

What hand was taught to women in the late sixteenth and early seventeenth centuries?

> Women were marginalized during this period and weren't working scribes; this was because of high illiteracy rates as well as social customs. Women were only taught how to write italic, because men who were writing masters believed that it was too difficult for women to learn the secretary hand. Italic was more legible and appropriate for low-literacy readers (including the aristocracy and royalty), and that's what women learned to write, if they learned anything beyond how to write their name.
> By Greg Johns and Michele Najarian,
> http://www.london.umb.edu/index.php/entry_detail/scribal_production/print_literature/

From *The Pens Excellencie* of 1618:

> "Italic is conceived to be the easiest hand that is taught with Pen and to be taught in the shortest time: Therefore it is usually taught to women, for as much as they (having not the patience to take any great pains, besides phantasticall and humorsome) must be taught that which they may instantly learn."

And yet, Anne Hutchinson's protégé, Mary Barrett Dyer, wrote in both cursive and italic hands. And Francis Marbury had time on his hands to teach his children, including his daughters, how to think critically, how to defend themselves with intelligence, and definitely, how to write.

Chapter 42

Aristotle's Complete Master-Piece: Midwifery and Childbirth in Anne Hutchinson's World

This 1820 edition of *Aristotle's Complete Master-Piece*, a book about copulation, coition, pregnancy, and childbirth published in New England, is not the *complete masterpiece* it claims to be. How do we know? Because when the 1684 first edition was published in London during the reign of Charles II, there was a section on how to have satisfactory lovemaking.

Apparently, that section was banned in Boston. The later edition acknowledges the "unlawful bed" (adultery) and illegitimate babies, but it's directed at the married couple only. Coition, as the anonymous author (not Aristotle) often refers to it, is for procreation.

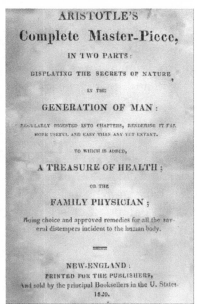

Aristotle's Complete Master-Piece book cover

In an article in *The Guardian* about the auction of the 1684 first edition sex manual, is a paragraph that doesn't appear in the PDF of the 1820 edition that I downloaded several years ago. The

1684 is much racier than the 1820 American version influenced by its puritanical founders. Here's the 1684 English version:

> The manual offers "a word of advice to both Sexes in the Act of Copulation." One passage advises that "when the Husband cometh into his Wives Chamber, he must entertain her with all kinds of dalliance, wanton behaviour, and allurements to Venery [sexual indulgence], but if he perceive her to be slow and more cold, he must cherish, embrace, and tickle her ... intermixing more wanton Kisses with wanton Words and Speeches, handling her Secret Parts and Dugs, that she may take fire and be inflamed to Venery."

Well, well, well! Cold shower, anyone? One can see why, with "Fifty Shades" passages like that, the book was a bestseller in 100 editions for more than two centuries.

By the time it made it through Boston editors in 1820, however, it was a medical book. The drawings of "monsters" looked like the females were wearing bikini tops. In fact, in my PDF is a passage that says this:

> Since nature has implanted in every creature a mutual desire of copulation, for the increase and propagation, of its kind; and more especially in man, the Lord of the creation, and master-piece of nature, that so noble a piece of Divine workmanship might not perish, something ought to be said concerning that, it being the foundation of all that we have been hitherto treating of, since without copulation there can be no generation. Seeing, therefore so much depends upon it, I thought it necessary, before I concluded the first part, to give such directions to both sexes, for the performing of that act, as may appear efficacious to the end for which nature designed it. But it will be done with that caution, as not to offend the chastest ear, nor put the fair sex to the trouble of a blush in reading it.
>
> It would be very proper to cherish the body with generous restoratives, that so it may be brisk and vigorous; and if their imaginations were charmed with sweet and melodious airs, and cares and thoughts of business drowned glass of racy wine, that their spirits may be raised to the highest pitch of ardour and joy, it would not be amiss.

And therefore I do advise them, before they begin their conjugal embraces, to invigorate their mutual desires, and make their flames burn with a fierce ardor, by those endearing ways that love can better teach than I can write. And when they have done what nature requires, a man must have a care he does not part too soon from the embraces of his wife... And when, after some convenient time, the man hath withdrawn himself, let the woman gently betake herself to rest, with all imaginable serenity and composure.

Page from the Aristotle's Complete Master-Piece,
half dog and half man.

As an editor myself, I'm sure that was the replacement of the text on women "taking fire and being inflamed to Venery." What, no fifty shades of blushing. Not only that, but I had to read half the book before I discovered that *this one had no naughty bits*. Publishers to Kindle and e-book sites know that they should put the hook or cliffhanger up front and put the acknowledgements at the back of the book, so readers can get the good stuff by browsing.

Dr. not-Aristotle, using classical medical literature, plagiarizing a 1554 text on midwifery, and showing personal experience as a seventeenth-century physician, described the anatomy of the reproductive organs, how to best conceive, and ways of dealing with problem deliveries. He used both superstition and contemporary medical knowledge in his book. Ovaries were called testicles, common terminology of the time, since they believed that both man and woman contributed "seed" in conception.

*Birthing chair, late sixteenth,
early seventeenth centuries.*

Perhaps he remained anonymous because he was very well acquainted with internal anatomy, and was surely conducting autopsies on both humans and animals. For that, he had to pay grave robbers to obtain cadavers, and perhaps hold his labs or demonstration lectures in secret locations.

On how "monsters" came to be:

"The agent or womb may be in fault three ways: firstly, in the formative faculty, which may be too strong or too weak, by which is procured a depraved figure. secondly, in the instrument or place of conception; the evil conformation or disposition whereof, will cause a monstrous birth. thirdly, in the imaginative power, at the time of conception; which is of such a force, that it stamps the character of the thing imagined on the child. And I have heard of a woman, who at the time of conception, beholding the picture of a Blackamore, conceived and brought forth an Ethiopian. I will not trouble you with more human testimonies, but conclude with a stronger warrant. We read, Gen. 30.31, how Jacob having agreed with Laban, to have all the spotted sheep for keeping his flock, to augment his wages, took hazel rods, and pealed white streaks on them, and laid them before the sheep when they came to drink, and coupled together three, whilst they beheld the rods, conceived and brought forth spotted young."

Based on the belief that the baby would resemble what the pregnant mother saw or imagined, I wove this into a scene in *Mary Dyer Illuminated* where Anne Hutchinson advised Mary Dyer on her pregnancy diet and to behold her husband's face intently when they made love so that the child would resemble its father.

Conception of a child, diet and posture

Though here he describes the best way to select the gender of a baby, a few pages after this, he explains that the baby's sex comes down to God's determination.

Then since diet alters the evil state of the body to a better, those who are subject to barrenness must eat such meats as are of good juice, and that nourish well, making the body lively and full of sap; of which faculty are all hot moist meats. For, according to Galen, seed is made of pure concocted and windy superfluity of blood we may therefore conclude there is a power in many things to accumulate seed, and other things to cause erection; as hens' eggs, pheasants, wood cocks, gnat snappers, thrushers, black birds, young pigeons, sparrows, partridges – all strong wines taken sparingly, especially those made of the grapes of Italy. But erection is chiefly caused by scuraum, eringoes, cresses, crysmon, parsnip, artichokes, turnips, asparagus, candied ginger, galings, acorns bruised to powder, drunk in muscatel, scallion, sea shell-fish, Etc, But these must have time to perform their operation, and must use them for a considerable time or you will reap but little benefit by them.

The act of coition being over, let the woman repose herself on her right side, with her head lying low, and her body, declining that by sleeping in that posture, the caul on the right side of the matrix may prove the place of conception, for therein is the greatest generative heat, which is the chief procuring cause of male children, and rarely fails the expectation of those that experience it, especially if they do but keep warm without much motion, leaning to the right, and drinking a little spirit of saffron and juice of hyssop in a glass of Malaga or Alicant, when they lie down and arise, for the space of a week.

For a female child, let a woman lie on the left side strongly fancying a female at the time of procreation, drinking the decoction of female mercury four days from the first day of purgation; the male mercury the like operation in case of a male;

for this concoction purges the right and left side of the womb, the receptacles, and makes way for the seminary of generation.

Aristotle's Master-piece also says that babies look more like their mothers because she "contributes the most to it," or they resemble their mother's (cuckolded) husband if, in an adulterous liaison, the woman imagines the face of her husband.

The author tasted human ovum. Oh, no he didn't! (Yes, he must have.)

> The truth of this is plain for if you boil them, their liquor will be the same colour, taste and consistency, with the taste of bird's eggs. If any object, that they have no shells; that signifies nothing: For the eggs of fowls, while they are in the ovary, nay, after they are fastened into the melus, have no shell.

The book goes on to describe why children look the way they do: it's because of what the mother thinks about most intensely, or with "fright or extravagant laughter." If she saw a hare cross the road before her, the baby might be born with a "hairy lip" (cleft palate, not a moustache). The author writes, "It therefore behooves all women with child if possible to avoid such sights, or at least not to regard them."

I depicted this common belief in my first novel, *Mary Dyer Illuminated,* and I used some of the information about midwifery to depict Anne Hutchinson's profession. In 1637, Mary Dyer miscarried the first recorded "monster" in America, an anencephalic and spina bifida female fetus. All babies born or miscarried with severe defects like that were called monsters, and were considered proof of the mother's heresy or evil thoughts.

You can read an 1846 (Victorian) version online at https://archive.org/details/8709661.nlm.nih.gov that's also a redaction of the jazzy release in 1684. But it, too, is missing the original how-to. Nothing to offend the most chaste ear.

Which begs the question, "What is a chaste ear?"

Chapter 43

The Midwife's Garden

In my biographical novel, *Mary Dyer Illuminated,* where Anne Hutchinson figured in Mary's story, I made use of sixteenth- and seventeenth-century literature on childbirth and midwifery, as well as herbal remedies and diet for keeping a pregnant mother in a good mood: dark leafy greens, chamomile and raspberry leaf tea, borage, beets, and foods we know to be high in Vitamin B. Obviously, they didn't know about vitamins or that their pewter tableware could give them lead poisoning, but they managed to treat and sometimes cure problems we'd be rid of with a pill.

Herb lore went back for millennia, and though it's largely been forgotten in the last century as we rely on prescriptions for synthetic chemicals, women have been known as healers, wise women, and midwives, and for good reason: they were closer to their kitchen gardens, and knew the best uses for their domestic and wild-foraged herbs.

Anne Hutchinson would have been well read on midwifery and herb lore, as well as experienced in her profession. And she did give birth at least fifteen times.

To increase a woman's milk.

To increase a woman's milk, you shall boil in strong posset ale good store of coleworts [cabbage], and cause her to drink every meal of the same; also if she use to eat boiled coleworts with her meat, it will wonderfully increase her milk also.

—*The English Housewife,* by Gervase Markham, 1568-1637

A midwife's garden would contain many foods and herbs we'd recognize today, including purple (not orange) carrots, turnips, beans, radishes, melons, onions and garlic, and greens of many kinds. We've often heard that they didn't have potatoes, but they were known in Connecticut in the 1630s as Virginia potatoes, and John Winthrop Jr. had a plentiful supply of them. The native Americans taught the English colonists to eat corn, of course. But the most important part of the garden would be the herbs and plants that a midwife needed throughout the pregnancies and neonatal periods of her patients.

"Sunflower buds, before they be floured, boiled and eaten with butter, vinegar and pepper, surpass the artichoke in procuring bodily lust [health and strength, not sexual desire]," wrote Thomas Johnson in his 1633 herbal encyclopedia *Herball - General Historie of Plants.*

He also wrote, "The woman with child which eateth many quinces during the time of her breeding shall bring forth wise children with great understanding." Quinces are hard, sour fruits that look like pears and apples, but can be cooked and sweetened. One recipe for preserving quinces involved three pounds of sugar to start, then more and more sugar, until the good housewife ran out of sugar entirely.

Some of the most familiar names to us today are comfrey to ease pain, lavender to calm and relax, and hyssop to purge afterbirth and as an aphrodisiac. Tansy, a pretty yellow flower introduced by European immigrants and now found all over the United States and Canada, was useful for a variety of purposes: purging intestinal parasites, reducing gas and easing abdominal cramps, reducing fevers and frequency of epileptic seizures, and for midwives' use, increasing female fertility and preventing miscarriage.

The opposite effect, inducing abortion, was illegal for midwives to administer, and some, on moral grounds, would refuse to provide pennyroyal for abortion. But the midwife Jane Hawkins may have given pennyroyal, as she was censured for giving mandrake and suspected of practicing witchcraft.

Growing the herbs was a matter of careful planting at a certain phase of the moon or time of the day. Herbalists used leaves, bark, blossoms, stems, roots, and seeds, depending on which treatment was desired. Herbs were harvested and stored after being dried, usually by hanging in bunches in a kitchen or shed.

There were various ways of administering the herbal medications. A remedy containing one herb was called a simple, and combinations were compounds. Decoctions were made by steeping the medical herb in hot water (what we'd call tea), and infusions were boiled to increase their potency. Some drugs were dissolved in alcohol, called a tincture, or boiled into a syrup of honey.

Pills could be formed in a lump of dough or wax, and eaten. When I was a child and had a severe cough, I remember being given crushed pills in applesauce. When I eat applesauce now, I still half-expect the bitter taste of those pills that were too large for my swollen throat. Some things never change.

Imagine organizing your last harvest in England, and packing the seeds, slips, or bare roots for a two-month voyage to Massachusetts, not knowing what soil or climate you'd find. And then after a long and severe winter, you'd nurse your seedlings and saplings, hoping for the same success you and your ancestors had known for generations.

One wonders how Anne Hutchinson managed her food and medicinal gardens, moving from Lincolnshire to Boston in 1634, then Portsmouth in 1638, and Bronx in 1642. Surely a woman of her talents didn't rake and hoe and fertilize on her own, and the family had children, relatives, and servants. But as the matriarch and professional midwife, she would be responsible for her garden produce and the medicinal stock, and would have taught her daughters and servants to carry on the special knowledge to the next generation of "wise" women.

Tansy is a yellow-flowered plant.

Chapter 44

Where's the Beef?

Anne and William spent most of their lives in England – into their early 40s. They had long traditions, just as you and I do. Hardly anything is more traditional than what we eat with our families.

An item like potato salad can be made several ways, with a vinaigrette dressing or with potato skins on, with mayonnaise, with or without mustard or eggs or pickle juice, and so on. The same goes for deviled eggs or the kind of pizza you prefer.

Some books say that the English diet was sparing of meat, and without much variety. They would eat bread and milk for breakfast and lunch, and then a bland stew of oats and peas or beans. But other authors point to a variety of fish and fowl and rabbit with the produce of orchards, gardens, and hedgerows. People lived close to one another in villages as well as the cities, and went out to the fields to work or care for their herds. They had generations-old connections and would have traded surpluses at the markets or shared at social gatherings.

We don't have the first clue about favorites of the Hutchinson family, but we do have cookbooks that were in circulation, including the aforementioned *The English Housewife*, by Gervase Markham, which contained recipes and menus for daily life and special occasions. Also, there were family recipes Anne learned from her girlhood, from her in-laws, and from exchanging dishes at church dinners, festivals, and at childbirth parties.

English food for the merchant class would have held more variety than for tenant farmers. They lived near the sea, so fish would have been commonly available, as well as rabbit, chicken, grouse, squirrel, and pigeon. They would have eaten pork more frequently than the lambs which were more valuable for their wool. And for special occasions, perhaps there was beef or turkey. They had parsnips, beets, purple carrots, peas and beans, onions, imported citrus, apples and pears, and many other fruits, vegetables and grains we're familiar with. They called their fresh or cooked vegetables "sallat," like salad.

Pottage was a savory oatmeal porridge that was flavored with herbs and onions.

In England, they had sugar from Caribbean plantations, and spices from the Spice Islands of Indonesia. As Boston and later, Newport, developed their ports and trade relations, there developed the Triangle Trade between Europe, the Caribbean, and New England.

When the Hutchinsons were on the ship *Griffin*, they'd have consumed stale water and beer, porridge, salt fish and pork, and if they were lucky, fresh fish caught at sea.

When they landed in Boston, their fare was much different. Cattle, sheep, goats and pigs (presumably young ones) were carried on the passenger ships, but up to a third of them died in passage, and the remaining animals were needed for breeding stock in the colonies. In some years, the slaughter of lambs was prohibited because the wool industry was nearly dead and the colony needed those animals for wool and further breeding stock.

Their meat was now venison, bear, squirrel, birds, fish and shellfish, and lobster. Yes, those massive Maine lobsters that make you salivate and start melting butter by the pound – were used by Indians for fish bait, and for dog food. The colonists gave lobster meat to their servants because it was inferior.

Hunting for venison and other game was dangerous because hunters could get lost or meet unfriendly natives in the forests, and muskets were dangerous to their own users, so the colonists traded European wampum shells (currency), cloth, buttons, and alcohol to the natives, for meat and furs.

They planted their English grains (rye, wheat, barley, oats) for bread and English grasses for livestock. Inclement weather often killed their first and second plantings of the year, or pests ate the grain before it could be harvested. At first, they imported more grain than they could grow for their own needs. But what worked best for those soils and climate was Indian corn. It could be eaten fresh, but even better, could be dried for future use.

In addition, they used pumpkins and squash, cranberries, wild berries, and other plants that could be cultivated or foraged. Another food source, a legume, grew in the same places as poison ivy – groundnuts. Like potatoes, they're tuber-like, but groundnuts are related to beans.

And that brings us to potatoes. Many of us learned that potatoes, a native of South America, didn't come on the scene until many decades later. But John Winthrop, Jr., ordered a large load of them for Connecticut in 1636, and they were well known in Boston before that. They were fairly expensive, when you compare their price to other commodities of the time, perhaps US$12 per pound, which is why they might not have been very well known to later history writers.

Girl Chopping Onions, by Gerritt Dou

Some of the foods Anne and her family would become familiar with were succotash (corn, onions, beans, bear or whale fat), boiled pumpkins, samp (a pancake made of milk and cornmeal), and pippin tarts.

Who did the cooking in the Hutchinson family? With that large brood, plus two unmarried female cousins of William's, and assorted guests at the table, Anne may have supervised, but it would take several people to prepare food, reconstitute the dry beans or corn, pluck the poultry and clean the fish, keep the various areas of the large hearth at proper temperatures for different foods, and to clean up later. Since single women relatives were not allowed to live on their own, and were required to live in families, they often became domestic helpers. And the Hutchinsons were wealthy enough to hire servants. Though they owned a large home in the town center (a restaurant occupies the site now), they also owned several valuable properties near Boston, including a farm at Mt. Wollaston (Quincy, Mass.), and at Pull-in Point. There would be laborers and employees to feed, clothe, and house in addition to the family.

Though the Hutchinsons had funds, and the towns of Massachusetts Bay were better organized for food than when the Winthrop Party had arrived in 1630, there were always famines and pestilences befalling the settlers, and the food supply was far from stable or easy. Roger Clap, a Devonshire man who lived from 1609-1691, was an early settler at Dorchester. He wrote in his *Capt. Clap's Memoirs* that he'd ordered provisions from his father in England. "But before this Supply came, yea and after too (that being spent) and the then unsubdued Wilderness yielding little Food, many a Time if I could have filled my Belly, tho' with mean Victuals, it would have been sweet unto me. Fish was a good help unto me, and others. Bread was so very scarce, that sometimes I tho't the very Crusts of my Father's Table would have been very sweet unto me. And when I could have Meal and Water and Salt boiled together, it was so good, who could wish better?"

The colonists brought seeds with them, and possibly small rooted slips from old plants. Within a few years, they'd have fresh fruit and nuts from their orchards. Well, most people would. The Hutchinsons would move too frequently to really put down roots.

Chapter 45

Hugh Peter, Inquisitor and Scoundrel

Hugh Peter, a Puritan minister who did good things for New England, was one of the accusers of Anne Hutchinson at her 1637 and 1638 trials and pushed for her banishment. He would have been aware of Mary Dyer and of both women's "monstrous" miscarriages.

His grandfather carried the name of a manor in Norfolk, England, called Dyckwoode, and it seems that for a time in the sixteenth century, the family lived in the Netherlands but moved to England for reasons of religious freedom. Hugh Peter (the surname his father changed from Dyckwoode, far be it from me to comment on the slang implications of both surnames) was born in Cornwall in 1598. He earned his MA at Cambridge University, which was favored by Puritans, and indeed, preaching became his career.

In 1625, he married a widow, Elizabeth Cooke Reade, who was 30 years older than Hugh and had adult children, one of whom married John Winthrop Jr. Elizabeth Reade died in England in 1637.

Rev. Hugh Peter
Portrait by Gustavus Ellinthorpe Sintzenich
Wikipedia

Hugh Peter criticized Queen Henrietta Maria, the Catholic wife of Charles I, lost his preaching license, went back to the Netherlands for a few years and was a military chaplain, then (when he was trying to slide past the English military that were looking for him) was persuaded by friends to go to New England. It's interesting that he mentions *The Book of Sports*, written by King James I and reissued by Charles I. *Sports* required the Puritans to play and enjoy themselves on Sunday afternoons, rather than sit in hours-long church services for the entire day. In other words, they had to break the sacredness of their Sabbath to do secular activities.

Hugh said of his decision to emigrate, "And truly my reason for myself and others to go, was merely, not to offend Authority [King Charles I] in the difference of Judgment; and had not the *Book for Encouragement of Sports on the Sabbath* come forth, many [would have] staid [in England]."

So in 1635, Hugh emigrated to Massachusetts Bay Colony and was appointed minister of the church in Salem, which was a more religiously fundamental town than Boston or most other towns. He was admitted as a freeman at the same time as Henry Vane and William Dyer. He excommunicated Roger Williams and banished him to the wilderness – during the vicious winter – so that Williams had to flee to the Narragansett Indians, where he bought land and founded Providence Plantation.

As the stepfather of John Winthrop, Jr.'s wife, Hugh Peter helped to make Connecticut a colony through his connections with the Winthrops and Rev. Thomas Hooker, whom he'd known in England. Winthrop Junior was Connecticut's governor or deputy governor for many years.

While in the Bay Colony, Peter was placed on a commission to develop the fishing industry from a gaggle of independent fisherman sending cargoes of fish to Europe or the Caribbean at great expense, into a confederation of fishermen, with coordinated cargoes, canneries for preserving, coastal stations for resupplying the fishing fleet with tackle and rigging, and regulations for what to do with fish: valuable cod, bass, and halibut were not to be spread as "manure" on crops, but preserved for sale abroad. Gov. Winthrop mentioned Hugh Peter's work as being helpful in the lean winters and springs before the crops came in: they had salt fish to keep them alive, and that Hugh organized funding to build a 150-ton ship to send Massachusetts goods to foreign markets.

In 1636, preaching at Boston, Rev. Peter urged several things of the church. Among them was that they would "take order for employment of people, (especially women and children, in winter time;) for he feared that idleness would be the ruin both of church and commonwealth." Winthrop's *Journal*, May 1636.

Mr. Peter was harshly critical of Anne Hutchinson's religious teaching and as one of her inquisitors, persuaded the General Court to banish her; he and other ministers visited Mistress Hutchinson during the winter while she was incarcerated at Joseph Weld's home. They preached to her, tried to get her to recant, and took her answers as evidences against her in her excommunication trial. He was also one of the founding board members of Harvard College in 1638.

Two years after his much-older wife died in 1637, he married Deliverance Sheffield – unwillingly – because it seems that members of the Boston and Salem churches didn't like having a single man as their minister, and they proceeded to arrange his marriage.

Hugh wrote to Governor Winthrop, "If you shall amongst you advise me to write to her, I shall forthwith, our town looks upon me contracted, and so I have said myself."

In 1641, three men were needed to return to England to be agents for the colony: Rev. Thomas Weld (who soon after wrote the vicious introduction to Winthrop's book about Hutchinson and Dyer), magistrate William Hibbins (whose wife would someday be hanged as a witch), and Rev. Hugh Peter. John Endecott stirred up the Salem church to deny permission for the hugely popular Hugh Peter to return to England, saying that he might never return.

Earl Charles Spencer, in *Killers of the King*, wrote that Rev. Peter had "extraordinarily infectious words, which could rouse men to fight with a courage reserved for those utterly confident in God's blessing." However, Peter did go to England as an agent for the colony of Massachusetts Bay, and they were right: he never returned.

Mrs. Deliverance Peter gave birth to Hugh's only daughter between 1639 and 1641, but it became evident that Deliverance was mentally ill. (With hindsight, one could see her scattered thoughts in her letters written before they married.) He left her in the colony when he moved back to England, and wrote from the old country, "Be sure you never let my wife come away from thence without my leave [if] you love me."

The three men, Weld, Hibbins, and Peter, were able to persuade Parliament to grant that the colony not pay customs or taxes on their natural resources like fish, timber, furs, or lumber. Sweet! That nifty patent stayed in effect for decades. And when another king, 140 years later, demanded customs and taxes, remember what happened? The Boston Tea Party.

Meanwhile, Rev. Weld was having less success with his efforts. He created a Narragansett patent and took it around the Council of State and other leaders for signatures. The patent said Massachusetts Bay Colony owned the northwesterly parts of Rhode Island. His fraud was discovered, and he was recalled to Massachusetts for disciplinary action, but he never returned, having conveniently found other employment. In the 1650s, he wrote tracts refuting the Quakers' radical theology.

Weld and Peter had another lucrative business in England: they took children and teens, orphans or the fatherless, from parish poor rolls and detained them in a camp until a ship could be made ready to transport them as "servants" (or slaves) to America. There were some reports that children were kidnapped from their beds or snatched in alleys. If parents tried to rescue their children, they were told that they'd been paid and given up their rights. An epidemic killed a large number of the detention camp inmates. When the children were put on ships, it was without minders or nurses – just the ship's crew were in charge for eight to twelve weeks at sea.

The human trafficking enlarged as the English Civil Wars raged in the 1640s and people were separated from families by death or displacement. Hugh Peter went with the Cromwell army to Ireland, too, so it's possible that he took part in or suggested the slaughter and deportation of Irish people to America and the Caribbean.

Hugh Peter was the chaplain for Oliver Cromwell and General Fairfax's army during the Civil Wars, and he counseled the Parliamentary politicians to try and execute the captive King Charles. Several diarists of the day wrote that Peter was theatrical, melodramatic, and absurd in the pulpit, with facial expressions and shruggings of shoulders.

Rev. Peter was critical of the Anglo-Dutch war (in which William Dyer sought and was given the commission of Commander-in-Chief-Upon-the-Seas), saying to the Council of State that the two Protestant powers should work together, and not blow one another apart on the seas.

He led the procession of King Charles I from Windsor to London for the king's trial. When the king's execution came to pass in early 1649 – meanwhile, back in Boston, Winthrop was suffering his final illness – rumor had it that Hugh Peter was the other man, besides the headsman and the unfortunate king, there on the platform at Charing Cross. They said they recognized his voice, though his face was obscured like the headsman's.

1647: Another side of Rev. Hugh (Dyckwoode) Peter.
In the Dictionary of National Biography, the historian Burnet characterized him as "an enthusiastical buffoon preacher, though a very vicious man, who had been of great use to Cromwell, and had been very outrageous in pressing the king's death with the cruelty and rudeness of an inquisitor."
On this satirical broadsheet, it looks like Hugh is peering through a keyhole, but one writer suggested that Hugh had a reputation for womanizing, and that in this cartoon from 1647, he was reaching under the door for a key when his fingers were caught in a mousetrap. When the husband startles awake, the duplicitous wife assures him that what he heard was the mousetrap.
"The Rat is catch't," she says.
Hugh Peter mourns, "Oh, my fingers."
The cartoon is 370 years old, and it still holds up.

At the restoration of Charles II to the throne in 1660, those who took part in Charles I's execution or the conspiracy to execute were called regicides. Most of them were caught and tried.

At Hugh's trial, one of his colleagues said that Rev. Peter had boasted of another reason beside colony business, that he was sent to England in 1641, and that was that the colonial agents Massachusetts Bay sent were to stir up war against the King of England. If that was true and not just a scurrilous accusation, Hugh Peter and his colleagues were successful.

After his trial, Hugh Peter was given the traitor's death: hanged to nearly strangle but taken down, emasculated, his organs drawn out while he was alive, and then dismembered, with his head set on a pike and his limbs sent around the country.

Hugh Peter was the butt of satirical songs and articles accusing him of drunkenness, adultery against his mad wife back in Massachusetts (adultery being a crime in the colony), embezzlement, and inappropriate jocularity against the king. He denied them; historian C.H. Firth, at the end of the nineteenth century, said that Hugh Peter didn't do those things, and that on the contrary, Hugh was honest and upright. In light of the many reports we can assemble in the twenty-first century, I'm of the opinion that Firth was a tad optimistic about Hugh's character.

Chapter 46

Cast Into the Wilderness

The Cottons, Wilsons, Winthrops, Hutchinsons, and Dyers lived 400 years ago. They spoke an English dialect which is archaic to us now. Their recent history, in their parents' and grandparents' time, was the reformation of the Protestant Church, and the horrors of torture and burnings made by Protestant on Catholic, and Catholic on Protestant.

In the early 1600s, in their childhood and young adult lives, the Crown and the Anglican bishops persecuted dissenters like Puritans, Anabaptists, and Separatists. Religion mixed with government was a violent business.

But worse than physical persecution was being isolated, excommunicated, and shunned. It wasn't being "unfriended" or blocked, or escorted out the door with a carton of personal items. Isolation in the wilderness was to be sent to hell.

Anne Hutchinson's banishment and hounding was meant to be a curse.

So how is it related to a parable in the New Testament?

You may have read the parable of the Rich Fool in the Gospels, and you probably learned, as I did, that we should never say, "I worked for this or gained this all by myself," and leave God, the Provider, out of the statement. We should always give thanks that God has blessed in his provision. But it's easy to miss a very important concept that appears twice in Jesus' words.

And [Jesus] told them this parable: "The ground of a certain rich man yielded an abundant harvest. He thought to himself, 'What shall I do? I have no place to store my crops.'

"Then he said, 'This is what I'll do. I will tear down my barns and build bigger ones, and there I will store my surplus grain. And I'll say to myself, "You have plenty of grain laid up for many years. Take life easy; eat, drink and be merry."'

"But God said to him, 'You fool! This very night your life will be demanded from you. Then who will get what you have prepared for yourself?'

"This is how it will be with whoever stores up things for themselves but is not rich toward God." Luke 12:16-21 NIV

The oldest stories in the Bible show us that people were meant to live in relationship with one another. When Adam and Eve were exiled from the Garden, they went together. When Abram set forth from Ur to go to a Promised Land he'd never seen, he took with him his wife, servants and their families and relatives, that might have numbered in the hundreds. They had a tribe for support. Jacob ran away to save his life, but he went to his uncle's settlement and came back years later with wives and sons of his own.

The wilderness was a place of isolation, death and despair. Every society and clan lived together in villages and extended families for protection, but also for the common good of sharing work at planting, harvest, herding, care of the sick or injured, care of the infants and elderly, feasting, worshiping, and every other function of human life.

In England in the 1620s, Rev. John Donne, the senior pastor of St. Paul's Cathedral, wrote his famous essay with the phrases "for whom the bell tolls" and "no man is an island."

All mankind is of one author, and is one volume; when one man dies, one chapter is not torn out of the book, but translated into a better language; and every chapter must be so translated; God employs several translators; some pieces are translated by age, some by sickness, some by war, some by justice; but God's hand is in every translation, and his hand shall bind up all our scattered leaves again, for that library where every book shall lie open to one another.

No man is an island, entire of itself; every man is a piece of the continent, a part of the main; if a clod be washed away by the sea, Europe is the less, as well as if a promontory were, as well as if a manor of thy friend's or of thine own were; any man's death diminishes me, because I am involved in mankind, and therefore never send to know for whom the bell tolls; it tolls for thee.

This deep sense of community was also true of early colonial New England. Widows and widowers were urged to remarry. Single adults, whether never-married or separated, were not allowed to live alone, but were placed in families for economic reasons, and to police their morals. In the first decades of the colonies, all people were required to live in villages for mutual protection and mutual assistance, and not allowed to homestead in the wilderness. Native Americans who were sentenced to colonial prisons withered and died because they were alone and separated from their people.

Brain research shows that humans need other humans to function in a healthy way. https://www.scientificamerican.com/article/why-we-are-wired-to-connect/

In the Great Depression of the 1930s, President Herbert Hoover pursued policies of "Rugged Individualism," which called for personal liberties with little state regulation. That sounds good until you realize that education, safety and health, infrastructure creation and management, and police/fire/military protection are institutions that must be administered by government. That movement evolved into the über-conservative John Birch Society. Hoover's individualist policies actually exacerbated poverty and worsened the Great Depression's economic conditions until President Franklin Roosevelt instated democratic policies like Social Security, organized labor, and a social safety net for the poor and disabled.

"No member of a crew is praised for the rugged individuality of his rowing." – Ralph Waldo Emerson.

Jesus told the Parable of the Rich Fool with the man being *alone*, speaking with his soul. And later, speaking to himself.

Notice that the Rich Fool was an individualist. "Everything for me, by me." His aloneness had been a dreadful concept to every society until very recently. He had no one to talk to but himself, having alienated everyone around him. That would have been a horrifying prospect to Jesus' listeners, for a person to be alone.

It would have been horrifying to Rev. Donne's audience and early Americans, too. No spouse? No children? No parents or siblings? No friends? No professional colleagues? Not even some toady to brag to? Just slaves to do your bidding but not good enough to socialize with?

The Rich Fool had done the unthinkable: he'd made himself an island.

On one level, we see that the Rich Fool was ungrateful to God and refused to give glory to him. But that's not the point of the story. God doesn't need to have his ego stroked. He's not insecure about whether or not we give him credit.

The parable is about an extraordinarily arrogant millionaire or billionaire, if you will, who lived only to acquire profit, and so many possessions that he couldn't consume them for many years, and that his warehouses needed to be rebuilt larger. God's dread answer was that the Rich Fool's life would be required of him because he had no one to share his goods with. "Who will get what you have prepared for yourself?"

There was supposed to be a family, a community, a clan, a village. The care of the widows and orphans that God calls pure religion. But there was no one. Just the clod of dirt that dissolved, washed away in the sea, meaningless, leaving no legacy.

There's nothing wrong with being wealthy. There is something wrong with that wealth destroying our environment, oppressing workers (whether on our shores, or in third-world countries) with slave wages and conditions, and filling the vast warehouses of the super-rich when the rest of us live with reduced circumstances even though we work harder and longer than we ever did. There's something wrong with unseen people using that money to overcome and overwhelm the single votes of citizens by donating from outside the constituency state, where the policies of an official can't touch them, or that the politician grants favors or access to special interests and lobbyists.

We can infer from what others said of them that the Hutchinsons, though wealthy, *shared* their bounty. They took in single female relatives of William's. They took in unrelated people like the midwife Jane Hawkins and the abused Barbara Sabire. Anne taught theology in her home; she was a much-valued midwife, nurse, and spiritual counselor. Their son Edward advocated for mercy and protection of Quakers like his aunt Katherine and others.

The Hutchinsons created a community of love and stability that angered those whose lives were set in hard, cold cement.

Where they went, others followed, and the "wilderness" retreated before them, becoming a Promised Land of community and brotherhood.

Chapter 47

A Good Name is to be Chosen
Above Great Riches

Proverbs 22:1, *1599 Geneva Bible*

Both Anne Marbury and William Hutchinson were born into very large families that used traditional names, and they named their many children after their own parents, aunts and uncles. The Hutchinsons also, by tradition, named later children for the ones who had died young, so they had two daughters named Susanna, and two sons named William.

But many Puritans of the late sixteenth and early seventeenth centuries, believing that the Second Coming was imminent, broke with tradition.

In Western culture, we know people with virtue names such as Hope, Faith, Irene, Zoe, and Joy, and those with biblical names like John, David, Jacob, Esther, Naomi, Mary, and scores of others. From ancient times, parents all over the world have named their children with religiously-significant meanings or prophecies in mind, names that would be something to live up to, names that could form a child's character and destiny. Many named their babies after kings, queens, and nobility, or after parents and other family members.

William and Mary Dyer named their children in this manner. William's father was William, Mary's brother was William (which means her father was probably William), and they named their firstborn William. He died within a day or two of birth, and a later son was named William – that one, at age 18, bore the news of Mary's reprieve of execution in 1659, and later was mayor of New York. They named one son Samuel ("Asked For"), another son Charles after the recently-executed king, another son Henry (probably after Sir Henry Vane), a daughter Mary, and a son Mahershallalhashbaz. It was shortened to Maher, but the name was bestowed based on Isaiah 8:4, after the death of their friend and mentor, Anne Hutchinson.

Only in the last few hundred years have children been named for popular figures or in an attempt to make unique sounds or word combinations.

As the Reformation gained ground in England, it splintered further when non-conformists insisted on "purifying" the Church of

England. There was a large pocket of Puritans (as one branch of non-conformists was known) in Essex, and they tended to name their children with virtue names. I found a list of jurymen in a PDF, with given names, followed by a comma and their surnames.

county of Sussex, a jury was empanelled whose names were

Accepted, Trevor	Return, Spelman
Redeemed, Compton	Be Faithful, Joiner
Faint Not, Hewit	Fly Debate, Roberts
Make Peace, Heaton	Fight the good Fight of Faith, White
God Reward, Smart	More Fruit, Fowler
Standfast on High, Stringer	Hope for, Bending
Earth, Adams	Graceful, Herding
Called, Lower	Weep Not, Billing
Kill Sin, Pimple	Meek, Brewer

Thousands of Puritan emigrants to New England came from Essex, including Governor John Winthrop of Massachusetts Bay Colony. So many of them left England with money and possessions that the government of King Charles I believed that the English economy would fail. Eight ships were stopped in the River Thames in 1634, and the emigrants were prohibited from leaving. Among the passengers was Oliver Cromwell, bound for Connecticut – who would make war on the royalists in less than 10 years, and have King Charles beheaded in 15 years.

The Puritans of England and America – self-described as the Remnant or Elect in the book of Revelation – thought that the "world" was evil and they were living in the last days (indeed, deadly plagues and famines, religious wars, economic depression, and vicious crime regularly swept Europe), and Jesus would come in his second advent, in their lifetime, to take them to heaven and destroy the earth. Some of their names reflect that apocalyptic expectation: Return, Hope For, Redeemed, The-Lord-is-Near, and Wayte-a-While.

Church members were encouraged to report those who didn't conform, or those who spoke against authorities, which was considered sedition. Hate-Evil, Obedience, and Zeal-for-the-Lord might be appropriate names given by families who believed that. The charge of sedition (for signing a mild remonstrance against the governor and assistants) prompted punishment and exile for about 75 to 80 families, including Anne and William Hutchinson.

Abstinence	Hate-Evil	Perseverance	Thankfull
Abuse-not	Hate-ill	Piety	The-Lord-is-near
Accepted	Helpless	Praise-God	The-Peace-Of-God
Amity	Hope-for	Preserved	Unfeigned
Anger	Hope-still	Promise	Verity
Battalion	Humble	Prudence	Vitalis
Be-faithful	Humiliation	Purity	Vyctorye
Buried	Increase	Redeemed	Wayte-a-While
Called	Joy-again	Redivivia	Weakly
Chastity	Justice	Remember	Wealthy
Clemency	Lament	Repentance	Weep-not
Continent	Liberty	Replenish	What-God-will
Creature	Lively	Restore	Wrestling
Die-Well	Love	Safe-deliverance	Zeal-for-the-Lord
Dust-and-Ashes	Loyal	Safe-on-high	Zeal-of-the-Land
Elected	Magnyfye	Seaborne	
Faint-not	Make-peace	Search-The-	
Faithful	Merciful	Scriptures	
Fear	Mercy	Silence	
Fear-God	Merit	Sincere	
Fear-not	More-fruit	Sin-Deny	
Fight-The-Good-	More-trial	Small-hope	
Fight-of-Faith	Much-mercie	Sorry-for-sin	
Flee-debate	Noble	Stand-fast	
Flee-Fornication	No-merit	Stand-Fast-On-	
Free-gifts	Obedience	High	
From-above	Obey	Steadfast	
God Reward	Pardon	Submit	
Handmaid	Patience	Supply	
Has-Descendents	Peaceable	Temperance	

Most of the awkward names faded away with the English Civil Wars and the restoration of the monarchy in 1660, which returned the nation to Anglican rule but with toleration of most religious practices. The strange names were replaced by virtue names such as Purity, Patience, and Faith. The vast majority of names we find in colonial archives and genealogies are what we'd consider "normal" names: names we still use 400 years later.

Chapter 48

Heretics, Seducers, and Nudists, Oh My!

A catalogue of the severall sects and opinions in England and other nations
With a briefe rehearsall of their false and dangerous tenents.
[London]: Printed by R.A., 1647. Public domain.

While researching my books on the Dyers, and this book, I found many books, images, and ballads from their time period, the early- and mid-seventeenth century.

This broadsheet, basically a paper periodical of the day, was written by an unknown author and published in 1647, during the English Civil Wars. The ECW had begun over royal authority (the divine rights of kings) and religious upheaval and reformation that had been fomenting for a hundred years, with the Puritan faction coming into the majority.

The author commends the worthy and pious Parliament, which was a different strain of Reform, Presbyterian, than the persecuted ministers and their flocks who emigrated to New England and formed a theocracy – but they were, still, theocrats themselves.

Anne Hutchinson and her followers, including William and Mary Dyer, were called by their Puritan contemporaries libertines, familists, anti-Sabbatarians, and antinomians.

Following is a verse that describes various groups the author considered heretical. Keep in mind that it's highly biased, but interesting to those who enjoy trying to understand the culture of our founders and ancestors.

Jesuit.
By hellish wiles the States to ruin bring,
My Tenets are to murder Prince or King:
If I obtain my projects, or seduce,
Then from my Treasons I will let them loose:
And since the Roman Papal State doth totter,
I'll frame my sly-conceits to work the better.

Socinian.
By cunning art my way's more nearly spun,
Although destructive to profession;
Obscuring truths, although substantial,
To puzzle Christians or to make them fall:
That precious time may not be well improv'd,
I'll multiply strange notions for the lewd.

Arminian.
Would any comfortless both live and die?
Let him learne free wills great uncertainty:
Salvation that doth unmov'd remain,
Arminian Logic would most maintain,
And faith that's founded on a firm decree,
Is plac't by them to cause uncertainty.

Arian.
What they dare to deny, Christians know,
Christ God and Man, from whom their comforts flow,
'Tis sad, that Christians dive by speculation,
Whereby they lose more sweeter contemplation:
Where Christian practice acts the life of grace,
There's sweet content to run in such a race.

Adamite.
Hath Adams sin procur'd his naked shame,
With leaves at first that thought to hide his stain?
Then let not Adamites in secret dare
Aparent sinful acts to spread; but fear,
Since Adams sin hath so defil'd poor dust,
Cast from this Paradise by wicked lust.

Libertine.

A pish at sin and open violation,
By wilfull lust, deserves just condemnation:
Repentance, though a Riddle, this I'll say,
Thou must unfold the same or perish aye.
Then least this holy Law thou yet dost sleight,
Shall press thee one day with a dreadfull weight.

Antiscripturian.

By cursed words and actions to gainsay
All Scripture-truth, that ought to guide thy way,
Without all question, were it in thy power,
Thou would it all sacred Rules at once devour:
Poor man, forbear, thou striv'st but all in vaine,
Since all mans might shall but confirm the same.

Soule-sleeper.

That souls are mortal, some have dar'd to say,
And by their lives, this folly some bewray;
Whilst (like the beast) they only live to eat,
In sinfull pleasures waste their time and state:
Meantime forgetting immortality,
To woe or joy for all eternity.

Anabaptist.

Poor men contrive strange fancies in the brain,
To cleanse that guilt which is a Leopard stain:
'Tis but a fain'd conceit, contended for,
Since water can but act its outward matter:
Regenerate, newborn; these babes indeed
of watery Elements have little need.

Familists.

Were all things Gospel that H.N. hath said,
A strange confused work were newly laid:
A perfect state, like Adams, is pretended,
Whilst outwardly each day God is offended:
No Sabbath, but alike all days shall be,
If Familists may have their Liberty.

Seeker.

All Ordinances, Church and Ministry,
The Seeker that hath lost his beaten way,
Denies: for miracles he now doth wait,
Thus glorious truths reveal'd are out of date:
Is it not just such men should alwaies doubt
Of clearest truths, in Holy Writ held out.

Divorcer.

To warrant this great Law of Separation,
And make one two, requires high aggravation:
Adultery only cuts the Marriage-knot,
Without the which Gods Law allows it not.
Then learn to separate from sin that's common,
And man shall have more Comfort from a woman.

Pelagian.

What Adams state had been with out a fall,
Is but presumption to contend withall:
But Adams state of deprivation
Profits by serious meditation;
Men it keep back, Christ's all in all to all,
Then live by faith obediential.

Separatist or Independent.

The Saints Communion Christians do profess,
Most necessary to the life of grace,
But whilst some shrowd them by this bare notion,
Condemning all the rest for Antichristian,
Preferring much confused sad destraction:
They thus disturb a settlement in the Nation.

Antinomians.

Under this name shrouds many desperate
Destroying Doctrines, unregenerate,
Express opposing grace in its true power,
And glories lustre some do much abhor;
Repentance and obedience are condemn'd,
And rarest Christian duties much condemned.

Anti-Sabbatarian.

This curst opinion long hath been on foot,
A Christian Sabbath from our Isle to root:
When for base pleasures or curst recreation,
On Lords days duties lost by profanation,
Divine example hints sufficiently,
A first days Sabbaths full Authority.

Anti-Trinitarians.

That dare to search into the Trinity,
And in divine distinctions much to pry:
Christs humane nature they would dare to stain,
As ours by Adams guilt, but all in vain:
Then let's beware, least diving thus too far,
We leese our love, and much increase sad jar.

Apostolicks,
That now expect a new revealed way,
Unknown in Scripture, they have dar'd to say,
Beyond the way of usual dispensation
Guists infallible with Revelation,
And miracles again with Ministry,
Thus men are lost, when they too far do pry.

Thraskites.
The Jewish Sabbath these would have remain,
As warrantable by command most plain:
But since the Priest and sacrifice are ceast,
That Sabbath Judaical is decreast:
The Lords days ravishment divinely is
Confirm'd by Practice which unerring is.

Hetheringtonians.
That Englands Church is false do firmly hold,
What truths are therein taught deny thus bold
Without true ground, there's many yet that say
As much as these that err and go astray:
Oh could we keep within a Christian bound,
That should such sad division not be found.

The Tatians
In what time that Eusebius lived, have
All Pauls Epistles dar'd reject and have
The Acts of the Apostles set at naught,
Thus strange opinions have confusion brought:
Not far from those are some now in our days,
That leave the Word and act contrary ways.

The Marchionites.
All Matthew, Mark, and Johns divine
Most sacred Writ, these Gospels trine,
Tertullian doth report, rejected were,
By this strange Sect, thus heretofore:
As now we see, division greatly spread,
And from the bounds of practice get a head.

The broadsheet continued:

We read how that in the last days many false Prophets shall arise, and many shall say, Lo here is Christ, lo there is Christ, and shall deceive many, 2 Pet. 2.1. there were false Prophets also among the people, as there shall bee false teachers among you, who privily shall bring in damnable heresies, even denying the Lord that bought them, and bring upon themselves swift destruction, therefore we had need to be established in the truth, as in 1 Cor. 16.13. stand fast in the faith, 1 Pet. 5.9. whom resist steadfast in the faith, 1 John 2.23. Let that therefore abide in you which ye have heard from the beginning, and ye shall continue in the Son and in the Father; Vers. 25.

These things I have written unto you, concerning them that seduce you. Many strange Sects and Opinions are held amongst us, so that it is to be feared, that what rule soever our wise and honourable Parliament shall establish it will not content the unquiet spirits of a lawless generation, which would have no rule; *for set any Rule in the Church they will call it persecution, and they say they dislike some things commanded because they are Imposed.*

Some there are that look for a Temporal Kingdom of Christ, that shall last a thousand years this opinion is most dangerous for all States, for they teach that all the ungodly must be killed, and that the wicked have no propriety in their estates. Others out of confidence that they are ruled by the spirit, despite all ordinary calling to the Ministry, all written prayers, all helps of study: Some make no conscience to hear and sing Psalms, but rather follow their own inventions, as he that would not believe the sun because it went not with his watch: Likewise this ordinary saying of theirs; Be in Christ and sin if thou canst; meaning, that regenerate men cannot sin; this is the Doctrine of the Anabaptists: also that to receive the Communion with a profane person, is to partake of his sin; that the Lords Prayer was never taught to be said; that the Gospel was never purely taught since the Apostles times; that a liberty of Prophesying must be allowed; that all humane Laws must be abolished; that Ministers of Gods Word should rule both the Spiritual and the Temporal; that distinction of Parishes is Antichristian.

Should these absurd and gross opinions take place, *what division and confusion would they work amongst us? but such is the wisdom and care of our worthy and pious Parliament, to provide an Ordinance for preventing of the growing and spreading of heresy.*

*****

There they go again: seeking laws to control beliefs and behaviors, in the name of peace and stability, yet going about it with judgment and punishment.

Text source:
https://quod.lib.umich.edu/e/eebo/A78343.0001.001/1:1?rgn=div1;view=fulltext
Public domain.

Chapter 49

Things You Just Can't Make Up

Anne Hutchinson died in the summer of 1643, on a Dutch property now called Pelham. The Hutchinson River Parkway, named for her, runs north from there, and the Boston Post Road, laid on a path used by her contemporaries, intersects the "Hutch," as the parkway is sometimes called.

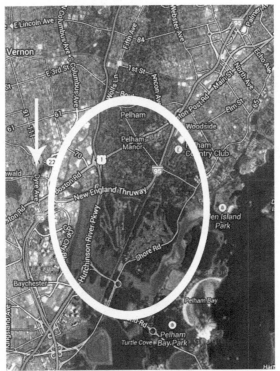

Arrow indicates Dyre Avenue in the Bronx; circle indicates approximate location of Anne Hutchinson's rented farm in Pelham-Eastchester, New York.

A mile or less to the east, in Mt. Vernon, New York, is a street called Dyre Avenue. It's not named for Anne's friend Mary Barrett Dyer, nor for Anne's grandson-in-law, Samuel Dyer, who married Anne's namesake. The streets are named for early colonial mayors and governors of New York; this one, in particular, is for

Samuel Dyer's next-younger brother, Major William Dyer, who was a royal customs inspector and mayor of New York City.

Surely there's no connection between the Hutchinson farm site, the Hutchinson River Parkway, and the naming of Dyre Avenue at some point many years later. But from the comfort of our homes, it's a fascinating coincidence to consider along with the deep connections between the Hutchinson and Dyer families.

As you've read, Governor Winthrop and his fellow founding colonists were zealous to preserve their 1629 charter that gave them virtual autonomy to govern and to worship as they chose. Winthrop and his family, John Wilson, John Cotton, Comfort Starr, and many others were buried in vaults or graves in the Burying Ground at what is now the corner of Tremont and School Streets in the heart of Boston.

THE FIRST KING'S CHAPEL.

But finally, their charter was revoked by King James II in 1684, and the royally-appointed governor, Edmund Andros, was stonewalled by Bostonians when he was shopping for land on which to build a Church of England chapel. (You know, the church the Puritan colonists had fled 55 years before.)

Frustrated in his plans, Andros had graves moved a short distance, built his house of worship over the Burying Ground, and called it the King's Chapel. That is its name to this day. Roll over, Mr. Winthrop.

R emember the story of Randall Holden, Samuel Gorton, and John Greene in early 1643, being abducted from their lands in Warwick, Rhode Island?

On July 18, 1972, Mick Jagger and Keith Richards of the Rolling Stones were jailed in Warwick for drug use and scuffling with a photographer.

Meanwhile, 15,000 eager fans awaited the Stones concert in Boston. There had been violence at other concerts in their other American venues, and Boston mayor Kevin White didn't want that happening in his city. So he persuaded Warwick police to release the Stones to his custody, and the band was given a state police escort, lights and sirens blaring, as they raced north on I-95. Stevie Wonder and Billy Preston entertained the crowd until the Rolling Stones rolled in at 1:00 a.m. They played for about 45 minutes and Boston concert-goers went home happy. Who knew that at one end of the time-space continuum, in 1643 Boston, there was violence, hard labor, and a silencing of dissent, while at the other end, in 1972 Warwick, there was jail for disorderly behavior? And connecting them both: a hurried police escort.

Chapter 50

Well, *That* Wasn't Very Nice

When the Hutchinsonian religious dissidents left or were exiled from Massachusetts Bay Colony in early 1638, they went first to the small town of Providence Plantations on the Seekonk River to meet with another dissident, Roger Williams, who had helped them negotiate with the Indians. Then they went on another few miles to the beautiful wooded island they'd purchased from the Native Americans during the extremely harsh winter when the women were preparing to move their households (children, servants, domestic animals), the men were selling properties in Massachusetts and surveying and exploring their new island and Narragansett Bay, Mary Dyer was recovering from her traumatic miscarriage, and Anne Hutchinson was under house arrest in the home of Joseph Weld.

The island was called by the Native American name of **Aquiday** or **Aquidneck** ("the floating mass" or "island"), and the town they founded at the north end was first called Pocasset, the native name for "where the stream widens." The Narragansett Bay is actually not an ocean bay, but an estuary for several rivers, so it does appear that you cross a river when you drive over the bridge from Massachusetts onto the island. Or in the seventeenth century, took a ferry or boat ride from the mainland.

Within two years of settlement, the island was renamed **The Isle of Rhodes** or **Rhode Island**, and the town officially became Portsmouth.

The city and harbor of Newport, Rhode Island were founded in 1639 by, among others, William Dyer and William Coddington, who were to be neighbors and political adversaries for decades. The deep-water harbor became the second-largest harbor and commerce center in New England after Boston, and traded in molasses and rum, horses and lumber, ship-building, food for the Caribbean plantations – and slaves. It was a center for smuggling and piracy. Mind you, Boston was no City Upon a Hill when it came to the same trade goods, piracy, and human trafficking, but Rhode Island had a bad reputation from the very beginning because of its religious tolerance and its rejection of a church-state government.

Other names for the first colony to encode full religious liberty as law:

- **Rogues Island:** This pun was an early name for the colony, used in the time of the Dyers. But its nickname was renewed at the time of the American Revolution, and its popularity continues today in websites, newspapers, and a restaurant name.
- Because of the heresy of the founders of Rhode Island, Governors John Winthrop and William Bradford called the place **"the Isle of Error,"** and that name was often used by other New England leaders in letters and journals.
- **Asylum to evil-doers.**
- **The sink into which the other colonies empty their heretics.** This is a direct reference to the Hutchinsons, Dyers, and Roger Williams.
- **The sink-hole of New England,** actually a reference to the morals of its residents, but now useful as a meme about roadway potholes.
- **A cesspool of heretics** (circa 1639).
- **The licentious republic.**
- Connecticut's Daniel Denison, writing on behalf of the Atherton Purchasers, punned that 'Roade Island is (pardon necessity's word of truth) **a rodde to those that love to live in order [and] a road, refuge, asylum to evil livers.**'
- Dennison also called it **an unhallowed sanctuary for capital criminals.**
- A modern nickname: **Rude Island.**
- **The receptacle of all sorts of riff-raff people.** In 1657, two Dutch Reformed ministers reported their encounter with Quakers to their religious board in Amsterdam, that "We suppose they [the majority of the Quaker missionaries] went to Rhode Island; for that is the receptacle of all sorts of riff-raff people. ... They left behind two strong young women. As soon as the ship had fairly departed, these began to quake and go into a frenzy, and cry out loudly in the middle of the street, that men should repent, for the day of judgment was at hand."
- **Caeca latrina.** Probably the same two ministers (of the colony of New Amsterdam) sent this report to the Classis of Amsterdam. The Classis was the religious arm of the Dutch West Indies Company (WIC). The WIC appointed the governor to administer the colony's business affairs, and the Classis provided Reformed,

Calvinist ministers to serve the WIC's towns and outposts. The Reformed doctrines were not far different from Puritan beliefs.

1658, Sept. 24th.
[from] Revs. J. Megapolensis and S. Drisius

Reverend, Pious and Learned Fathers and Brethren in Christ:
—

Your letter of May 26th last, (1658,) came safely to hand. We observe your diligence to promote the interests of the church of Jesus Christ in this province, that confusion may be prevented, and that the delightful harmony which has hitherto existed among us here, may continue. At the same time we rejoice that the Hon. Directors have committed this matter to you, and we hope that God will strengthen you in your laudable efforts. Last year we placed before you particularly the circumstances of the churches both in the Dutch and English towns. And as this subject has been placed by your Rev. body before the Hon. Directors, we hope that their honors will take into earnest consideration the sadly destitute circumstances of the English towns. ...The raving Quakers have not settled down, but continue to disturb the people of the province by their wanderings and outcries. For although our government has issued orders against these fanatics, nevertheless they do not fail to pour forth their venom. There is but one place in New England where they are tolerated, and that is Rhode Island, which is the *caeca latrina* of New England. Thence they swarm to and fro sowing their tares.

The letter went on to complain about a Lutheran minister that they didn't like interfering with their Reformed churches and people.
Source: (Abstract of, in Acts of Deputies, Jan, 13, 1659. xx. 391.)
https://books.google.com/books?pg=PA433&lpg=PA433&dq=caeca+latrina&sig=JVSVCS9zqu10HX u_CjS95XKfnYo&id=U3EAAAAAMAAJ&ots=2P2AE1C-z2&output=text

The Classis, and indeed the Netherlands government, was very tolerant of various religions in their country and colonies. The Reform church was prominent, but they tolerated Jews, Catholics and Protestants, Lutherans, Musselmen (Muslims), and English Separatists like the Pilgrims who came from England and later moved to Plymouth, Massachusetts. And Rev. Megapolensis himself had redeemed a French Catholic missionary who had been captured by the Mohawks of the Hudson River Valley. But it seems they had no tolerance for Quakers or rogues!

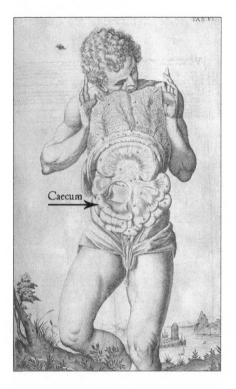

What did they mean by calling Rhode Island a caeca latrina? *Caecum*, in seventeenth-century anatomy, was the colon or rectum (they used the term interchangeably). *Latrina* was the public toilet or sewer used by a military barracks. So the epithet of *caeca latrina* meant, basically, the outdoor toilets for feces, a.k.a. "number two" or "poop." (One could go on, but surely you've heard other slang terms.)

Well, *that* wasn't very nice.

Chapter 51

Up Close and Personal With the Hutchinson and Dyer Statues

Hutchinson statue seen from Beacon Street over the iron fence.
That's as close as most people get.

The memorial statue of Anne Marbury Hutchinson was cast in bronze in 1915, and placed on the grounds of the Massachusetts State House in 1922. For generations, it was a landmark easily visited by descendants and admirers of Hutchinson. But after the terror attacks of Sept. 11, 2001, the state raised an iron fence around the statehouse, and no access is granted except by permit. For most people, the best they can do is shoot photos with a long lens, from Beacon Street. (The Mary Dyer statue, on the east wing of the State House, is fenced but open to the public during business hours.)

But lucky ticket holders had a chance to get up close and personal on July 20, 2016, the 425th anniversary of Anne Marbury's baptism. The Anne Marbury Hutchinson Foundation held a ceremony at the statue in Anne's honor. Honored guests included biographer Eve LaPlante and former Massachusetts governor, the Honorable Michael Dukakis, who granted a pardon to Mistress Hutchinson in 1987, 349 years after she was convicted of heresy and banished from Massachusetts Bay Colony.

Anne Hutchinson statue at the Massachusetts State House on July 20, 2016, the 425ᵗʰ anniversary of Anne's baptism. Former Massachusetts governor Michael Dukakis (at the podium) spoke at the ceremony. Behind Gov. Dukakis is Hutchinson descendant Dr. Eric Nielsen.

The statue honoring Mary Barrett Dyer is located to the right of the Hutchinson statue, on the north wing of the State House. It was placed in July 1959, and was created by Sylvia Shaw Judson, based on a descendant of Mary Dyer. This statue is behind a fence also, but there's public access during business hours on weekdays, and it's closer to the sidewalk on the corner of Beacon and Bowdoin, so it's easier to see from the many tourist buses that round the corner there.

Both statues face the Boston Common and the city center where the First Church, courthouse, and prison were, and beyond that, the Massachusetts Bay and England.

Mary Dyer statue

BIBLIOGRAPHY

You probably wouldn't be much interested in the books I read on sociology or women's influence in the seventeenth century; one of the few films I've seen in the last couple of years was on a plane coming home from Boston. But one of the best pieces I've read in months was a portion of a seventeenth-century book I read *about* in the footnote of a college textbook published in 1982, that I'd bought from Amazon. I searched for its author, its title, bits of text, and people mentioned, and after hours of research over several evenings, I found it. It had only been scanned/digitized in 2016, six months before I found it. It was one book in a university library in the Boston area, and I doubt that the person who scanned it bothered to read it. If I'd looked for it earlier, I wouldn't have found it. But the fact that this letter exists in a book, mentioned in a textbook footnote, tells me significant things I wanted for this book. It's the stuff of private happy dances, or toasting some long-dead Quaker with my berry tea in the wee hours. It's the thrill of the nerd hunt. If you're a golfer, you just won the tournament. If you hike, you just summited Mt. Whitney.

And that, my friends, is why bibliographies are *exciting*. Yes, I said it. What will you find in this bibliography 35 years from now, that will fire a neuron and help discover more facts that have lain dormant for hundreds of years?

As the Countryman of *The Great Frost* said, "We old men are old chronicles, and when our tongues go they are not clocks to tell only the time present, but large books unclasped; and our speeches, like leaves turned over and over, discover wonders that are long since past."

Go ahead: unclasp these books!

Boorstin, Daniel J., *The Americans: The Colonial Experience*. Random House, 1958.

Breen, Louise A. *Transgressing the Bounds, Subversive Enterprises among the Puritan Elite in Massachusetts, 1630-1692*. Oxford University Press, 2001.

Bremer, Francis J., ed. *Anne Hutchinson, Troubler of the Puritan Zion*. Krieger Pub. Co., 1980.

Brinsley, John. *How the Master may direct his Scholars to write very fair, 'though himself be no good penman.'* Chapter iv of the *Ludus Literarius*, 1612.

Bush, Jr., Sargent, editor, *The Correspondence of John Cotton.* The University of North Carolina Press, 2001.

Chapin, Howard M. *Documentary History of Rhode Island, Vol. 2, Being the History of the Towns of Portsmouth and Newport to 1647 and the Court Records of Aquidneck.* Providence, Rhode Island: Preston and Rounds Co., 1919.

Clapp, Roger. *The Memoir of Capt. Roger Clapp of Dorchester,* 1640.

Cressy, David. *Agnes Bowker's Cat: Travesties and Transgressions in Tudor and Stuart England.* Oxford University Press, 2000.

Cressy, David. *Birth, Marriage & Death: Ritual, Religion, and the Life-Cycle in Tudor and Stuart England.* Oxford University Press, 1999.

Davis, Tom. 'The Practice of Handwriting Identification' in *The Library: The Transactions of the Bibliographical Society,* Volume 8, Number 3, September 2007, p. 269.

Dekker, Thomas (attributed). *The great frost. Cold doings in London, except it be at the lotterie. With newes out of the country. A familiar talke betwene a country-man and a citizen touching this terrible frost and the great lotterie, and the effects of them.* London, 1608.

Donoghue, John. *Fire Under the Ashes: An Atlantic History of the English Revolution.* University of Chicago Press, 2013.

Emerson, Everett, *John Cotton,* G.K. Hall & Co. Revised edition 1990.

Endicott, Charles M., *Memoir Of John Endecott, First Governor Of The Colony Of Massachusetts Bay,* 1847.

Evenden, Doreen. *The Midwives of Seventeenth-Century London,* Mount Saint Vincent University, Cambridge University Press, 2000.

Famous Kin website. Famous *Kin of Anne Marbury Hutchinson.* Accessed October 2017.
https://famouskin.com/famous-kin-menu.php?name=8872+anne+marbury

Groome, S. *Glass for people of New England, in which they may see themselves and Spirits (etc.).* London,1676.

Guillemeau, Jacques. *Child-birth or, The happy deliuerie of vvomen VVherein is set downe the gouernment of women. In the time of their breeding childe: of their trauaile, both naturall, and contrary to nature: and of their lying in. Together with the diseases, which happen to women in those times, and the meanes to helpe them.* London: Printed by A. Hatfield, 1612.

Hall, David D., ed. *The Antinomian Controversy, 1636–1638: A Documentary History.* Second Edition. Duke University Press, 1990.

Hall, David D. *Worlds of Wonder, Days of Judgment,* Harvard University Press, 1989.

Holden, Randall. *Letter of Randall Holden to the Massachusetts Bay Court,* Collections of The Massachusetts Historical Society.

Howard, Sharon. "Imagining the Pain and Peril of Seventeenth Century Childbirth: Travail and Deliverance in the Making of an Early Modern World," *Social History of Medicine,* 16:3 (2003), pp. 367-382.

Johnson, Edward. *Wonder-Working Providence of Sions Saviour.* 1654.

King James I. *The Book of Sports.* 1618, 1633.

Koehler, Lyle. *A Search for Power,* University of Illinois, 1980.

LaPlante, Eve. *American Jezebel: The Uncommon Life of Anne Hutchinson, the Woman Who Defied the Puritans.* HarperCollins, 2004.

M'Clure, Alexander Wilson. *The Lives of John Wilson, John Norton, and John Davenport,* Boston. 1870.

Mack, Phyllis. *Visionary Women: Ecstatic Prophecy in Seventeenth-Century England.* University of California Press, 1992.

Markham, Gervase. *The English Housewife,* 1612.

Morgan, Edmund S. "The Case Against Anne Hutchinson." *New England Quarterly* 10 (1937): 635–649.

Morison, Samuel Eliot, *The Founding of Harvard College,* Cambridge, Mass., 1968.

Peckham, Stephen F. "Richard Scott and his Wife Catharine Marbury, and Some of Their Descendants," *New England Historical and Genealogical Register,* Vol. 60 (1906):170

Raisz, Erwin. *The Founding of Harvard College,* Harvard University Press, 1935.

Rhode Island Historical Collection III.

Robinson, Christy K. *Mary Dyer Illuminated.* CreateSpace, 2013.

Robinson, Christy K. *The Dyers of London, Boston, & Newport.* CreateSpace, 2014.

Thwing, Annie Haven. *The Crooked and Narrow Streets of the Town of Boston, 1630-1822*, Marshall Jones Co., 1920.

Twichell, Joseph Hopkins, ed. *Some Old Puritan Love Letters – John and Margaret Winthrop, 1618-1638*. New York: Dodd, Mead and Company, 1894.

Ward, Nathaniel, *Simple Cobbler of Agawam*, 1647.

Watson, Foster, M.A., Professor of Education in the University College of Wales, Aberystwyth. *The English Grammar Schools to 1660: Their Curriculum and Practice*, Cambridge University Press, 1908.

Wheelwright, John. *Mercurius Americanus*. London, 1645.

Williams, Roger. *Letters of Roger Williams. 1632-1682. Now first collected*, Oct. 28 1637, (Providence: Printed for the Narragansett Club, 1874) pg. 70.

Williams, Selma R. *Divine Rebel: The Life of Anne Marbury Hutchinson*. Holt, Rinehart, and Winston, 1982.

Wills, Garry. *Head and Heart: American Christianities*. Penguin Press, 2007.

Winship, Michael P. *Making Heretics: Militant Protestantism and Free Grace in Massachusetts, 1636–1641*. Princeton University Press, 2002.

Winship, Michael P. *The Times & Trials of Anne Hutchinson*, University Press of Kansas, 2005.

Winthrop, John. *History of New England*, (a.k.a. *Journal*) Vols. 1 and 2.

Winthrop, John, and Weld, Thomas. *Short Story of the Rise, Reign and Ruin of the Antinomian...* London. 1642, 1644.

Winthrop, Robert Charles, *Life and Letters of John Winthrop, from 1630 to 1649*, Ticknor and Fields, Boston, 1867.

Acknowledgements

Thanks to **Valerie Debrule**, whose support of the memory and honor of Anne Hutchinson has been so effective over many years, and who so kindly and generously took in strangers who became friends. Her painting of Anne Hutchinson graces the cover of this book.

Thanks to my research friend, beta reader, and "sister from another mother," author **Jo Ann Butler**. Her expert eye, her expert commentary, and intimate knowledge of the people of colonial Massachusetts and Rhode Island were essential to the success of this book.

Thanks to **Stephen Lillioja**, a physician-scientist-professor who introduced me to the concept of Antinomianism in the 1980s (for the record, he was not in favor of it), which led me to study the backgrounds of Mary Dyer and Anne Hutchinson in the 2000s. From there I wrote a few books…

Thanks to **Susan Higginbotham** for giving me her Toshiba laptop when my old (really old) laptop was having fits.

Thanks to **Kevin and Sharon Crockett Walker** for giving me their desktop Mac when they moved house.

Thanks to **Bob and Patti Cottrell Grant** and **Cate Linrud Biggs**, for supporting my writing efforts on a regular basis; and other amazing supporters like **Phil and Christine Berkland, Dennis Petticoffer,** and **Cliff and Freddie Harris**. Their gifts arrived at the *perfect* time. They might not have known, but they heard and obeyed the Voice within.

Thanks to **Dr. Ken Horn**, a descendant of Anne Hutchinson and Mary Dyer, who is a minister, an editor and author, and has supported my efforts by reading advance copies of my books. He is at once a distant cousin through ancestry, and a brother in the faith and a shared profession.

Thanks to **Cindy S. Manning**, whose vision and moral support have buoyed me up many times, particularly when I was considering writing this book.

Thanks to the friends and distant relatives in the Facebook groups "William and Mary Barrett Dyer Descendants," "Descendants of Anne Marbury Hutchinson," and the several groups of New

England and Rhode Island history and genealogy where I post my research nuggets. I appreciate your support and your questions that sharpen my research focus in my books and blogs.

The Partnership of the Historic Bostons and President Emerita **Rose A. Doherty** have brought me new colleagues and friends who are immersed in the same time periods and places I am. Sharing expertise, photos, and factoids about old and new Boston and its people has been exciting, and were great background for this book. A few people of the group have been beta readers for my drafts, and have agreed to provide images and articles for my history blogs. Thank you, Rose, for your dedication.

To the nameless university student **library workers** who scanned antique documents, letters, books, broadsheets and chapbooks that may have seemed boring to them, but are invaluable to researchers, my proverbial hat is off to you. The Gutenberg Project, Google Books, UK archives and British Library, the Library of Congress, the Massachusetts Archive, and many university libraries that provide the documents are the backbone of research today.

More thanks are due to readers and critics of drafts of this book, **Joyce A Lefler** and **Martha Bruneau**.

Thanks to the people of the churches of various denominations where I've worshiped, studied, and served as a musician, teacher, or elder over the last three decades. Your perspectives and your spiritual gifts have broadened my horizons and made me a better researcher, thinker, and writer.

Meet the Author

Christy K Robinson's books are found at
http://bit.ly.com/RobinsonAuthor,

*and the author may be contacted about book
clubs (in person or by Skype) or speaking appointments at*

http://ChristyKRobinson.com,
*where you may read a brief biography of the author
and connect with her history blogs.*

*If you believe that this book has added to the wealth of information contained in
other books about the Hutchinsons, please review it on Amazon or another
bookseller.*

For ongoing research into the early seventeenth century
first founders, the Titans of New England,
with entertaining and informative articles and images,
bookmark Christy K Robinson's history site

http://MaryBarrettDyer.blogspot.com

**More than half a million page views
200 illustrated articles focusing on**

- Dyers and Hutchinsons
- Winthrop, Cotton, Endecott, Wilson
- Roger Williams and John Clarke
- New England colonies of the 1600s
- Old England homes of New England colonists
- nature (earthquakes, climate, comets, storms)
- art, music, literature
- fashion and food
- medicine, midwifery, and healing
- the supernatural (witches, unexplained phenomena)
- and more …

Other books by Christy K Robinson

Mary Barrett Dyer, 1611-1660, was comely, dignified, admired for her intellect, and known in the court of King Charles. But how did she become infamous in England and America as a heretic who gave birth to a monster? Were she and her mentor/friend Anne Marbury Hutchinson responsible for curses falling on colonial New England in the form of great earthquakes, signs in the heavens, and plagues? What possessed the ultra-righteous Governor John Winthrop to exhume her baby before one hundred gawkers, revile her in his books, and try to annex Rhode Island to get its exiles back under Boston's control? In *Mary Dyer Illuminated,* follow William and Mary Dyer from the plague streets and royal courts of London to the wilderness of America where they co-founded the first democracy of the New World 135 years before the Declaration of Independence. They were only getting started.

In the second volume, *Mary Dyer: For Such a Time as This*, the Dyers return to war-torn England and their lifelong association with **Sir Henry Vane,** and lay a foundation for liberty that resonates in the 21st century. Why did beautiful, wealthy Mary Dyer deliberately give up her six children, husband, and privileged lifestyle to suffer prison and death on the gallows?

The two novels and the nonfiction companion book, *The Dyers of London, Boston, & Newport*, are compelling, provocative, and brilliantly written, blending historical fact and fiction to produce a thoroughly beautiful work you won't want to put down. The author has reconstructed a forgotten world by researching the culture, religions, and politics of England and America, personal relationships, enemies, and even the events of nature, to discover who they were.

Order the books and view the 5-star reviews at
http://bit.ly/RobinsonAuthor

She was warned.

From 1657-1659, she was jailed numerous
times for supporting prisoners who were fined,
tortured and imprisoned for their religious beliefs.

She was given an explanation.

Banished from Massachusetts on pain of death.
Returned anyway, to protest.
Sentenced to death.
Reprieved on the gallows.

Nevertheless, she persisted.

She advocated separation of church and state.
She was determined to use her death to
shock the theocratic government.
She timed her return to Boston during their
elections and court sessions.
Died by hanging on June 1, 1660.

Her death stopped further deaths over religion
and inspired the wording of Rhode Island's
1663 charter of liberties, which was a template for

The First Amendment

guaranteeing free speech, free assembly, free press, freedom to
petition, and freedom of religion
without government interference.

Mary Barrett Dyer

http://MaryBarrettDyer.blogspot.com

Mentored by Anne Marbury Hutchinson,
Mary Dyer was one of the titans of New England.
Read her story in the books
Mary Dyer Illuminated and
Mary Dyer: For Such a Time as This,
by Christy K Robinson.

Effigy Hunter

Effigy Hunter, by Christy K Robinson, is a literary genre-bender.

It's nonfiction medieval **history, genealogy, monument photography, travelogue**, a **bucket list** of where to go on your effigy hunt, **anecdotes about the people** behind – or under – the effigies, and a lesson in **medieval religious symbols and what they meant to the people who made them**. This book contains more than **60 original images**, and tables with **more than 900 medieval names and burial places in Great Britain and Europe**. Many of the subjects were royals or aristocrats, and others were famous or forgotten – until now. If you're interested in ancestry research, this book is indispensable: you'll learn what some of your ancestors looked like, and chances are great that you share many of these ancestors with millions of people living today, so you can find out more about what kind of people they were as you extend your lines.

You need *Effigy Hunter* as your trail guide.
http://bit.ly/RobinsonAuthor

What reviewers have said about *Effigy Hunter:*

"**The book you didn't know you need, but you do**! A must for medieval lovers."

"Effigy Hunter was an **impeccably well-researched** read..."

"**Very highly recommended** for genealogists, historians, novelists, & travelers."

"A **superb** medieval travel experience! For travelers, as well as those of the armchair variety, it is a **fabulous book** to enjoy. I loved it."

"It brings to life real people who are usually only remembered as epitaphs. I would **recommend this book to anyone who is interested in medieval history/genealogy as I am.**"

"**What an adventure**! *Effigy Hunter* breaks the mold; it is time-travel writing, history, genealogy, yet it takes the reader to the United Kingdom, Paris, and other places in Europe giving new insights to those places while invoking the experienced traveler of good memories. **Try this book!**"

"Is this **intriguing** book a history, genealogy, or personal memoir? All that, and more. Ms. Robinson's meticulous charts provide readers with locations and descriptions of tombs and effigies, interspersed with unique photographs and lively travel anecdotes."

"I can't tell you enough how fascinating this book is! It's **like Rick Steves meets Indiana Jones**! Its engaging, historical and utterly relevant information is a traveler's absolute "must have" if you're an individual researching your family tree or even just hitting the road less traveled by tourists. Even if you're an armchair or virtual traveler, don't leave this book behind as you go traipsing back in time, exploring who you are and where you came from!"

"**A must-read.** *Effigy Hunter* **teaches the language of the dead**: the words, symbols and history of the medieval departed. Christy helps you decipher the world of the medieval person of means: what they believed, what they meant to tell us of themselves and even of ourselves. **No, it isn't spooky and scary** but the sobering, boastful, hopeful beliefs of those lying within these sacred spaces requesting a final intercessory prayer on their behalf."

Last Words on Anne Marbury Hutchinson: American Founding Mother

Religious liberty for all is the freedom to believe and act one's conscience, even if the majority disagrees with an individual or group. It's not freedom or justice for all if some are excluded for their belief – *or their non-belief*. In the United States, besides those who do not believe in a god or higher power, there are approximately 2,000 religious sects, and the variety of adherence and buy-in to their individual creed or dogma runs from weak to strong. Infinite variety! Who gets to choose which strain gets prominence or receives government financial support?

It's not freedom for one branch of believers to have privileges from the government while others are denied based on their religious beliefs, or their choice to not believe in any religious system.

Because Anne Hutchinson and Mary Dyer, Roger Williams and John Clarke, and almost every co-founder of Rhode Island, were very religious people (zealous Puritans, Antinomians, Baptists, Quakers, etc.) who sacrificed worldly goods and even their lives for their faith in God, we might think of these "Founders before the Founders" as desirous of a religious utopia in the New World.

Not. At. All.

They'd faced religious persecution by their governments in Europe, to such a degree that they'd fled to the wilds of North America. But the people who governed the new society were theocrats who based their laws in the Old Testament laws given to the Israelites in the wilderness of Sinai. Ministers and magistrates locked arms and wills to accuse and prosecute, imprison, torture, and execute in the name of God. This marriage of religion and government is called theocracy.

Williams, the Hutchinsons, the Dyers, and scores of others were banished from Massachusetts Bay Colony, reviled as heretics, and ridiculed for the rest of their lives, for insisting on liberty of conscience and separation of church and state. In the 1630s, though they believed and practiced their deep faith, they were the first people in Western civilization to form a secular (non-religious) government. They insisted on it, to the degree that religious liberty is encoded in the charter (constitution) of Rhode Island, which was central to the formation of the First Amendment to the US Constitution in the next century.

The problem is not that people have strong religious beliefs. The problem is *enforcing* one set of beliefs on another person or a community, or discriminating against another because of their beliefs or behaviors.

Liberty of conscience is what Anne Hutchinson, Roger Williams and John Clarke lived for, and in Mary Dyer's case, died for. They didn't impose their beliefs on others, but advocated for the full rights of others. They were the great-great grandparents of the revolutionaries of the United States and authors of its Constitution – which is by design a secular document.

Even today, our rights to freedom of religion and freedom from oppression are under sneak attack. As an admirer or descendant of Anne Hutchinson or Mary Dyer, I hope you will work to protect the rights of all people, as fought for by our *first* founders, Roger Williams, William and Anne Marbury Hutchinson, Richard and Katherine Marbury Scott, William and Mary Dyer, John Clarke, and many others. Because it's a never-ending struggle in every government agency, every state and territory, and every municipality, to allow freedom for all, and not just freedom for the powerful.

"Those who would renegotiate the boundaries between church and state must therefore answer a difficult question: why would we trade a system that has served us so well for one that has served others so poorly?" – Sandra Day O'Connor, conservative Supreme Court Justice.

Join me in support of liberty.

Made in United States
North Haven, CT
03 October 2022